D1598711

All the Bright
Young Men and Women

A PERSONAL HISTORY OF THE CZECH CINEMA

Peter Martin Associates Ltd.
In Association with 'Take One' Magazine

All the Bright Young Men and Women

A PERSONAL HISTORY OF THE CZECH CINEMA

Josef Skvorecky

Translated by Michael Schonberg

Translated and published with the assistance of the Province of Ontario
Council for the Arts and the Canada Council.

We would like to thank the following individuals and organizations for
stills and information: Barrandov Film Studios, Canadian Film Institute,
Pat Harris, International Film Distributors, Seth Willenson, New Line
Cinema, New Cinema of Canada, Kent Carroll, Grove Press Films, Mr.
Jerry Brejcha, CBC Picture Service, Mrs. Olga Dimitrov, Forman-Crown-
Hausman Productions, Mrs. Marie Haas, Muky, Mr. Antonin Prazak,
Mr. Alfred Radok, Mr. George Voskovec, Mr. Zavis Zeman, Film Canada,
United Artists, and several people in Czechoslovakia whose names we
thought better to withhold for reasons only too obvious.

Library of Congress Catalog Card Number: 73-174568
ISBN: O-88778-056-3

Printed in Canada by John Deyell Limited

Designed by Pat Dacey, assisted by Susan Fothergill

The Take One Film Book Series is published by Peter Martin Associates
Limited, 17 Inkerman Street, Toronto 5, in association with *Take One*
magazine, Post Office Box 1778, Station B, Montreal 2, Quebec.

General Editors: Peter Lebensold
                 Joe Medjuck

Acknowledgement

This book is a product of nostalgia: for the country which I left when others entered, and for the friends I had there who have made so many fine films, sometimes due to, and sometimes in spite of, the local conditions. It began in a course I gave at the University of Toronto in 1969-70. Then, Joe Medjuck of Innis College asked me to write an article for *Take One;* after which he and Peter Lebensold decided to begin their film book series with a book on the Czech New Wave, and Peter Martin liked the idea. So I wrote the book, in the hope that it might help a little to keep the memory of certain things alive, in this fast forgetting world.

It is not a scholarly work, just a personal remembrance, and therefore I have not referred to sources. Nevertheless, I would like to thank all those brilliant, and often courageous, Czech film critics and historians without whose work, as it appeared in the sixties in *Filmove Noviny* weekly, in *Film & Doba* magazine and elsewhere, the historical sections of this book could not have been written, and whose analyses helped me greatly to see many things I would not have otherwise understood.

My thanks go also to Dr. C. T. Bissell, President of the University of Toronto and to the Board of Governors of that University, whose understanding enabled me to write this book during my year as writer in residence.

Josef Skvorecky

To Kathryn

who loves to watch the late late show

Contents

It is an indisputable fact and not just chauvinism when I say that one of the most important pioneers of film was Jan Evangelista Purkyne (1787-1869). This great Czech physiologist, with an unusual sense of humour, came up with a number of original ideas. Being a theoretician, he didn't bother putting all of them into practice. The invention of dactylography, for instance, has been ascribed to a doctor of the British Colonial Service, although Purkyne had noticed long before the uniqueness of the fingerprints, and thought that they might serve as an excellent tool for identification. He then promptly forgot about them.

His film exploits, however, are better remembered. Around 1840, having decided to provide a little entertainment for his students, he glued several grimacing daguerreotypes of himself onto a stroboscope equipped with a shutter of his own design—a system which is still used—and became perhaps the first jester ever to appear on a photograph-come-to-life. He went on to invent a pull-down system which he used to illustrate the systole and diastole of the heart. In this respect he had advanced further, technically, than the younger Edison. As he observed himself revolving around his own axis on the strosboscope—or as he learnedly called it: kinesiscope—he pondered about the future of his toy: "It may be presumed, that in time this thing will develop into a new form of artistic expression. When this happens it will not suffice to simply show a single phase of the passing motion. Instead it will be necessary to show the motion in its entirety."

The real grandfather of Czech cinematography was the handsome architect, Jan Krizenecky, who in 1896 brought from Paris the Lumiere camera and began to take moving pictures of interesting scenes: firemen running around a fire-engine, with the water really jetting out of the hose; a group of bearded gentlemen very rapidly laying the corner-stone of a monument, etc.

The young bon-vivant was a far too enthusiastic visitor of the Prague cabarets to be contented with shots of arriving locomotives or jogging labourers. He hired a popular comedian, Josef Svab-Malostransky, and made a short called *Laughing and Crying,* which incidentally contained another "first" for the Czech cinema: as far as I know it was the first time close-ups were used in the same manner as they were to be by others much later. Krizenecky's work culminated in two very short comedies, *The Exhibition*

1

Czech Heaven: *the prominent standing Frankenstein on the left is historian F. Palacky; the mad doctor on the extreme right is the composer Antonin Dvorak.*

Sausage Vender and *A Rendez-Vous at the Grinding Room,* both of which were shown at the Exhibition of Architecture and Engineering in 1898. The humour of these shorts, like that of the classical American comedies, consisted of people falling into food and of Victorian-styled *in flagranti* situations.

The lonely pioneer Krizenecky found no understanding among investors, but the first commercial film companies began regular production some ten years later, in 1908, and from then on they were very successful. The average yearly feature film production in Czechoslovakia in the 1920's was about twenty films; after the Prague studios at Barrandov were built it increased to between thirty and forty, occasionally reaching as high as fifty. Early Czech films contained very little art, as was the case everywhere at this time when film was primarily a new business venture. The majority of the productions consisted of comedies of a type easily identified by their titles: *The Pink Slip, Annie Is Jealous, Saxophone Suzi, The Prague Adamites**; they generally dealt with the comic events preceding the wedding night. Others were highly popular melodramas such as *The Light of his Eyes, The Silver Clouds* or *Hearth Without Fire,* mostly based on the enormous sufferings of enamoured millionaires. Two smaller categories were adventure

---

*Adamites were 15th century Czech nudists (another "first" for the Czechs); they were the most radical sect of the Hussite religious movement, one of whose claims to fame lies in the introduction of the word 'pistol' into several European languages. The Hussite movement preached the return to the Bible a hundred years before Luther. The Adamites, however, took it so literally that they discarded their clothes and walked around like Adam and Eve before the Fall. The Hussite leader Jan Zizka mercilessly slaughtered every one of them, thus setting an example of how to best deal with deviationists. This film described the amatory adventures of a turn-of-the-century playboy, and took place at a Prague public swimming pool. The Don Juan's adventures were complicated by a double, which constituted the first use of double exposure in Czech cinema. The film was made in 1917.

Jan Krizenecky (1868-1921), the handsome lonely pioneer.

The Kidnapping of Banker Fux: *Anny Ondra imitating Mary Pickford, Eman Fiala as Sherlock Holmes.*

films and, after World War I, patriotic super-films. In the latter, the audiences were treated to mass appearances of giants of Czech history who, for purposes of greater verisimilitude, wore stiff masks made after ancient portraits. The result resembled a congress of Frankensteins (*Czech Heaven,* 1918). In a film made to commemorate the millennium of the martyrdom of St. Wenceslas, the first Czech saint, costly armies of extras pretended to be fiercely engaged in deadly battle and the good king reached out to Heaven with his sword-bearing hand. He shouldn't have done that because the close-up of the hand revealed a wrist-watch on the actor's arm, whereupon my father burst out laughing. This is my oldest personal memory related to film as *Saint Wenceslas* was the first movie which my pious parents took me to. That was in 1929, and I was five.

The adventures were movies of the Bulldog Drummond type about international conspiracies (*The Poisoned Light,* 1921). Since the country never did have a particularly high private crime rate, such films were usually parodies (*The Kidnapping of Banker Fux,* 1923; *Lelicek in the Service of Sherlock Holmes,* 1932). Even horrors appeared, for instance, *The Arrival from Darkness* (1921), a story about a count who after three hundred years in a grave awakened and fell incestuously in love with a female descendant. Sometimes the film-makers reached out to themes from foreign classics, as with *The Feathered Shadows* (1930), based on a story by Edgar Allan Poe about madmen who murdered a psychiatrist. Sometimes they used non-actors with some natural disposition for a

3

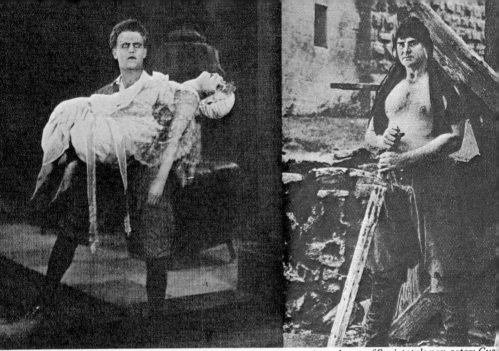

Anny, this time in the arms of a drugged corpse that came to life in Arrival from Darkness.

An early use of Soviet-style non-actor: Gus Fristensky as The Prague Executioner.

particular part; for instance Gustav Fristensky, the Czech world champion in catch-as-catch-can wrestling, gave a stellar performance in the title role of *The Prague Executioner* (1927).

The colourful adventure genre brought about the first attempt at Czech-American co-production. Two rich American Slovaks, the Siakel brothers, decided in 1921 to make a movie, *Janošik,* about the Slovak Robin Hood. The film was shot simultaneously in two versions with two cameras. The more historically accurate version, which was shown in Czechoslovakia, had Janosik captured and executed. The other version, intended for the more sensitive American public, showed Janosik escaping from under the gallows and marrying a beautiful girl from the mountains. Both versions contained long western-style chases on horseback more appropriate to Arizona than to the valleys of the Tatra mountains.

Film-making was evidently an excellent business, operated according to the customers' demands. Despite this, a handful of enthusiasts decided to validate Prukyne's prediction and turn film-making into an art. The early beginnings were comical. Charmed by Méliès, Stanislav Hlavsa made *Faust* (1912); it was based on Gounod's opera and had Mephistopheles appear, disappear and then, astoundingly, re-appear. After the film's completion, the director travelled with it through the country and, hidden behind the screen, sang the part of Mephistopheles, thus creating one of the first sound films in history. The Faustian

4

The Song of Gold *(1920): I love the early-twenties atmosphere of this still, with Anny Ondra on a period chair looking like a baroque shepherdess.*

theme was used again in *The Builder of the Cathedral* (1919)—the story of a Gothic architect who offered his soul to the Devil in order to be able to complete a daringly conceived cathedral. For the first time in the history of Czech cinema, the word art does not have to be used in quotation marks. The film was even more successful abroad than at home: it had a long run in France under the title *La Cathedrale*.

But it was socially critical themes that brought some consistency into the efforts to turn film into an art form. One of the first was Vaclav Binovec's *The Grey-Eyed Demon* (1919), a story about the labour unrest of the 1870's; later came Premysl Prazsky's *Battalion* (1927), a biographical film about the early Czech socialist, Dr. Frantisek Uher. The trend culminated in a film described by Maurice Bardeche and Robert Brasillach as "the swan song of the silent film era". Called *That's Life,* it was made in 1929 by Carl Junghans.

Junghans, although German, has a place in the history of Czech cinema. He made his film in Prague with Czech money provided by the popular Czech comedian, Theodor Pistek, who being fed up with petit-bourgeois farces raised the funds, invested his own savings (despite the warning of the film merchant Mr. Auerbach

5

Vera Baronovskaya, Pudovkin's Mother, in Karl Junghans' That's Life *(1929).*

that nobody in the world would ever buy it), and persuaded Czech actors to work without pay.

The social drama of a washer-woman who slaved to keep her family alive was made very much in the style of the left-oriented German school of that time; the German Social Democrats and Communists promised to finance the film, but in the end failed to keep their promise and backed instead Piel Jutzi's *Mother Krausen's Road to Happiness* (1929). Jutzi's film bore a rather striking resemblance to an original idea Junghans had been offering since 1925. It seems that Jutzi had simply "borrowed" Junghans' theme.

As Mr. Auerbach had predicted, *That's Life* was a total financial flop and it disappeared. One copy was discovered after the war. It was shown in numerous film clubs and was highly acclaimed. In 1957, Elmar Klos (*Shop on Main Street)* made a sound track for the film, but when Junghans saw it in 1964 he did not like it. Klos used brass band music, whereas Junghans thought Richard Strauss would have been more suitable.

However, at least one country did notice the film at the time of its original release—the Soviet Union. Junghans went there with very high hopes in 1931. He was interested in the problems related to the use of sound in film; he wanted a functional utilisation of sound rather than the popular chatty intoxication. At that time, however, a socialist-realistic code began to be felt in Moscow; Eisenstein and Pudovkin were already experiencing difficulties and the bureaucrats did not seem very interested in the functional utilisation of sound. Instead of "futile" experiments, Junghans, upon their suggestion, wrote a scenario based on Langston Hughes' novel *Not without Laughter;* criticism of foreign oppressions was a safe and fashionable topic in the Moscow of the early thirties. In the end, the bureaucrats changed their minds even about criticism of foreign oppressions and Junghans did not receive any money to make his anti-racist film. They explained that "a film dealing with such delicate internal problems of the USA might endanger Soviet-American commercial relations".

After this hard lesson in socialist realism, the disgusted Junghans returned to Prague. His old friends, this time with the aid of a Yugoslavian company Presvetni Film, secured some moderate capital and Junghans began shooting *Life Goes On* on location in Yugoslavia. Then came the Marseille assassination of Alexander II;

political disturbances followed; the shooting dragged on and the capital dwindled. It took years to finish the movie.

In Germany, meanwhile, the National Socialist German Workers' Party, in its vociferous building of the New Order, was using slogans expressing the necessity to fight for peace and for the defeat of Anglo-American war-mongers. Junghans seems to have been tricked into cooperation as, after all, were many others. He returned home and made a commercial hit, *Through the Desert* (1936), based on Karl May's novel; then he created something which he later, very unconvincingly, tried to conceal. Whatever the real truth may be, the fact remains that the film *The Years of Decision* (1939) bears his name among the credits. Later he maintained that it was an anti-war film, which is possible, particularly since the Nazis were very vehemently against war—and cleverly manoeuvered the Western "war-mongers" into declaring it. But the film is also a eulogy to the NSDAP's revolutionary ascent to power.

Junghans, himself, apparently caught on very quickly; in April of 1939 he escaped to France and then to the United States. He never returned to film-making. Instead he opened a photographic studio, secured exclusive rights to the manufacturing of coloured photos of Disneyland, made money and retired to Munich.

As I have pointed out, he was a German who made an outstanding Czech film. His life reveals the formula of a typical Central European fate. Hollywood has seen all sorts of tragedies, but this one is specifically Czecho-German. The lives of famous people of this corner of the world are not marred so much by disease, change of taste, or loss of youth, as by battles of ideology which, under ominous threats, compel them to absolute loyalty. Many actresses have slept with influential politicians, but they rarely had to pay for it with exile, as did the beautiful Czech film star, Lida Baarova. She was chosen by Josef Goebbels, the Nazi Minister of Propaganda, the limping "gentleman" who wielded absolute power in the Protectorate of Bohmen und Mahren. This power extended to film stars as long as they did not commit suicide, as did Baarova's sister Zorka Janu, driven by shame. Many directors have failed in other parts of the world, but very seldom because of overenthusiastic audiences. This, however, was the fate of quite a few directors east of the Ore Mountains.

That European specialty affected the career of Gustav Machaty —the first Czech director to enter film histories. He was truly

The eager young man with the wicker chair is Gustav Machaty, the high-school drop-out who later made Extasy. *Here at work in an early Prague film studio.*

reared by the movies. Thrown out of high school for disobedience at the age of sixteen, he became a side-kick in the mini-studios of the pre-war Czech producers. In 1918, he acted in his first comedy; the title, *Alois Won the Sweepstakes,* indicates the level of the film's humour. From then on he acted, wrote scenarios, assisted in skits like *The Enraged Groom* (1919), *Gilly's First Visit to Prague* (1920), and even got to direct a farce called *Teddy'd Like a Smoke* (1919). Being a youth by film possessed, he obeyed the calling of Hollywood and left for California as soon as the Great War ended. He arrived there in 1920 and, according to unconfirmed accounts, worked as assistant to both D. W. Griffith and Erich von Stroheim. In 1921, Machaty returned to Prague as the manager of Eddy Polo, a famous movie cowboy of that time. Trying to increase the popularity of Polo, Machaty spread the story that he was in fact a Czech from Karlin (the Prague version of Soho). It didn't impress the public. During a performance of *The Massacre of Farmer Cook's Family* Polo behaved so arrogantly that the audience booed him off the stage. The furious cowboy slapped Machaty's face and then fired him on the spot.

Machaty was an artist and the two years near Griffith equipped

9

him with a fine film sense. After his return to Czechoslovakia he spent several years peddling his ideas for art films among the Prague rich. Finally one of them, who made his money selling canned fish, wrote a check and Machaty was on his way. Shooting in Prague and Vienna, and using Czech and Austrian actors (one of them was the son of the gentleman who wrote the check), Machaty made a film of Leo Tolstoy's *Kreuzer Sonata* (1926). The cast was indicative of Machaty's enthusiastic cosmopolitism—he believed that film was an international art. *Kreuzer Sonata* bore the markings of the German expressionistic style and earned the canned fish manufacturer a goodly sum. Machaty was no longer forced to offer his services to any taker; instead he accepted an offer to shoot a version of *Good Soldier Schweik in Civilian Life*. Inspired by Hasek's classic Czech novel, the film was made in Vienna, and was a total failure. It was evident that the serious young man had absolutely no sense of humour.

After two years of studying foreign movies, he atoned for this failure by making the first of his two erotic films, *Eroticon* (1929). For the first time in Czech cinema a completely naked actress appeared on the screen. Her name was Ita Rina; she was Yugoslavian, and played the part of a train watchman's daughter; the watchman was played by a Czech actor, Karel Schleichert. The girl was seduced and lured away from her father's house by a rich young man—a German actor with a Norwegian name, Olaf Fjord—was abandoned in the big city, and finally properly married to a rich man, played by an Italian, Luigi Serventi. Thanks to Machaty's talent this "true romance" turned into a work of art, although admittedly a somewhat eclectic one. The text books of cinema quote the first of Machaty's many famous symbols: two drops of rain slowly slide down the window-pane until they finally merge into one—inside the room a debauchee is seducing the watchman's daughter.

Eroticon's story was written by the great Czech surrealist poet, Vitezslav Nezval, who was obviously not being quite serious. He was more serious in the script for Machaty's next feature, *From Saturday to Sunday* (1931), which has been unfairly neglected probably because it was sandwiched between the two erotically scandalous pieces. It was a poetic and socially-critical story of young sales girls, who worked hard during the week and on Saturday night tried to grab a little bit of the "rich" life at one of the night spots. Machaty turned the film into a test case for his theory that, in

10

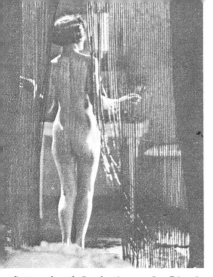

e first nude of Czech cinema: Ita Rina in
»tikon.
e most successful nude of Czech cinema:
dwige Kiesler-Lamarr in Extasy.

movies, speech should be used as little as possible, and even the
talkie film should remain primarily a visual medium. That year he
returned for the second and last time to comedy, only to once more
realize that he was no good at it. He produced *Naceradec, the King
of the Kibitzers*, based on a humorous character created by the
Prague Jewish author, Karel Polacek. Then came his lifetime
triumph—*Extasy* (1933).

The history of this scandalous and beautiful cinematographic
work is well known. The film was admired by such giants of erotic
art as Henry Miller [*viz.* "Reflection on Extasy" in his book *Max
and the White Phagocytes* (1938)]. The unclothed heroine, Hed-
vige Kiesler, launched her great Hollywood career as Hedy Lamarr
from it. Her husband, an Austrian millionaire, tried unsuccessfully
to prevent the scandal from spreading by buying up prints of the
film and the pictures of his nude wife which appeared in magazines.
Later, Hedy Lamarr wrote about it in the book, *Extasy and I*
(1966). In it she maintained that she had undressed only after
Machaty had pressured her with threats that, unless she stripped,
the film would be a financial failure and her husband would have to
pay. Unfortunately for Miss Lamarr, the still surviving cameraman
of *Extasy,* Jan Stallich, declared in an article, "*Extasy and Hedy
Kiesler*", that Hedy had disrobed quite voluntarily and performed
the daring scenes with youthful enthusiasm. After the performance
of Lena Nyman in *I Am Curious Yellow* and other public
cohabitors such "daring", of course, has completely faded.

Despite the Pope's protests the film triumphed at the 1934
Venice Festival and subsequently became one of the classics of

11

world cinema. After World War II, certain critics, particularly the leftists (Georges Sadoul, Chiarini) described it as over valued. They accused it of cosmopolitism, empty formalism, and eroticism. When I saw *Extasy* after twenty years, in 1969, in Toronto, I got the impression that these critics were paying tribute to the holy war of A. A. Zhdanov against beauty and love-making. *Extasy* is a charming and poetic film of classical perfection, and however cosmopolitan it might be in aesthetic principles and cast, its lyricism continues an old Czech tradition.

The remainder of Machaty's life is a typically Czech tragedy, although it takes place predominately in the United States. Notwithstanding his triumph in Venice, he was unable to obtain money at home, and had to turn to Austria, and later to Italy, where he first made *Nocturne* (1934) and then *Ballerina* (1936). The latter was sent to Venice, but the audience expected another *Extasy* and rejected it. At that time Machaty already had a contract with MGM and escaped the shame by going to Hollywood. However, MGM sent people to Venice and had second thoughts about the contract. Machaty was allowed to shoot only one short *(The Wrong Way Out,* 1938) for the series *Crime Does Not Pay,* and a single B-movie, *Within the Law* (1939). Other than that Machaty barely subsisted in Hollywood; he received no offers from Czechoslovakia, was not allowed to enter Italy (he had offended Mussolini), and did not want to work in Nazi Germany. He made a living as a specialized side-kick: whenever a famous director felt under the weather, Machaty was sent for to become a director for a few days: so he, for instance, substituted for Sidney J. Franklin in *The Good Earth* in the scenes where the locusts attack the harvest; for Clarence Brown in *The Conquest* with Charles Boyer and Greta Garbo; he stood in for Sam Wood in *Madame X,* where, as an "expert" on the erotic, he shot scenes in the South American brothel. His last chance came after Herbert J. Yates, the owner of Republic Films, married a Czech figure skater Vera Hruba Ralston. Vera probably put in a word for Machaty and he was given a Dalton Trumbo script, which he shot and titled *Jealousy* (1945). The story of a Czech immigrant was so naive that nobody dared to show it in Prague—it was not supposed to be comical.

After *Jealousy* came the long skid; Machaty became financially dependent on his wife Maria Ray, a costume designer, and when in 1950 she committed suicide, he had to leave Hollywood. He settled

12

Vancura's Before the Matriculation *(1932). The brooding handsome student is Antonin Novotny: when I referred to him as "an empty beau" the censor confiscated the article although the actor was no relation to the President.*

in Germany, where in 1955 he wrote the script for G. W. Pabst's *It Happened on June 20th.* Later he directed his only German film *Missing Child 312* which resulted in a professorship at the Munich Film School. Under his guidance, the students made *New Year's Eve 1957,* but then the school closed. There were only two more glimpses of hope before the end of his life. In 1957 he negotiated in Prague about the possibility of shooting two scripts. The first had a telling title, *The Career in Rome,* and it was a tragedy about young embittered film-makers; the second was to be a new version of *Extasy.* I don't know why nothing came of either. I cannot, however, imagine *Extasy* being produced in the prudish fifties at Barrandov. It would have been possible after the arrival of the New Wave, and Machaty did come to Prague again in 1963. During the negotiations he became ill, was taken to Munich and there died on December 13th, 1963.

It was a creeping drama with an unhappy end, but in that sense no particular exception. The fates of Czech film-makers-artists are often variations of a sad theme. One of the most promising creators of the thirties was Vladislav Vancura, who did not live to see his best films: that is films based on his books, Jiri Menzel's *The Capricious Summer,* 1968 and Frantisek Vlacil's *Marketa Lazarova,* 1967. Vancura was shot by the Gestapo after Czech commandos assassinated Reinhard Heydrich, the Nazi *eminence grise* of the Protectorate, in 1942. His name headed the endless columns of vic-

13

tims listed on the laconic blood-red posters; the posters which were the only obituaries of the men of Lidice*, and of thousands of innocent people.

Vancura was primarily a novelist; he was a virtuoso of the vocabulary, a master of the rhythm and timbre of the Czech language, but since he did not write in English, he remained virtually unknown outside of Czechoslovakia. Along with the other modernists of the 1920's he loved the wonderful moving pictures—a Douglas Fairbanks styled script written in 1926 and called *The Incorrigible Tommy* survives. He finally got his chance in 1932, when he made a student drama about the "generation gap", *Before the Matriculation*. He directed it in collaboration with the experienced Svatopluk Innemann, who provided the necessary craftsmanship, while Vancura gave it the gently lyrical artistic quality.† His second film, *On the Sunny Side* (1933), illustrated the more sympathetic of the two opposing opinions—both apparently marxist—regarding human character. Two children meet in an orphanage—one is a son of a poor widow, the other a daughter of a rich stock-broker. Under the guidance of a progressive teacher both of them grow up to become sensitive, model people. The film echoed the theories of the Soviet educator Makarenko, which were later considerably neglected by socialist realism. In its fictive world, ruled by predestination of social origin and class hatred, there was not much room for them.

A year later Vancura made a film in the Carpatho-Ukraine region of Czechoslovakia, which was quietly annexed in 1945 by the Soviet Union. It was called *The Unfaithful Marijka;* Vancura for the first time used non-actors in this visually beautiful study of the life of orthodox village Jews. His last two films, *Love and People* (1937)

---

*Lidice was a village near Prague razed by the Nazis in retaliation for the assassination of Heydrich.

†The male star of the film suffered from a different kind of typically Czech fate. He was Antonin Novotny, and was the Czech answer to Robert Taylor. Around 1936, Louis B. Meyer received a high Czechoslovakian medal of merit; he was so touched by this appreciation that he offered the handsome young actor a Hollywood engagement. His emotions lasted for three months; Novotny did not manage to learn English in that time, so he subsequently had to return the borrowed swimming pool and villa, and return home without glory. He continued his career as a screen lover as long as he could, and then completed a degree in engineering. In a 1963 article on film history, I referred to him as "an empty beau"—and the censor confiscated the article. Then I discovered that some Western women's magazine had selected Antonin Novotny—the President, not the actor—the most handsome statesman of the year.

14

Jirina Stepnickova (kneeling) as Rovensky's Marysa. *She later spent ten years in a concentration camp for attempting to travel abroad without an exit visa.*

from a car-racing milieu, and *The Swaggerers* (1937), a village drama based on a classical Czech play, were made in collaboration with another competent practitioner Vaclav Kubasek; both were good, although not excellent films. The inspiration provided to young film-makers by Vancura's enthusiasm for this youngest art was the greatest contribution that the famous author could have made. His fame established a degree of respect for the hitherto lightly regarded art form. He fought against kitsch, and during the war led a group which planned the nationalization of the Barrandov studios. It must also be remembered that his fantasy gave birth to the masterpiece of Czech historical film, *Marketa Lazarova,* made from his novel 25 years after his death.

Josef Rovensky, another of the grandfather generation, did all sorts of things related to film, but most of all he spent his time trying to raise money to carry out projects which, in the end, usually never did get under way. He often made money as an actor—he even co-starred with the American actress Louise Brooks in Pabst's *Diary of a Lost Girl*—and once in a long while he intelligently directed a negligée comedy or a B-movie. The first one, made in 1919, was called *The Vanished Writing,* and Rovensky introduced in it a

15

young Prague dancer, Anny Ondra, who went on to become the greatest star of first Czech, and then German, pre-war film. Later she married Max Schmelling, one of the two men who managed to knock out Joe Louis. Contrary to the tradition of great stars, she is still married to him.

Rovensky's *opus maior* was *The River* (1934), a gentle, lyrical visual poem, and a harbinger of the lyricism of one of the fathers of the New Wave, Vaclav Krska. Together with *Extasy* it was the sensation of Venice 1934. Rovensky next directed two lesser films, but then the young Otakar Vavra adapted for him a classical play of Czech naturalism, *Marysa*; it is a story of a village girl who is forced to marry a rich peasant, and finally poisons him. The part of Marysa was given to another future great star of Czech cinema, Jirina Stepnickova. Probably under Vavra's influence, Rovensky emphasized the socially critical aspects of the old repertory piece. In 1937, he began filming *Watchman No. 47* but he never completed it; it was later made in Hollywood during the war as *Pickup* by Hugo Haas. He also started *Virginity,* a movie about a shop-girl who promises to sleep with a lecherous old man in order to be able to pay for her sweetheart's medical treatment. During the second day of shooting, Rovensky suddenly died. The film was completed by his pupil and the author of the script, Otakar Vavra.

Vavra is the only member of the founding generation who survived all the changes in taste, aesthetics and politics, and is still making movies. From the very beginning, his films bore the trademark of determined rationalism and willingness to learn. While others were self-taught improvisers, visionaries or faltering seekers, Vavra was the first Czech professional film-maker. In comparison to Machaty or Rovensky, he never made anything that would stand out in the history of Czech cinema as a beautiful exclamation mark; on the other hand he never lowered his high artistic standards. With the exception of two symptomatic pauses, not a single year has passed since *Virginity* (1937) without a new film by Vavra. His last movie, *Hammer Against Witches,* was released in 1970. The two exceptions were the years 1950 to 55, and 1962 to 65. Both unproductive periods coincided with the arrival of new trends, and both must have shocked Vavra's artistic spirit. The first was the era of raging socialist realism, and the intelligent communist Vavra could hardly have been expected to digest the fact that his life-long

efforts towards the creation of an artistic socialist cinematography*
were turning into an embarrassing parody. Vavra never made a
socialist-realistic movie, having escaped the requirements of propaganda by a retreat into history. The second pause coincided with
the arrival of the New Wave. Vavra's films are traditionally precise,
rational, and professional work. His own students (he was the most
successful teacher of the Film Academy) emerged suddenly with
anti-traditional experiments, which they did not learn from him, but
rather from industrious examination of Western films. In this they
followed Vavra's example in his earlier years. Vavra in turn began
to study the works of his students; after three years of silence he
came up with two beautiful formalistic films, and proved that he still
knew how to do it. In this context it should be remarked that his first
work was a little experiment in social criticism called *We Live in
Prague* (1933). It was set in the Great Depression period. His last
work to date, *The Hammer Against Witches,* describes the witch-
craft trials of the Czech baroque era, but is obviously directed
against trials of a much later period. In between, there was a Golden
Lion from the Venice Festival for *The Guild of the Maidens of
Kutna Hora* (another historical cryptogram, banned immediately
after the arrival of the Nazis) and more than twenty other films. In
the end Vavra outdid both Machaty and the New Wave in erotic
daring. One American critic wrote about the frolics of a nude thirty-
year-old lady in *The Romance for a Fluegelhorn,* saying that it was
the most daring nude scene he had ever seen. In addition to its
serious overtones, *The Hammer Against Witches* can also be seen
as a black mass of nudity, functionally utilized.

Vavra's exact opposite is the great improviser Martin Fric (before
the German occupation, and after it until the Communist takeover
in 1948, called "Mac" Fric). He started at nineteen with the comedy
Why Aren't You Laughing (1922), and ended after forty-six years
and almost twice that number of films with the comedy *The Best
Broad of my Life* (1968). An absolute majority of the films in that
mountain of fun were conceived as comedies—nevertheless some
involuntary socialist-realistic funnies do appear among the
multitude. Unlike Vavra, and despite the occasional lapses, Fric
made a few films which, after so many years, remain very vividly in

*For instance, the Prague Film Academy was his brain-child.

Another early still I love: a perfect study in black and white with Anny Ondra and Vlasta Burian in The Sweethearts of an Old Jailbird.

one's mind, as do the eternal gags of *Modern Times. Kristian* (1939) became symptomatic of the spiritual atmosphere of its time, in a way comparable to Humphrey Bogart's movies; then came the first, and only good, Czech screwball comedy, *Eva Is Fooling* (1939), and a parody on kitsch, *The Poacher's Ward* (1948), which many took seriously, and as a result suffered considerable attacks of melancholia. Last, but certainly not least, should be mentioned his films with the comic genius, Vlasta Burian (*Catacomb,* 1940), and with the duo of Voskovec and Werich (*Heave-Ho!* 1934, and *The World Belongs to Us,* 1937).

Fric departed after a career as the most successful Czech film entertainer, although some of his serious films were also remarkable. Yet even he was affected by the Central European fate: he died of a heart attack on August 21, 1968, as the first Soviet tanks rolled into Prague.

For those who somehow managed to escape anonymity, this small piece of land in the heart of Europe prepared strange surprises and unwelcome adventures in a period shorter than the average life-

The White Sickness: *Haas in white coat; sitting: Karel Capek with wife O. Schein-pflugova.*

The man who felt: *1) A soccer fan, 2) A Czech, 3) A Jew – Hugo Haas in* Men Off-Side.

span. This is well illustrated by the careers of the four great comedians of Fric's films.

Best known on the American continent is a Jewish actor from the Moravian capitol Brno, Hugo Haas. He was, at heart, a serious artist, a subtle psychological comedian somewhat in the manner of Charles Laughton, with whom he appeared as Pope Urban in the Actors Laboratory production of Brecht's *Galileo Galilei,* directed by Brecht himself. This was preceded by a life full of ironic little tragedies which became progressively greater, until they culminated in the final tragedy of a premature death.

Haas was a full-blooded Jew, and only half Czech (his mother was a Jewish-Russian emigré), and yet the family felt completely Czech and did not even speak any other language until they were reminded of their "race" in a typically Central European way: Hugo in January 1938, when a production of Karel Capek's *R.U.R.* and *The World of Beggars,* a socially critical film directed by Miros-lav Cikan, were viciously attacked by the fascist paper *Vlajka,* mainly for Haas' participation in them. Hugo's father and brother Paul, a talented musician, were given an even more tragic reminder during the war in Auschwitz.

For some ten years, at the beginning of his career, Haas was viewed by the critics as just one of many handsome, dark-haired stage-and-screen gigolos; but then, in 1931, in a film based on a humourous novel *Men Off-Side,* by another Czech-Jewish artist, Karel Polacek (who died in a Nazi camp), the audiences suddenly witnessed the birth of a comic actor of the first magnitude. So thorough was the identification of the young Jewish actor with the main character of the film, the Czech-feeling Jewish shopkeeper and soccer fan Mr. Naceradec, that the success of the movie made

19

Hugo with a very young Gregory Peck in Days of Glory.

Hugo Haas with Charles Laughton in Brecht's Galileo, *directed by Brecht.*

Machaty shoot a rather poor sequel to it, *Naceradec, the King of The Kibitzers* (1932). In 1933 Haas joined forces with Mac Fric, and they produced a series of first-class comedies, based often on their own ideas and scripts (*A Dog's Life,* 1933; *The Last Man,* 1934). Later they used Otakar Vavra as screenwriter in another series of memorable films (*A Lane in Paradise,* 1936; *Morality Above All,* 1937), and finally Haas started to direct his movies himself; first with the help of Vavra *(Camel Through the Needle's Eye,* 1936), and then independently in an outstanding adaptation of Karel Capek's anti-Nazi science-fiction drama, *The White Sickness* (1937).

In 1939 the tragedy set in: Haas was thirty eight, and he had never spent one day outside of his native Czechoslovakia. In spite of the impending, and rather obvious, holocaust he did not want to leave the country. His wife, however, knew better. The experience of similar holocausts was in her bones for she, like Haas' mother, came from a family of post-revolutionary Russian emigrés. First she fought the French consul, then she fought the Gestapo, finally she had to leave their new-born baby with her non-Jewish sister-in-law and force her husband to flee in the very last minute before the brown iron curtain fell down. They went to France where Haas appeared in one film, *The Sea in Flames,* and made a documentary about the Czech cause, *Our Combat.* But soon they had to flee again: France fell to Hitler in the summer of 1940.

It is undoubtedly a sign of Haas' extraordinary abilities that from his first American movie (*Days of Glory,* in which he co-starred with the young Gregory Peck) until the day he left for Europe in the early sixties, he was featured in some twenty Hollywood films, and

20

Hugo with Linda Darnell in Chekhov's Summer-storm.

Hugo with Nat King Cole in Night of the Quarter Moon *(directed by Haas).*

in 1950 he was even able to form his own company and buy the old Chaplin studios (where he found an abandoned huge cog-wheel, a remnant of *Modern Times,* which he kept as a memento). He directed fourteen films, and appeared in all of them but one, the most memorable ones being *Pickup* (1951), based on a novel by the Czech novelist Josef Kopta, which had been started but never finished by Rovensky in Prague in 1937; *Thy Neighbour's Wife* (1953), an adaptation of a story by another Czech-born writer Oskar Jelinek; *Lizzie* (1957); *One Girl's Confession* (1953); and particularly the delightful *Edge of Hell* (1956), an Americanized version of his and Fric's *A Lane in Paradise,* which, occasionally, can still be seen on TV.

The war ended and he had a strong desire to go home—but the feared news about the death of his brother and father in Auschwitz came and shocked him into staying. The only consolation was his seven year old son, who survived, protected by courageous relatives, and was sent now to join his parents in the USA. And yet, the nostalgia proved to be too strong. He resisted it, but eventually, after more than twenty years, he embarked on a slow and hesitant journey home. It lead him first to Rome, then to Trieste, then to Vienna. There he settled, full of indecision: for things were rather different at home from what they had been when he left. His good friend Jan Masaryk had died under mysterious circumstances; the shamefully anti-semitic Slansky affair had not yet been explained; and there were camps in the country so reminiscent of those where his family had met their death. He waited in Vienna and, in the meantime, made several TV films. Finally, in 1963, he came for a tentative visit. The people welcomed him with love and nostalgia;

21

Vlasta Burian: "... if Czech cabaret ever had a genius..."

neither he nor his times were forgotten, even after twenty-four years. But he did not feel quite at home any more. He refused a part in Jiri Krejcik's adaptation of some short stories by Karel Capek, and was gravely disappointed when the National Theatre declined to accept his play; it did not quite meet all the requirements of the new times. Discouraged, he returned to Vienna and made another TV comedy, *The Crazy Ones* (1967). In 1968, with the developments of the Czechoslovak spring, hope flourished once again and he planned a final and definitive homecoming. But the tanks were faster. He died, broken-hearted, on December first, 1968. Only his ashes returned to Prague; they were buried there near the remains of Franz Kafka.

Another great comedian of Mac Fric's pre-war movies, Vlasta Burian, was a very different personality from Hugo Haas, but shared with him, in a certain respect, the Central European fate. He was something of a Czech Groucho Marx. He had the same mercurial energy, was capable of similar verbal floods, and stupefied the audience with wise-cracks, explosive gags, aggressive conquests of women, fantastic mimicry; besides that, he had a great vocal range. If the Czech cabaret ever had a genius, it was Burian; unlike the intellectual Groucho's, his was a strangely warped genius, something in the style of the idiot savants, the miraculous mathematician-fools. He lived exclusively for the theatre; for years he appeared on stage nightly, and three times a week in the afternoon; in the mornings he made movies. Considering this enormous workload, it is doubtful that he ever knew what was happening to the world around him. His films took place outside time and space, although they were accurately delineated historically. Burian represented in them the eternal idiotic wiseguy—the exact opposite of the Good Soldier Schweik, who assumed the masque of an idiot to protect himself from the dangerous insanity of constantly battling ideologies. The political awareness of this "holy simpleton" was that of a preschooler.

When the Nazis arrived, the idiot-savant, loved by the nation, allowed himself to be tricked into collaboration; in a radio sketch he offered his genius as a parodist to satirize Jan Masaryk. The nation cringed and friends explained to the simpleton what he had done. He slowly began to realize what was happening, became careful, and remained so till the end of the war. Notwithstanding his subsequent prudence, he was tried after the war ended; he cried at his trial, but was sentenced to a large fine, given a suspended jail sentence and, worst of all, he was forbidden to act. For a while he tried to live without the theatre, but then he broke down. He started to write self-humiliating supplications and tearful requests to various agencies, ranging from the actors' union to the head of state, until he was finally allowed back on stage. He acted for a while, sometimes even in movies, fighting for yet another, completely different ideology (*The Hen and the Sexton,* 1950) together with Rovensky's Marysa, Jirina Stephnickova, who shortly after tried to escape to England but was caught and sent to a concentration camp for ten years. He remained the idiotic genius, living outside his time and world, and died during a travelling engagement.

When Burian passed away, George Voskovec was back in the United States; unlike Burian, he knew perfectly well what was happening around him. It was his second trip across the ocean—he had sailed for the first time shortly before Burian parodied Jan Masaryk on the Prague Radio. That time, he had travelled with Jan Werich.

Voskovec and Werich appeared after the First World War as an indivisible comic duo, in the tradition of Pat and Patachon or Laurel and Hardy. However, with all due respect to Stan and Ollie, Voskovec and Werich mean much more to Czech culture—they are the most revered symbol of a great era. Together with Jaroslav Jezek, the father of Czech jazz, they moulded dadaism, circus, jazz,

23

V + W in a ballet parody from Powder and Petrol: *"to say 'the Prague cultural atmosphere of the thirties' is almost equal to saying V + W."*

Chaplin, Buster Keaton, and American vaudeville into a new art form. They created a new form of intellectual-political musical. Never before had anything like that existed in Bohemia, and it was a quarter of a century after the Nazis had closed the Voskovec and Werich theatre, before it appeared again in the Semafor Theatre of Jiri Suchy and Jiri Slitr (S + S). To say "the Prague cultural atmosphere of the thirties" is almost equal to saying V + W. In the late sixties Milos Forman mentioned during an American interview that the average young person in Prague might not know the name of the current Prime Minister, but he would certainly know the names of Voskovec and Werich.

They made four films which surpass anything made before them in Czech film comedy; *Powder and Petrol* (1931) and *Money or Your Life* (1937) were directed by the director of their plays, Jindrich Honzl; *Heave-Ho* (1934) and *The World Belongs to Us* (1937) were made by Mac Fric. After the films and their anti-fascist musicals it was easy to calculate what they could have expected had they waited for the Nazis, and so they went to the USA. They returned after the war, and when in 1948 the political system turned another somersault, the tired Jan Werich remained in Czechoslovakia, while Jiri Voskovec moved, this time permanently, across the ocean. There he became—as George Voskovec—a

Early American talkies hired European actors to attract Europeans: V + W in a Paramount musical.

Voskovec and Werich in the brilliant comedy of the Great Depression Heave-Ho! *(1934)*

24

Burian + V + W the only time they met on stage: in a one-act farce written by V + W for a New Year's Eve production.

Jiri Voskovec as George Voskovec in Henry King's The Bravados.

Jan Werich today — with a reminder of the past in the background.

distinguished Broadway actor. He appeared for instance in the title role of Chekhov's *Uncle Vanya,* for which he won the Obie Award, in the Gielgud-Burton *Hamlet,* as Einstein in Peter Brook's production of Dürrenmatt's *The Physicists,* as the Pope in Brecht's *Galileo* and most recently in Edward Albee's *All Over.* He also starred in many films, e.g. *Twelve Angry Men, Butterfield 8, The Spy Who Came In From The Cold, Mr. Buddwing, The Boston Strangler, The Bravados* etc. Jan Werich, meanwhile, fought for several years against "difficulties"; he was attacked for a motley selection of sins, such as delivering political anecdotes on stage*, but he survived, because in Czechoslovakia V + W are not just another couple of actors; they are the object of love, which the nation, deprived of any political illusions, shows only to some of its artists.

But V + W belonged together; each one of them on his own is but a half. They are also Central European. Their fate foreshadowed what is happening today, a generation later.

*One of his most famous ones—Question: What's the difference between impressionist, expressionist and socialist-realist painting? Answer: the impressionist paints what he sees; the expressionist paints what he feels; and the socialist-realist paints what he hears.

Czechs began to make films as early as the classical film nations of the West; they made many, and several received world acclaim both before and after the war. Despite this, the "World" acknowledged the existence of Czechoslovakian film as an art form only at the beginning of the sixties. At that time, the films of the New Wave started to accumulate prizes at Western Festivals, and this appeared to the world to be almost a miracle. Czechoslovakia was thought of as some East European country—political schizophrenia had long before replaced geography—*eo ipso* technically undeveloped and culturally impoverished. As late as 1966, I was asked by a friendly gentleman in New York whether Czechoslovakia had manufactured anything besides Pilsner Beer, before being industrialized by the Russians. When, on another occasion, I mentioned to another gentleman a story by Ambrose Bierce, he was so impressed that he spent the rest of the afternoon collaring his friends and pointing me out as some kind of rarity from the distant steppes of the Elbe region, who knew the name "Bierce". I came to understand his amazement when I taught at Berkeley, where most of my students had never heard of the San Francisco scribe. The students of the Faculty of Journalism in Prague used entries from *The Devil's Dictionary* as political slogans in their underground mimeographed anti-Novotny magazine.

The New Wave was clearly no miracle. It was a synthesis, evolved from a dialectic situation formed by four factors of the post-war development.

The first factor was nationalization. This meant the end of financial worries for the most important element of film production—the directors. Not that they were suddenly able to burn money (although some, for instance Vavra in the Hussite Trilogy, tried it successfully), but they could certainly afford to do more than they managed under the private producers. The old boys were never as rich as their Hollywood colleagues, and consequently the average shooting time of a comedy ranged from a record two to a very decent six weeks; most of the time was spent arguing about production costs. When the state assumed the role of the producer, the production time extended to between two and six months (and frequently longer), which was naturally the first prerequisite of higher quality.

The second factor was the establishment of the Prague Film

Academy in 1947, two years after the nationalization. Not only were the students of the Academy equipped with all the tools necessary for their art, given expert instruction and enabled to make short study films, they could also attend bi-weekly, all-day showings of excellent old films from the well-stocked Prague Film Archives, as well as good contemporary Western films; to this factor I attribute paramount importance. The majority of foreign films were sent to the Czechoslovakian Film Board of Trade, which held the national film distribution monopoly. After viewing the films, the Board usually rejected them as unfit for showing in Czechoslovakian cinemas. However, before they were sent back, the Film Academy "borrowed" them and showed them for "study" purposes in the school's small screening room. Thus, unlike the rest of the public, the students acquired a solid knowledge of the history of cinematography, as well as of its contemporary trends. Simultaneously, they gained immunity against the third factor in the game.

This was what I would call the nationalization of aesthetics. The artists of a nation with a long and sophisticated artistic tradition were being forced to conform to a mandatory aesthetic system of socialist realism in its most primitive form. The reign of this twentieth century cultural curiosity in Czechoslovakia was in fact short—some five or six years—a little-known fact in the West. Despite the monster's evanescent life, the Barrandov studios helped to give birth to some of its most delightful progenies. The unequal marriage of cynical opportunism and naive enthusiasm can be credited with such dandies as *DS-70 Is Not Starting* made in 1950 by Vladimir Slavinsky, the most notorious pre-war director of sentimental petit-bourgeois comedies about the loves of millionaires and servant girls. A group of saboteurs try to destroy the hero of the film, a monstrous walking dredger, but are only partially successful, and are subsequently apprehended and arrested. The workers repair the good machine and fulfil the production quota. Another pre-war manufacturer of sentiment who quickly became nationalized was K. M. Wallo. In his *The Great Opportunity* a gang of evil-doers also fails pitifully, discovered this time by a character called Tonda Buran (in English this would be Tony Uncouth, or Joe Hillbilly), an ex-hooligan, who while doing time in a socialist prison saw the light so clearly, that he turned into a model shock-worker (a Czech equivalent of the Russian stakhanovite).

The thematic range was not limited to direct sabotage. In *Thirst* (1949), the co-operative farm workers decide during a very dry summer to build an irrigation system, but the local "kulak" (rich peasant) dissuades them from the idea; his sinister intentions are finally unmasked and the water flows freely towards a somewhat unexciting happy ending. Another contemporary problem was aired in *Seagull Is Late* (1950). Here Mr. Seagull, a rather conservative baker, despises miners, because they are "dirty"; in the nick of time he is sent with a group of volunteers to the mines, where in the comradely subterranean atmosphere he rapidly changes his opinions. The easy accessibility of Marxism to even the most backward characters is clearly revealed in the film *The Hen and the Sexton*. A group of agitators attempt to persuade some hard-boiled villagers to stop farming privately and form a cooperative. They encounter interference from the local church authorities, who are in cahoots with the kulaks. The villains are ruthlessly apprehended, and the more folksy types among them repent. The most enthusiastic repenter is the cleverly stupid sexton, played by the repentant, almost-collaborator with the Nazis, Vlasta Burian.

These, and similar heavy-handed didactic fairy-tales, were served to an audience, who from their own experience knew the real problems of the transitory period, aggravated by the bloody eccentricities of the declining Stalinism. This points towards the fourth factor in the game: the audiences lost interest in Czech films and crowded in to see the few imported samples of French, Italian and British comedies, and the erstwhile rare, but later more frequent, products of Italian neo-realism.

A truly dialectical situation developed: never before did the technical and artistic education of the young film-makers reach such high standard—the amount of material resources at their disposal was also unprecedented; on the other hand, with the exception of the Nazi occupation, there were never so many aesthetic and political restrictions. The inevitable result of such contradictions is, of course, revolution.

The revolution was preceded by some colourful and complicated developments. In the early post-war years Barrandov production rose quickly from three films in 1945 to ten in 1946, eighteen in 1947, sixteen in 1948 and twenty-one in 1949. This was still considerably less than the pre-war thirty to forty films per annum; the

Jiri Krejcik in studio *Jiri Weiss*

decrease indicated more than anything else the shift in emphasis from quantity to quality, although the latter still wasn't overwhelming. Production was concentrated on comedies and war movies. The first international success came when Karel Stekly received the Golden Lion at Venice for a social drama of striking workers called *The Strike* (1947). Besides the middle-aged generation of artists represented by Vavra, Krska and Fric, five new names came into prominence in 1947. Young Jan Kadar wrote the story and scenario to a witty comedy *Know of a Flat?* Elmar Klos, eight years older, authored the script of a psychological drama *Dead Among the Living.* Jiri Weiss, who had worked before the war as a documentarist, and as a British soldier worked with the Crown Film Unit during the war, made his first feature *The Stolen Frontier,* which dealt with the mobilization of the Czechoslovakian Army during the Munich crisis. This surprisingly mature work began a long career which was consistently marked by perfect professionalism (*Romeo, Juliet and the Darkness,* 1960, *Ninety in the Shade,* 1964). Jiri Krejcik, who also started out as a documentarist, directed a lively version of Jan Neruda's classical book of short stories *A Week in the Quiet House.* Some of his later films ideologically foreshadowed both the first (*Conscience,* 1949) and second (*Awakening,* 1959) revolt against the canons of socialist realism of the mid-fifties and early sixties. The fifth of these new film makers was Jiri Trnka, who in 1947 made the puppet feature *The Czech Year.* To do justice to the achievements of Trnka, one of

31

the greatest artists of animated film, one would have to write a separate book.

A year later the Communist Party took over the country and its Cultural Department presented the film-makers with two requirements: the majority of films should be set in the present, and all the films must stress the educational aspects of a work of art—they must have a propagandistic value. The film-makers followed the "true direction" so enthusiastically that after seeing the results of two years' production the Party was forced to issue a declaration. It stated, "it is necessary not to take the problems from schematic theorems but rather from real life"—which would have been nice if the same theorems were not always used to evaluate the "real problems", provided that some mad dare-devil wrote them into a script. In addition, everything had to pass through an intricate network of approval commissions, which invariably confused dramaturgy with censorship. It is difficult to assess to what extent the catastrophic harvest of socialist realism was attributable to the cynical drive to fulfil Government orders, and how much should be contributed to the general aesthetic insanity of naive zealots. Both factors certainly added to the cause. It is quite possible to believe that young Vaclav Gajer was serious when he created the model kulak in *The Smiling Land* (1952); it is certainly less possible to give the same benefit of sincerity to someone like Mac Fric who went from anti-fascist satire with V + W, to German films for the Nazi companies during the war (*The Second Shot,* 1943, and *Out of Love for You,* 1944)*, to socialist realism *(It Happened in May,* 1950).

The same applies to Vladimir Slavinsky who was, according to the Nazi press, considering making German movies under the name of Otto Pittermann. (He actually made two: in 1943 and 1944.) The fact remains that at that point the desire to serve the people or the Party (this was synonymous) was not just an empty expression; the big axes had not yet stricken, and the radical youth still believed that revolution was made of poetry, flowers, enthusiastic work on voluntary projects, and an evening of love in a communal dormitory. Many a head was muddled by enthusiasm. Under the relentless barrage of hypnotising propaganda many film-makers chose to learn from zealous bureaucrats rather than from the fathers of modern

*I have not found this aspect of his career satisfactorily explained in the official apologetic histories of the Czech cinema under Nazism.

32

Jana Brejchova in Krejcik's Awakening *(1959) which foreshadowed the New* Wave.

cinema. There may have been cynics even among the bureaucrats, but I believe that an overwhelming majority of them were sincere. Quite a few were ex-workers; the directors saw in them the true authority, and listened to their wise voice of class instinct, in keeping with the sanctified slogan, "I am a miner and who is more?" The directors themselves did not possess that particular instinct: they, as almost everybody who ever meant anything in Czech culture, came from the petit-bourgeoisie. Some interesting stereotypes developed in their subconsciousness; these led to the habit of public autocriticism (a Marxist term for flagellantism), and to the practice of solving all kinds of problems (including private marital problems) at Party meetings under the watchful eye of the collective (this progressively satisfied their needs for exhibitionism). When the bureaucrats later became old and cynical, they consciously attacked these subconscious stereotypes during the first clashes between the new revolting forces and the old conservatives.

Despite all their unintentional comedy, it would not be fair to assume that the strange adventures of Joey Hillbillies and walking dredgers did not have some foundation in reality. Shock-workers did exist, although the endings of their real dramas were usually not as happily optimistic as the films would have it. The women weavers in my home town would literally run the soles off their shoes, and ruin their hearts in the process, as they tried to service eighty looms; at the ripe age of forty some were forced into disability retirement. The wealthy peasants who sometimes sabotaged things also existed—even a few retaliatory murders occurred—and once in a while an angry ex-businessman probably poured some sand into the gears of a fine lathe. The films, however, gave the impression that the country was faltering under the terror of the kulaks, while at the same time developing successfully. The real dramas of a truly dramatic period were reduced by the socialist-realists to a crude puppet show. Its characters were squeezed into stereotypes with unchangeable attributes: class-conscious workers, understanding Party officials, wavering small peasants, intellectuals who started out as reactionaries but soon unerringly recognized the truth, villainous kulaks and factory owners—the real incarnations of Satan. The workers wore caps, while intellectual noses were adorned by spectacles; Party officials always appeared tired and chain-smoked cigarettes—their fatigue coming from over-devotion; kulaks had bristles in their hat-bands and thermometers in their pockets—they used the mercury to poison cows at the collective farm. The former factory owners secretly listened to records of Duke Ellington and Count Basie. After some time the characterizations deepened: shock-workers were allowed a few human weaknesses such as a mild indulgence in beer or an occasional curse; the kulak was given a son who saw the light and became a progressive.

People in the cinemas laughed at dramas and slept through comedies. The workers complained that their arms ached from watching Czech films, and the Party's Central Committee had to intervene in 1950 with the declaration in support of real life problems. Official surveys of Czech film often call this proclamation "the great impulse to further efforts" or "the great initiative". If it was any kind of an impulse at all, then it was towards greater thoroughness; the production in 1951* fell from twenty one films in the previous year to eight—the lowest number ever, including the period of the Nazi occupation. Of the eight movies, four were based in the present and they managed to surpass the standards of socialist-realistic imbecility—if that is possible. *Road to Happiness* was about a female tractor driver, who discovered the inevitable kulak and persuaded the peasants to form a cooperative. In *We Love,* a group of mining apprentices apprehended a band of saboteurs, and *The Pike in the Pond* showed a young female bricklayer teaching the stupid old bricklayers how to lay bricks progressively. In the following years the production volume rose, but it nevertheless remained far below the capacity of the studios; the number of contemporary films fell, and seldom constituted half of the total output. The following was the approximate score:1952: 14 historic to 5 contemporary; 1953: 15 to 8; 1954: 13 to 7; 1955: 14 to 5; 1956: 18 to 9. It should also be pointed out that the present was almost exclusively represented by escapist comedies, in which the socialist-realistic theme was replaced or touched-up by the usual boy-meets-girl scheme (*Word Makes a Woman,* 1952, *It's Still Before the Wedding,* 1953). Another acceptable variation was the espionage-detective entertainment (*The Nuremberg Express,* 1953, *The Northern Port,* 1953). Contemporary reality simply trickled out of

*Figures cited do not include the Slovak films which were made since 1947. Their numbers are: 1947—1; 1948—2; 1949—1; 1950—3; 1951—1; 1952—2; 1953—3; 1954—1; 1955—2; 1956—3; 1957—3; 1958—5; 1959—5; 1960—4; 1961—8; 1962—6; 1963—6; 1964—7; 1965—7.

Otakar Vavra shooting The Hammer Against Witches

the films, and the better directors retreated *en masse* into the past, both historical and literary.

Vavra retreated farthest, although at first he took only a small step backward into year 1945 in *The Drive* (1952), a drama about the resettlement of the Sudeten region of Northern Bohemia. Then he leaped straight into the Middle Ages; in the trilogy consisting of *Jan Hus* (1955), *Jan Zizka* (1956) and *Against All* (1957), he created an incredibly dull spectacle inspired by the worst side of Cecil B. de Mille, complete with battling armies of knights on horseback. He secured three years of full employment for the Barrandov wardrobe. On the other hand a few of his equestrian draftees crippled themselves by falling in full armour off galloping horses. In the late 1950's, when the first critical wave arrived, Vavra dared to move all the way up to 1949. He made *Citizen Brych* (1958) which deals with the transformation of a reactionary into a communist in the course of a few months after the takeover. A year later he back-tracked to 1937, but he made up for it by choosing a work of Karel Capek, a friend and admirer of Masaryk; at that time Capek was not quite kosher, but Vavra compensated for that by selecting from the multitude of the author's works an appropriate mining drama *The First Squad*. After a further relapse into the past with *The Closing Hour* (1960) Vavra finally arrived at the demanded present. He filmed a play by Frantisek Hrubin (*A Sunday in August,* 1960), which two years earlier constituted a bold thematic experiment on the stage of the National Theatre. It spoke about what was really happening in the minds of people during the transitory period, instead of presenting the "how-little-Johnny-imagined-it" view. But at that time the first impact of the New Wave was rapidly approaching. Members of the New Wave were mostly Vavra's somewhat unruly students from the Film Academy.

Although a succession of directors undertook the popular pilgrimage into the past, a number of them did not really help themselves. The almost insignificant, but nevertheless unforgettable, retreat of Ivo Toman into the last months of the war, resulted in *The Tank Brigade* (1955). Its memorability is attributable to the fact that for the first time since *The Czech Heaven* (1918) statesmen appear in a film, with similar results. At this time Soviet cinema indulged in showing Lenin and Stalin, along with other historical personalities who were frequently still alive. For that purpose, the Moscow studios had actor-specialists who resembled the living and the dead, so that with a little bit of good will from the audience the total fantasy was completed. Following the fashion of his time, Toman bore in mind the Soviet example*, and included in the screenplay the figure of Klement Gottwald, the first worker's President and Chairman of the Communist Party. When a double could not be found, the part was given to an actor from the National Theatre, who performed in a face mask made of the material used in Hollywood for Frankenstein's. The mask was very stiff and permitted the actor to move only his lower jaw. It was rather like Chaplin's *A King in New York*.

*The limits of "learning from Soviet examples" were reached by the Czechoslovakian Sound Newsreel; it had been sounded since the 1930 introduction of sound film. A shot of workers dragging a fiery noodle out of a blast furnace would appear on the screen accompanied by an enthusiastic voice saying, "The workers in Nova Hut carry out a record-breaking cast" or something of this sort. In the 1950's, two newsreels began to be shown in Prague—the Czech one and one produced by the Soviet *Novosti Dnia* (Daily News). The Soviet newsreel also had sound, but it retained the introductory titles from the silent era. A title in a Victorian style frame would appear on the screen with the words: "The workers in Krasnodarsk carry out a record tapping of a furnace". The writing remained for a while, soundless, to give everyone an opportunity to read it, and was then replaced by moving images of the workers with the fiery noodle. For some time the two newsreels appeared in succession. Then one day I went to the movies, the lights went out, and the well-known credits of the Czechoslovakian Sound Newsreel appeared, only to be followed suddenly by subtitles in a Victorian frame which read: "The Delegation of the Supreme Soviet visit Prague". To make doubly sure, it remained on the screen a little longer than the Soviet newsreel. This was followed by the shot of the delegates kissing each other like aged homosexuals. This was when I first realized that the greatest enemies of even the best things are toadies.

Vaclav Krska directing

Mac Fric* was carried by the time machine much further into the past, albeit on an incomparably higher level. In a two part comedy, *The Emperor's Baker* and *The Baker's Emperor* (both parts were made in 1951), he went all the way to the seventeenth century. The movie kept the year following that of the Resolution of the Central Committee of the Communist Party from being a total disaster. It was undoubtedly the best comedy of the socialist-realistic period—mainly because it had nothing to do with it. The scenario was written by Jan Werich and Jiri Brdecka, who later gained renown in puppet films and who also wrote the Western spoof, *Lemonade Joe* (1964). Amidst the female bricklayers "educating" the old hands and the escapades of walking dredgers, this

*First names went through an interesting development. Before the war it was fashionable to use English names or to anglicize Czech ones, Mac for Martin, Fred for Bedrich, etc. Harry Macourek, a good and very well known composer of popular melodies, went through the following development: after the communist takeover in 1948 he started to sign his name as Karel Macourek and, though a one time advocate of jazz, became its enemy, because of the association of jazz with capitalism. Years passed, Macourek once again turned from a jazz-hater into a jazz-lover, and started to use the name Harry. I don't know which name he uses currently, but the piquant part of the story is that his real name is Harry. The jazzmen, however, adopted another name for this eminently adaptable musician. I think it was invented by the saxophonist, Strudl, who died in a car accident in Mongolia on the day of the Invasion: Strudl called him "Karel-Marx Courek née Harry Mac Courek". Needless to say, it caught on.

Vladislav Vancura

humanitarian and common sense movie appeared like a message from another world. It was based on *Maharal,* a sixteenth century Prague legend of the Golem, a clay robot made by Rabbi Low ben Beaalel, and it was the greatest box-office hit of the fifties. Encouraged by the success Fric moved three hundred years forward and made an excellent biographical film set at the turn of the century, *The Secret of Blood* (1953), about the Czech doctor, Jan Jansky, who discovered blood groups.

Often "Time's wingèd chariot" didn't help. Vaclav Krska, a delicate artist, began during the war with two films related to the somewhat irrelevant present: the sensuous *Fiery Summer* (1939) and a children's film, *Boys on the River* (1944). Then he devoted himself exclusively to the past. First he made a series of biographical films about great men of the 19th Century, (for instance *The Messenger of Dawn,* 1957, about the Czech inventor of a steam car); later he produced two film adaptations of works by the greatest Czech erotic poet of the early twentieth century, Frana Sramek. The first was *Moon above the River* (1953), the second *The Silver Wind* (1954)—which was where he ran aground. The film was found to be overly erotic, and even homosexual motives were discovered, (naked behinds of youngsters swimming in the river flashed across the screen)* and a ban followed; it lasted several

*The late Mr. Krska, one of the really great directors of the fifties, apparently was a homosexual. What is paradoxical about the troubles of *The Silver Wind* is that a few years afterwards Czechoslovakia became one of the first countries in the world to legalize adult homosexuality.

39

Alfred Radok

The Long Journey *"the motions of actors changed into a terrifyingly poetic* danse macabre.*"*

months, if not years, before the work was finally released for showing. Krska quickly returned to the great men of Czech history and made *Of My Life* (1956), about Bedrich Smetana, after which he "spun" a Turkish fairy-tale, *The Legend of Love* (1957).

The expression "difficulties" gradually became a house-hold word in the Czech film industry, and those who were having "difficulties" carefully changed the subject of their conversations in front of those without them. A children's film, *The Green Notebook,* based on a novel of the pre-war communist author Vaclav Rezac, had them, because it featured a good-humoured policeman—and socialist realism did not grant capitalism the right to have good-humoured cops. As late as 1960 Jiri Weiss and I wanted to escape into the future with a fiction against nuclear war, *Where Will You Be, When that Trumpet Sounds?,* which was to take place in a coffin factory. Barrandov dramaturgists finally threw the project out, fearing trouble from the elderly comrades in key positions: what would those comrades say if they had to watch coffins for two hours? It wasn't always as funny. The most tragic victim of difficulties was a man, who was the immediate, highly influential, predecessor of the New Wave. He was, and probably still is, the best director of the Czech theatre—Alfred Radok.

Radok's first film *The Long Journey* (1949) was as much of a

"I am not aware of any comparable work created at that time in world cinematography."

revelation to all of us as were the films of Vera Chytilova, Milos Forman or Jan Nemec fourteen years later. It was a tragically premature and anachronistic work of art. It dealt with the fate of the Jews in the Third Reich; as far as artistic influences are concerned one might perhaps find traces of German expressionism. I am not aware of any comparable work created at that time in world cinematography. The film presented highly unorthodox camera work by Jan Strecha, non-realistic nightmarish stylization of the phantasmic world of warehouses, where the Nazis accumulated stolen Jewish property. Years later these scenes still inspired Brynych in *The Fifth Horseman Is Fear.* The motions of both the individual actors and the extras became a terrifyingly poetic *danse macabre.* In addition, the socialist-realist critics said that the film reflected "only" humanitarian philosophy. It possessed as little "class approach" as the Nuremberg Laws. It was simply not comparable to anything else produced at that time. The appropriate official places exploded: the film was labelled "existential" and "formalistic". After a very brief run, it was withdrawn from public showing and for almost two decades was locked away in the Barrandov vault.

Only twice was Radok able to return to the Studios. In 1952 he made *The Magical Hat,* an adaptation of an early 19th Century classical comedy, and in 1956 he directed *Grandpa Motorcar,* about car races from the beginning of this century. Both were very good films, which far exceeded the contemporary average; never-

The film "possessed as little class approach as the Nurenberg Laws."

theless it was hardly what Radok—by nature a very serious artist—wanted to do. The latter film could probably still surpass the much later and costlier *Those Daring Young Men in Their Flying Machines,* which resembles it in time, action and setting. Radok's assistant for this movie was a young graduate of the Film Academy, Milos Forman. When Radok started the Laterna Magica, he took Forman with him and entrusted him with the direction of some of the sequences.

Laterna Magica became one of the greatest triumphs of Czech cinema: in 1958 it amazed people at the Brussels Expo, and nine years later it was still one of the major attractions at Expo 67 in Montreal. For all these laurels Radok did not receive many thanks. For the second program of Laterna Magica, Radok filmed a magical story *The Opening of Springs* inspired by the music of Bohuslav Martinu. The film was previewed by the influential stalinist minister Vaclav Kopecky, who banned it on the spot for being the quintessence of pessimism. Radok had to leave Laterna Magica—the show which he conceived and created. He suffered his first heart attack and then, while directing in the small Chamber Theater in Prague, he had two more. In 1968, tired and disgusted, he left the country after the Soviet Invasion, and is currently working in Sweden. The Laterna Magica was taken over by more "reliable" people, who converted it into a commercial attraction for foreign tourists.

42

"as much of a revelation to all of us as the films of the New Wave."

The Long Journey was not the only example set by Radok: his personal influence was certainly just as important. People like Milos Forman, Ivan Passer, Vladimir Svitacek and Jan Rohac (*End of the Clairvoyant*), as well as the dramatist Zdenek Mahler, all learned from him; his ingeniousness inspired Raduz Cincera (*Kinoautomat*) and many others. However, in 1956, new and important factors entered the game: the Twentieth Congress of the Soviet Communist Party caught the advocates of pure Stalinism so badly off guard that they remained groggy for years after. This opportunity was seized by some of the more daring film-makers (among them were some of the first graduates of the Film Academy), who quickly made the first socialist films about the "real" reality. The cultural and political bureaucracy was so punch-drunk that it awarded the National Prize to one of them.

The film was *The School of Fathers* (1957), made by young Ladislav Helge, who had earlier assisted Jiri Krejcik. It told a story of a teacher who, after discovering certain discrepancies between the ideal theory and the somewhat less ideal practice, took a rather unorthodox ideological stand. As a result he became (almost—at the end a *deus ex machina* in the form of a gentle Party secretary intervenes) the victim of a well organized "will of the people". The award convinced Helge that his was a step in the right direction; consequently he made another ideologically courageous film, *The Great Seclusion,* a psychological portrait of a communist director

43

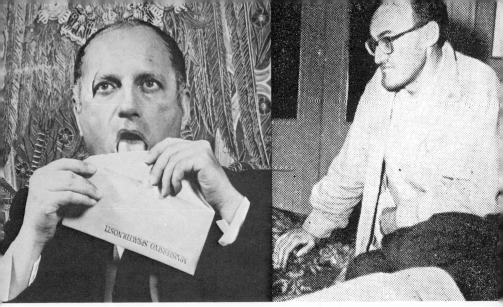

Blazek in Crime in the Night Club   *Ladislav Helge*

of a village cooperative. The director is a devoted worker and an honest communist, with an incurably dictatorial personality: he arranges a number of improvements in the cooperative, but in doing so behaves ruthlessly, hurts and offends all the villagers, and finds himself in a "great seclusion".

Another graduate of the Film Academy, who forgot about the pink colour when he made his first film, was Vojtech Jasny. The film was *September Nights* (1957), and showed various abusive practices in the Army. It was based on Pavel Kohout's play, which the Minister for National Defense, General Cepicka, failed to ban only because he was named Head of the Office for Inventions before he managed to do so.

Even ancient Vaclav Krska emerged from the safety of the costumed past and, lo and behold, dared the farthest. *Hic Sunt Leones* (1958) was a story of an engineer battling against stupidity and the ill-willed bureaucracy. The bleak and harshly portrayed cheerless environment made it one of the most realistic films of that period. An essentially similar rugged picture of contemporary life was offered in Zbynek Brynych's first movie, *The Local Romance* (1958) which bore visible traces of neo-realistic influence. The socialist-realistic critics tolerated the trend in Italian films, but were allergic to it in Czech cinema.

These serious, even tragic, films may be linked to a comedy made in 1958 by Kadar and Klos. *The Third Wish* was the film version of a play by Vratislav Blazek, which dealt with the problem of personal morals and the conflict between an individual's conscience and the knowledge that things which were not supposed to be done were

44

being done. Similar problems were, of course, at the centre of *The School of Fathers, The Great Seclusion,* as well as *September Nights* and *Hic Sunt Leones.* Unlike these films however, *The Third Wish* presented similar themes in the form of a musical entertainment, which was considered especially dangerous. The film has a fairy-tale plot: a young man in a street car offers his seat to a senior citizen, who is so surprised by the unusual courtesy, that he rewards the young man with a small bell. He may ring it three times and the old man will fulfil any three wishes. The young man first takes the old man for a fool, but is soon convinced of the opposite, and uses the bell's magical powers to achieve a miraculous career. A strange transformation occurs with the increase in his income. The enthusiastic critical socialist gradually turns into a conservative supporter of the *status quo.* Then his best friend loses his job for criticizing the management. He asks the hero—now an important comrade—to intercede on his behalf. The official rings the bell, but the quota of three wishes is exhausted. Despite that, the Grandpa of the Bell promises to help—naturally at the hero's own risk. The important comrade asks for time to consider it. He calls a family gathering, where all contemplate whether to ring or not to ring. The film ends without disclosing the resolution of this dilemma.

The novelty of all these films did not lie in experimental form, as was the earlier case with Radok, but rather in their realistic view of the situation. Although their method may have been archaic, it was important in the given situation to simply discover truth, and history shows that it is always more important for the artists to show the truth of human suffering rather than the truth of what is in order. Eulogies are most frequently written by senile laureates or by sycophants. Artists hold out the mirror to the bruises on the face of the world.

All the creators of the Ur-Wave were members of the Communist Party; this is why they took the questions of public conscience more to heart than the non-members, who, having no claim to the merits of the revolution, did not feel responsible for its less meritorious facets. Although later, under the influence of the New Wave, some of the old guarders did experiment with form, their predominant concern was always "what", and not "how". The question of personal conscience remained till the very end their trauma and obsession; fundamentally it is the old dilemma of obedience,

Vojtech Jasny

Helge's Shame: *the hero committed so much e'* *the name of the Good that he changed into a Mr. F*

voluntarily promised to the Party, coming into conflict with the impossibility of obeying the Party, when it either demands unethical action, or orders its members to remain silent. The bureaucrats resolved the dilemma quite simply: whenever something positive took place it was credited to the Party; if something negative happened "certain individuals in the Party leadership were guilty". Politicians have an easy life. Artists don't.

As seems to be the case with all revolutionaries, the lives of these Solzhenitsyn souls with party membership cards affirm the tragic formula. In 1960, Helge's *Great Seclusion* received the Prize of Czechoslovakian Film Critics. However, after the prize was awarded to the film, two cultural correspondents and the Cultural Attaché of the Soviet Embassy arrived, and explained to the committee the impropriety of their decision so thoroughly that one female jury member rescinded her vote, and the prize was finally cancelled. Then a special committee viewed the film. Helge was not invited to the showing, but hid in the projection booth and listened. His testimony speaks for itself: "It was dreadful. I had the feeling that I would never make it home that night, that they were certainly

46

waiting for me somewhere. The word 'anti-communist' was probably the mildest term used. In time they persuaded me to reshoot the end. Originally, the hero remained alone and started weeping. Instead, the film presents a mockery of which I am still ashamed: the members of the cooperative come for the director, and accept him into their midst...." The officials finally got their *deus ex machina,* and the stereotypes planted in the early fifties began to function: "Worst of all was the feeling inside me. Today it would be no longer possible, as the developments and experience immunized us, but at that time I really started to think that maybe I had really done something anti-social. Mlikovsky and I had finished a script about the pseudo-nihilism of the young, called *The Tower;* you should have seen how they set us straight...at that time I was...a walking complex...."

That is when, as Helge says further, the trouble really started: the next films were catastrophic. Only in 1964 did he attempt to express his obsessions—under the influence of the New Wave—with the aid of the magical camera of Western formalism. He made *The First Day of my Son*—but he exaggerated so badly that the movie turned into a parody. Depressed, he for several years looked for a theme, and as the saying goes, "devoted himself to organisational work". He became the *spiritus agens* of F.I.T.E.S. (The Union of Film and Television Artists). In 1968 he finally returned with a new film, *Shame,* a thematic variation of *The Great Seclusion.* (Helge even contemplated giving the hero the same name.) Once again there is a political functionary alienated from his fellow citizens. The honesty which so significantly characterized the hero of *The Great Seclusion* is present in a pitifully derelict form in the protagonist of the latter film. He had committed so much evil in the name of "the good cause" that he changed into a Mr. Hyde. Then came the invasion, and Helge, the citizen, adhered to the convictions he professed as an artist: with a truly super-human effort he organized the "Coordinating Committee of Creative Associations". This organisation was for a long time the main stronghold of the ideas of that idealistic enterprise, whose viability in a world governed by the politics of super-powers, was probably a self-delusion. What Helge now had to listen to far surpassed the private discussion of the cultural overseers in the Barrandov projection room. He became one of the "leaders of the counter-revolution". He did not manage to shoot either the script about Czech political prisoners, which he was preparing together with the "Czech Solzhenitsyn" Karel Pecka (who, unlike his Russian colleague, at the last moment managed to publish his works at home), or another script *How Bread Is Made* written by the screenwriter of his film *The Great Seclusion* and other films, Ivan Kriz. According to unconfirmed reports, the new rulers of Barrandov prepared several lists ranging in political colouring from white, past several shades of gray, all the way to black. Helge is on the blackest of them all.

As far as the advent of the young film-makers in the early sixties is concerned, the most important member of the Ur-Wave was Vojtech Jasny: all of the young ones considered him an older brother. In his second film, *Desire* (1958), he abandoned the formal traditionalism of the *September Nights,* and made a film-poem. Although based on the conventional parallel between the four seasons and the four ages of man, it nevertheless utilizes modern forms of expression. For the first time since Radok, the camera was used as a poetic and metaphorical device; after a long pause non-actors appeared, and for the first time "a topical social theme" based on contemporary material retired into the background. Then followed a concentration camp drama, *I Survived my Death* (1960), where in the crucial scene of the film an imprisoned opera singer sings Gounod's "Ave Maria" instead of the usual "The Internationale". I thoroughly disliked Jasny's next film—the anticlerical *Pilgrimage to the Virgin* (1961) which is highly valued by the Czech critics. The first period of his work culminated in *That Cat* (1963), which had Jan Werich in the lead. Under the stare of the cat's magical eye, people changed colours according to their concealed vices. It was a nice idea, which, somewhat incongruously, combined poetry with satire; the film was successful abroad and brought Jasny a contract for the international super-film based on Erenburg's *The Pipes*. According to an advertisement blurb, "It was shot on locations all over Europe, and boasted a cast of the greatest international stars". All of this only proved the old holistic finding, that the whole has to be more than a simple summation of the parts. *The Pipes* bombed, and Jasny withdrew into himself.

He returned to the subject on which he had started to work after *Desire*; first he could not see it through due to "difficulties", and then, overwhelmed by his rise and fall, did not dare to. The film was *All Those Good Countrymen;* at Cannes in 1969 Jasny received

Werich in Jasny's That Cat — *people changed colours according to their concealed vices.*

for it the prize for best direction. Once again it was a directorial poem, but this time lyrico-epical, with the theme of socialist realism having been transposed onto a level of wise sophistication. This was at last the film which actually fulfilled the demands of the Party resolution of 1951 about the portrayal of the present in its struggle for the future, which "extracted problems not from the schematic theorems, but from real life". However, Novotny's cultural arbiters, having thrown their ex-protector overboard, were once more back in their positions, and they again preferred theorems to reality. F.I. T.E.S. gave Jasny its annual prize for the film; it was the last gesture of the organization. The Cultural Secretariat took it as a personal insult, and F.I.T.E.S. was dissolved. Jasny, unlike Helge, was too well known abroad, and never really did get involved organizationally; he was therefore allowed to make another film—this one about the relation between men and dogs. It is difficult not to recall in this context a saying attributed to Madame de Sévigné: "The more I see of men, the more I admire dogs." It appears that while dealing with dogs, Jasny could no longer bear his knowledge of people, and in the summer of 1970, without finishing the film, he left Czechoslovakia.

Vratislav Blazek, another important member of the Ur-Wave, is not a director, "only" a screen-play writer. However if anybody besides Voskovec and Werich ever tried to lead Czech comedy out of the trashy forest of inanity, it was the stubborn Blazek. As a small boy

49

in my home town of Nachod he performed the duties of the local enfant terrible. Our friendship was somewhat symptomatic of Blazek's later relation to the Communist Party and its doings. It did not prevent me—a conforming boy from a good family—from being the frequent target of this habitual dissident's full-blooded humour. Naturally I was not the only one. Blazek's first literary problems began after the war, when he published in a literary magazine a few Leacockian stories in which some of his friends appeared under their real names. A number of them promptly ceased to be his friends.

Blazek's scholastic career at the Nachod gymnasium ended rather abruptly when he was kicked out of the fourth grade for insufficiency in the then most important language, German. I have the feeling that his ill manners also had something to do with it. He became a druggist's apprentice. Following a series of mishaps reminiscent of film gags*, he was caught smoking on a barrel of gasoline, and finally fired by the owner of the store. Then he took up amateur painting; the local minister of the Church of Czechoslovakia (a kind of an equivalent of the Church of England) commissioned him to paint a picture of his church, but Blazek made it too experimental.

The ensuing litigation concerning payment was won by the minister, after expert opinions by various parties were submitted. Blazek got back at him in a venomous story about an acolyte, whose singing surpassed the priest's performance during mass. The story failed to have the necessary impact because Blazek, unfortunately, was ignorant of the fact that acolytes do not sing during mass, and that the Church of Czechoslovakia does not have acolytes. After the war, Blazek became a Party member because its dissident character appealed to him. He studied painting at the School of Arts and Crafts in Prague, which is where he seems to have embarked upon the career of a dramatist. At this time the Czech forests were being attacked by the bark-scarab. University students had to battle the harmful bug during their summer vacation as a part of their compulsory summer work. Blazek was sent to the Ore Mountains where,

*The best one would have been suitable for coloured film: for some reason carbonated soft drinks were stored, at that time, lying flat on high racks, which were stacked one above another. On top of the racks the druggist kept cans of paint. Standing high on the ladder, Blazek tried to get one of the cans for a customer. He slipped and dropped the can, which, as it was falling, knocked off the necks of about fifteen bottles in a vertical row. Blazek, whose body followed the can's progress, was drenched by a multi-coloured carbonated fountain, and then was sent to sweep excelsior in the yard as a form of punishment.

in a small village with the charming name Mountain of St. Catherine, he wrote a play. Had it been shown in a professional theatre instead of a student camp, it would have been termed pessimistic and therefore noxious, if not outright anti-socialistic. In *Tragedy of the Bark-Scarab* (1946) it is the scarab and not the socialist work-force, who finally wins. The bug's victory is quite convincing—along with the forest, he devours the workers and the gamekeeper.

Even this student farce is indicative of a soul that was not created to praise. In Prague, Blazek established close contacts with the semi-professional Theatre of Satire, the post-war sensation of the capital. Many of the famous creators of comedy began there: men such as the directors Ladislav Rychman (*The Hop-Pickers,* 1964) and Oldrich Lipsky (*Lemonade Joe,* 1964), his brother, the actor Lubomir Lipsky, and the comedians Vlastimil Brodsky and Miroslav Hornicek. The latter is known in Canada as the host of Kino-automat at Expo 67. Blazek wrote for the theatre a comedy *The King Dislikes Beef* (1967); it was essentially a conglomerate of satirical sketches which were the specialty of the theatre, and which the actors of this collectively talented group wrote themselves. The most famous, created in 1947 by Miroslav Hornicek, was *Duna Latrina Zaryetchnaya,* one of the very earliest contributions to the socialist-realistic thematic range: the Theatre was as a rule either clairvoyant or premature. The heroine, Comrade Zaryechnaya, inspired by the shock-workers' movement also decides to come up with an improvement. She is a Public Toilet Assistant, also known as a washroom attendant. In order to raise the productivity in her working area, she organizes the work in the following manner: she collects the money from all the customers, but she admits them into the booths only when their number guarantees the full utilization of the toilet's capacity. With a special device she then simultaneously opens all the doors, the customers enter and sit down. After a precisely limited time period (three minutes, I believe), the assistant presses a button, and all the toilets simultaneously flush. Another precise time period elapses and the mechanism reopens the doors. A new shift of customers take their places.*

*The deadly serious shock-workers' movement was accompanied by all kinds of excesses, which turned this economically dubious enterprise into mockery. Everybody cited—rather maliciously—an ode on the Pig-Feeder, which equated the vision of Communism with that of workers' faces glistening with the fat of the eternal porcine spread; evidently a vision of "The Big Rock Candy Mountain" taken seriously.

While the Theatre audiences laughed, the bureaucrats were frowning. This assumption is born out by the fate of Blazek's second full length play, *Where Is Kutak* (1948). Both the play and the Theatre of Satire survived only the first preview for the "worker's" cultural officers. The heroes of this allegory based on the Biblical story of the Flood, are building an Ark. They are using the well-known method of late Stalinism: incapable unqualified idiots make decisions from stem to stern, self-appointed characters review people and decide who will be left behind; a class of new aristocracy emerges, which only gabs and never does anything. Three months after the communist takeover, the play presented delightful songs, such as the following:

> To make the new gentry
> Help with the sails
> Is what our new counter-plan
> Briefly entails

The metaphor was more than clear; what Milovan Djilas much later understood and described in his book, *The New Class,* Blazek saw—in the tradition of Mayakovsky's farces *The Bedbug* and *The Bathhouse*—much earlier through his satirical eye. Like Miroslav Hornicek's piece, *Kutak* was, to say the least, a somewhat premature piece of satire, written twenty years before the economists began discovering similar practices in the Czech economy. It was taken off the repertoire and the theatre was closed. For a while it appeared that the author might go the same way, since one of the songs proudly presented:

> Captain or Private
> Make him do the dishes
> Who muddies the water
> Feed him to the fishes.

With a little bit of good will the most ardent toadies or faithful worshippers could have equated the Captain even with the Head of State. Fortunately the First Worker's President must have, after all, been a better man than the later Novotny, that is if he was ever informed of the affair, and so the numerous and talented group of the Theatre of Satire was spared the Uranium experience of the concentration camp. Many of them went on later to create works which spread the fame of socialist Czechoslovakia throughout the world.

Hop-Pickers, *popularly known as* The Hop Side Story – *this great Czech musical turned into a kind of festo of the young generation who placed character above class origin. Later they supported Dubcek.*

In 1954 Blazek tried a safer topic in the play *Karlstein for Sale,* about an American millionaire who is conned into buying the fourteenth century dwelling of the Czech kings and wants to take it apart and transport it stone by stone to the United States. Blazek's second attempt at screen-play writing was the scenario for *Music from Mars,* directed by Kadar and Klos. (His first script was *Katka,* 1950, directed by Klos alone.) *Music from Mars* was a story about the problems of a factory dance band (called after the Soviet fashion "a variety orchestra"). It gave the impression of refreshing novelty, mainly because for the first time in many years it used something vaguely resembling jazz. After a string of comedies, the best of which was *The Third Wish,* Blazek's film career culminated in 1964 with the film *The Hop-Pickers,* which was directed by Ladislav Rychman, his old friend from the Theatre of Satire. In the context of Czech musical comedies, *The Hop-Pickers* (or *Hop Side Story* as it was called in Czechoslovakia) bore the same weight as the first films of the New Wave in the area of serious films. The theme is typical and well known: a story of human character, of honour and principle, taking place during the late summer hop harvest. Instead of killing the bark-scarab, the students gather hops—the product so eminently important for the manufacturing of that eminently important export article, Pilsner Urquel Beer. The film presented a fresh and fast moving entertainment, full of rock music with Blazek's excellent lyrics. The songs reached such popularity among the young people of Czechoslovakia that their aesthetic and philosophical impetus became comparable to the effect of the best songs by the Beatles. The film turned into a

53

manifesto of the young generation, which later supported Dubcek, because the leader emphasized the questions of human character. In the crisis accompanying the end of Novotny's era, this was obviously more important than political theories.

Blazek's progress was marked by an almost incessant chain of greater and lesser mishaps. His three heart attacks at the age of 42 are symptomatic of the life of this born satirist who, even under socialism, could not have become anything else. In 1968, true to his own high moral standards, he supported the Director of the Barrandov Studios, Alois Polednak, whom some ultra-radical radicals wanted to oust, but who, although with a hesitance understandable in a general director working in a country with a long history of continuous "difficulties", nevertheless facilitated the emergence of the New Wave. The arrival of the Soviet tanks was as great a shock to Blazek as it was to so many other communist idealists. He left the country and works now in West Germany.

Just as the New Wave of the early sixties did not spring from a cultural desert, so the wave of socially critical films of the 1957-59 period was not an isolated occurrence within the context of Czech culture. In all branches of art the artistic common sense gnawed at the glazing of officious socialist-realism from the very beginning. The representatives of Novotny's regime naturally interpreted the development their own way: they liked to talk about the wise directions provided to culture by the Party (by which they meant themselves). The fact remains—and let someone try to disprove it—that anything positive produced in Czech culture during the twenty years of socialism had to surmount the stubborn resistance of the Party (if we mean by it the Stalinist and Novotnyist bosses). The Party was of course an historically unprecedented benefactor of the arts; unprecedented also was the way the Party imposed its taste on the artists. The cultural bosses bestowed their true love only on the performers for the most part, and even there only when they performed works of the dead and recognized classics. Lillian Hellman's comment on Soviet cultural life is very appropriate in this context: "Russian production, directing and acting is often wonderful. But that's a dead end. When the major talents are directors, actors and set designers—that's dead-end theater. Fine to see, but it ain't going nowhere. You have to turn out good new writers." The banning of one new outstanding satirical play is more significant in the cultural

54

life of a nation, than a hundred performances of Beethoven's symphonies. After all, the classics flourished uninterruptedly (and indeed unprecedentedly), even in Nazi Germany.

The culture of the fifties had to battle the resistance of people, who knew everything better, and besides that also wielded the power. The best example was the fate of jazz, whose most extraordinary property is that it is considered subversive wherever it is played. After the Communist takeover and the acceptance of Zhdanov's canon, jazz was naturally declared to be bourgeois and decadent music. This was argued even with Langston Hughes who defended jazz during his visit to Moscow. His counter-argument: "It is my music!" (which reminds one of LeRoi Jones' reasoning), was not considered marxistically sound. How then could the Czech imitators of the Soviets ascribe any validity to the argument used by band-leader Karel Vlach, who walked out of a "model performance of Czech dance music" (with limited syncopation and predominantly in major), with the comment that if they didn't give him anything better than Stan Kenton, he would keep on playing Stan Kenton. As a punitive measure he was forced to leave the theatre where his band had an engagement, and perform in a circus.

During the first years jazz survived only in dixieland form. An important and influencial communist stage director, E. F. Burian, (in his younger days a jazz singer and theoretician) liked it, and a few enthusiasts headed by the apostolic personality of Emanuel Ugge succeeded in persuading the suspicious officials that dixieland is really folklore, which cannot be decadent. Its limited practice was permitted, together with Polynesian music and the Society of Medieval Instrument Players, with the provision that each performance of bands such as The Czechoslovak Washboard Beaters would be preceded by a scholarly lecture on the subject of the class roots of dixieland among the impoverished New Orleans creoles. And so dixieland somehow survived.

Swing had a much harder time. When, during a concert at the Prague "Lucerna" Hall, the naive queen of Czech swing, Inka Zemankova, (after a five year absence during which she studied singing techniques) permitted herself a little scat, she was not allowed to return on stage after the intermission. She disappeared for fifteen years into obscure provincial nightclubs and more liberal Poland. The reverence for the securely dead classics affected even the work of the Czech pioneer of jazz, Jaroslav Jezek*. It led to the founding of what was probably the only orchestra in the history of jazz founded by bureaucrats and not by enthusiasts. Karel Vlach played new arrangements of Jezek's old compositions and swung. The bureaucratic orchestra was strictly ordered to obey Jezek's classical heritage. That is, it was supposed to play his songs in their original arrangements, the way they sounded on the old records. Jezek wrote his arrangements in the early thirties, before the swing era. In the 1950's, after the war-time swing craze, which deeply affected the generation of young musicians, the imitation of the thirties sounded ludicrously anachronistic. Wild opinions were ventured: some glum theoreticians decided that the use of mutes in brass instruments was decadent because it perversely deformed their healthy timbre. According to others, the hybrid sound of the saxophone was a typical product of the decayed bourgeoisie, and they recommended that it be replaced in the dance orchestras by cellos. So, for a while, the bureaucratic band tried to harmonize the fortissimo of the unmuted trombones with the intimate whisper of cellos; it didn't last very long since nobody, including the musicians, was interested.

Jazz is an exemplary *pars pro toto;* similar grotesque trends were (officially) perpetrated in all areas of art. In the creative arts this trend culminated in the well-known sculpture of Stalin, which is said to have been born under the strangest circumstances. The creator, a young sculptor, relied on not winning the closed competition and submitted a slap-dash proposal. The more distinguished artists, however, made even worse proposals, and the young man was awarded the prize. When he saw the completed sculpture, towering over Prague like King Kong, he committed suicide. All of this might be a typical Prague underground story—except for the suicide. Proposals were made for ballet performances in which the Generalissimo would celebrate himself in pirouettes, but fortunately were never realized. Composers of classical music wrote symphonies which were indistinguishable from the works of Bedrich Smetana (*The Bartered Bride,* etc.); nobody imitated Anton Dvorak (*New World Symphony,* etc.), because he was disliked by the ancient Minister of Culture, Professor Zdenek Nejedly. Dvorak supposedly did not allow Nejedly to marry his daughter, who preferred the composer, Josef Suk. This might have been another story from the

*Jaroslav Jezek died in the United States during the war.

56

Czech underground, if it were not true that Nejedly did indeed dislike Dvorak pathologically.

Beneath all of this the creative souls of the country industriously corroded the absurd foundations. Without government support and against the wishes of the bureaucrats, the important movement of the small theatres emerged. Among the founders of the movement was the mime, Ladislav Fialka, who abandoned a lucrative engagement in order to perform pantomime, which at that time was also suspected of formalism; others included the absurdist writer and actor, Ivan Vyskocil, the dramatist, Vaclav Havel, and above all the duo of Jiri Suchy and Jiri Slitr, whose songs helped to form the emotional world of the young generation of the 1960's in a truly revolutionary fashion. Their revolution—perhaps for the first time in history—lay in the separation of their songs from any political involvement. It was a natural reaction to the compulsory political awareness, which was so brutally demanded by the bureaucrats.

Underground literature also flourished. Stories by Bohumil Hrabal (author of the novel *Closely Watched Trains,* which Menzel later made into a movie), by the avant garde Vera Linhartova, and others, were read at private and semi-private gatherings. The first abstract painters crawled slowly out of their cellar studios. Once in a while they exhibited, and then quickly disappeared back into the cellars after the angry explosions of Novotny's guards in the press and radio. Typed anthologies were put out by the underground surrealistic group of Vratislav Effenberger which existed throughout the period.

The Stalinists were, however, slowly recuperating from the blows inflicted by Khrushchov, and planned a counter-attack. Events ripened in 1958. The counter-attack was prepared, and the forces waited for the proper pretext, a truly exemplary case. In a closed competition two submissions reached the final round: my novel *The Cowards,* and a parcel of films by the first critical wave. *The Cowards* fell under the well organized attack of a battery of cultural officials in January of 1959, and the films were crushed a month later at the film conference in Banska Bystrica.

*The Cowards** and the defeated films had to compete for the unwanted prize with other works. Karel Ptacnik had published earlier a novel, *The Town on the Border* (1956), which was also con-

*An English translation of *The Cowards* was published by Grove Press in the United States in 1970, and simultaneously in London by Gollancz.

sidered for the prize. It described the deportation of German settlers from the Sudeten region to West Germany, and the simultaneous influx of a mixture of idealists and carpet-baggers into the region and the Party, accompanied by the rise of careerists in the Party hierarchy. The book contained all kinds of murders of Czechs by Germans and vice versa, with the score in favour of the Czechs (there were more murdered Germans than Czechs). Ptacnik supposedly refused to correct the score to at least half and half, and thus became a serious candidate for liquidation. Since Ptacnik had already received the State Prize for his first novel, and was a Party member, the committee selected a beginner who had, among other things, translated from English an ideologically unbalanced satire, *Fahrenheit 451* by Ray Bradbury. And so it exploded. For two whole weeks, day after day, I was pummelled by a succession of reviewers; some indicated sinister connections with Tito's Yugoslavia, and Radio Free Europe. One day the President himself spoke about me at a private meeting of Party Secretaries. While the speech was still in progress one friendly lady official phoned my mother-in-law, who immediately rushed to my apartment (a one-room sublet with the landlady occupying the kitchen—a typical dwelling for a young married couple) to at least salvage the savings-books. My mother-in-law was a simple woman who went through the hard school of the Great Depression, the poverty during the Occupation when the Nazis jailed her husband, and the poverty after the People's Takeover when her son was given a ten-year sentence for helping a boy-scout friend of his across the border, and her husband, after getting out of jail, defected to the U.S.A. where he lived on welfare.

In the end her precaution proved unnecessary. I was only fired from the position of editor of a literary magazine. Along with me went the director, the editor-in-chief and a few other editors of the publishing house which published my book, as well as Jiri Lederer, a reviewer for an evening paper, who dared to support my book in a short review.

In February they attacked the film-makers.

As with *The Cowards,* the final film nomination was preceded by some cunning reasoning. Helge's *School of Fathers* was eliminated because like Ptacnik's book it held the State Prize. (*The Great Seclusion* had not yet been completed.) The choice fell on Jasny: he

58

came in handy, since *Desire* could be attacked for its decadent formalism, which was more reasonable to attack than social criticism in a country whose regime was, after all, the product of the greatest socially-critical movement in history. However, in November of 1958, Novotny's henchman, Jiri Hendrych, previewed the first print of *The Third Wish,* and the strategic plans were immediately revamped. It was decided to carry out the campaign as a "battle against the remnants of bourgeois thought". This had an interesting consequence: it was logical to accuse of such a sin people who remembered the bourgeois society, such as Kadar (then 31 years old), Klos (39), and particularly Vaclav Krska (49 years) for *Hic Sunt Leones.* It did not make such sense to accuse the 24-year-old Jasny. Besides, both leads in *The Third Wish* were played by Yugoslavian actors. This was an expression of ancient, pre-Tito, sympathies towards the southern Slavs, traditionally held by the Czechs, and facilitated by Khrushchov's rapprochement. Meanwhile Khrushchov's relations with Tito cooled, and the whole thing could now be interpreted as an expression of the influence of Yugoslavian revisionism. As strange as this reasoning may sound, it pales in view of a performance given by another maniac, who attacked *Hic Sunt Leones* on the grounds that the actor Karel Hoger playing the part of a frustrated engineer performed his part too well, thus gaining sympathies for the not quite unequivocally positive character.

The main speeches of the Conference were delivered by the Minister of Culture, Vaclav Kahuda, and the film "theoretician", Jan Kliment, invited to provide theoretico-aesthetical justification to Jiri Hendrych's strict commands. It will be useful to remember Kliment's name, since it emerges in similar roles several times throughout the next decade. Kahuda used the generally accepted scheme, and first brought out the "successes", before passing on to the mistakes and insufficiencies. The successes were unquestionably present though Kahuda of course spoke only about the harmless ones: Zeman's *An Invention for Destruction* (1957), a charming work made through a sophistication of Melies' style, which received the Grand Prix at Brussels' Expo 1958; Weiss' *Wolf Trap* (1957), a psychological drama based on Jarmila Glazarova's pre-war novel was awarded the FIPRESCI prize at the Venice Festival of 1958. But the Minister was more interested in the mistakes, which he saw mainly from a

The beautiful Madla Drahokoupilova in Vaclav Gajer's Flirting with Miss Siberstein *(1969). With this story of a modern Antigone based on my novel* The Lion Cub *I said goodbye to Czech film.*

sociological point of view. First he accused unnamed directors (it might have been Brynych for *The Local Romance,* 1958, or Vaclav Gajer for *The Guilt of Vladimir Olmer**, 1956), of limiting their contemporary films "to themes taken almost exclusively from private life" (the Minister did not ask why this was the case) and of using "stories which are not exactly optimistic. It would be an interesting and simple statistical account," he added further, "which would show how many films find their contemporary setting exclusively among old decrepit tenements, where life goes on in corridors and dirty flats." In the portrayal of that milieu the Minister recognized the definite influence of Italian neo-realism. It did not occur to him that it also might have been the influence of Czech

---

*I said my involuntary good-bye to Czech movies with a film directed by this director of the now middle-aged generation. It was *Flirting with Miss Silberstein,* made in 1969-70 and based on my novel *The Lion Cub,* to be published in English by Grove Press. The freudian girl-of-everybody's (or mine, at any rate) dreams was played very convincingly by Madla Drahokoupilova.

reality, one of whose main features at that time was a hopeless housing crisis.*

Kahuda was followed to the lectern by Jan Kliment who delivered an exemplary speech. He simply read the socialist-realistic formula (positive hero, optimism in every situation, and joyful discipline, instead of independent thought), applied it to the films selected for condemnation, and found them to be, let us say, unsatisfactory.

The third speaker, Stanislav Zvonicek, then tried to combine serious aesthetic thought with the demands of the Cultural Secretariat, but since no one has ever been able to square a circle,† he became

---

* This was captured very realistically in *The Third Wish,* where the family shares a one-bedroom apartment in the following fashion: Grandpa and Grandma live in the kitchen, Mom and Dad in the living room, and the Granddaughter in the bedroom. Housing projets were practically non-existent, the allocation of apartments was riddled with corruption, and only too frequently did the young couples' only hope of getting their own apartment rest in the early departure of the grandparents. When I began writing detective stories, and carried out some criminological research, I discovered several cases where children speeded up their parents' exit to the eternal resting grounds.

† Zvonicek tried to square the circle again in 1970, in a booklet entitled *Czechoslovak Film 1945-1970.* There are two interesting passages in this mellowing transcript of the rough stalinist clichés of the Soviet *White Book on Counterrevolution in Czechoslovakia* into a quasi-serious politico-esthetical evaluation. One deals with Schorm's *Courage for Every Day* (see page 143) and Zvonicek bases his arguments on a real gem of establishment philosophy: "The objective truth...is but one..." but "a ruthless truth, if said at an improper time, in an improper place and in an improper manner can betray its objective . . . " and so "the screenwriter and the director found themselves in the situation of their hero who tries to alarm in vain the people in the tavern . . . . Not even half a million of cinema-goers went to see their film." To my mind, this very fact shows how exact were the observations of Schorm and Masa. And as for the appropriateness of time, place and manner, however interestingly aristotelian this may sound—who was to decide what was appropriate in the arts at that time in Czechoslovakia? Novotny? Would there ever have been, for instance, the excellent Forman whom Mr. Zvonicek (and after the triumph of *Taking Off* at Cannes in 1971 also Mr. Kliment) cautiously praises, had Novotny's Cultural Department been in full control of what was, and what was not, proper at Barrandov in the early sixties?
    The second interesting passage (a little contradictory to the one mentioned above) is from the Preface where Mr. Zvonicek, with a symptomatic air of exhausted resignation, expresses his doubts as to whether there is "anything objective in the world in general, and in the world of art in particular". I am glad he has his doubts because this, to a certain extent, exonerates my book from the sin of subjectivism. However, if this is so—and perhaps Mr. Zvonicek has come to his sad conclusion after reading Lenin's definition of the "objective truth" in *Materialism and empiriocriticism*—is it not a strong argument for artistic freedom which alone guarantees that ideas freely enter the dialectics and artistic revolutions are real revolutions, not pogroms on the artists?
    As for Mr. Vrba: this excellent translator of, among many others, Geoffrey Chaucer and Ernest Hemingway and one-time film critic of the Literarni Listy, was—according to underground sources in Prague—sentenced to four years in jail, in the spring of 1971.

confused. One of the attacked critics, Frantisek Vrba, pointed out the injustice of being chastised for a positive review of *Hic Sunt Leones,* while Zvonicek went unpunished, despite writing an equally positive review of the same film in the Party newspaper *Rude Pravo.* The confused Zvonicek told him to read the review more carefully. Vrba didn't bother, but Jiri Hendrych did, and shortly after the conference Stanislav Zvonicek's association with *Rude Pravo* ended.

Despite all of this, one important reality came out at the conference: Khrushchov had deprived the militant Stalinists of the most potent arguments which could have transposed the aesthetic controversy to the level of treason and counter-revolution. No one was accused of intentional enmity, or of plotting schemes injurious to socialism; the Jews, Kadar and Jasny, were not accused of a Zionist plot, and even the well-worn CIA failed to get into the speeches. Everything was reduced to the remnants of bourgeois thought, represented by Yugoslavian revisionism, and influenced by Italian neo-realism. Even so, the campaign shook many of the Communists; it consciously attacked the old stereotypes formed during the period of socialist realism and based on the conditioned reflex of guilt. When a conditioned artist arrived at a dilemma between the official truth as it was proclaimed by the Cultural Secretariat, and the concrete truth as he experienced it in everyday life, he began to doubt not the proclaimed truth but his own progressiveness. "Do I have enough class-consciousness? " he would ask himself according to the account of one of the film critics, Jaroslav Bocek. "Are not my doubts just the remnants of intellectualization, or some other individualistic anachronism, which I must negate? "

Naturally these disrupted souls were for several years incapable of further struggle; "they turned into walking complexes, into anything other than crystalized characters" (Helge). The fight was continued by others—and the fact that members of the New Wave did not suffer from these feelings of metaphysical guilt was one of the main reasons for the surprising freshness with which the New Wave arrived on the scene, traditionally overburdened by such complexes. For the New Wave, socialism was not something new and desperately fought for. It was not the great divide of their lives, but rather the *status quo;* they saw no reason for calling rot "insufficiency", a gangster "an atypical exception", and incompetence "developmental difficulties", nor why they should

An Invention for Destruction — *a charming work made through a sophistication of Méliés.*

repent for liking beautiful things (including naked girls) because they are "only" beautiful. Unlike the film makers of the Ur-Wave, few of the New Wave were Party members. Of the thirteen leading representatives of the group only four belonged to the Party, and of the leaders (Forman, Passer, Schorm, Chytilova, Nemec, Menzel, Krumbachova) none were Communists. This had a greater importance than is generally admitted. It does not mean that these young men and women were not socialists. They were socialists without complexes. The Fathers of the Revolution are members of strict brotherhoods, bound by the inhibitions of their beliefs for which some of them died—ironically, in greater numbers after the revolution than before it. The Sons of the Revolution are protestants who want to marry life.*

In Banska Bystica social criticism was no longer considered treason, but the penalties were nevertheless hard. The manufacture of further copies of *The Third Wish* was stopped, and it was prohibited to show the film to anyone; consequently most of the delegates never actually saw the work—still they rejected it. The censorship banned any mention of the film in the media, and removed it from the list of Barrandov productions for 1958—even today, it is missing from the statistics. Kadar and Klos were not allowed to direct for two years, and Blazek was fired from his

*Similar phenomena are evident in other areas. The tone of renaissance is given by non-Communists, and surprisingly frequently by Catholics. For instance, in prose, Hrabal, Linhartova, Paral, Fuks, Vyskocil; in poetry, Holub, Zabrana, and Holan; in drama, Havel, Topol and Smocek; in the area of musicals and pop-music, Suchy and Slitr, and of course a slew of rock composers, musicians and singers.

position as a Barrandov screenplay writer. * The production unit responsible for the banned film was dissolved, and the General Director of the Studios, Jiri Marek, was replaced by Alois Polednak.* The film *Hic Sunt Leones* was immediately recalled from distribution. *September Nights* and the *School of Fathers* were also carefully manoeuvered out of the cinemas. The distribution of *The Star Goes South* was also stopped. (This was a rather unimportant musical comedy, but it was shot in Yugoslavia.) The new management of the Barrandov studios upheld the decision made earlier by the fired director, Jiri Marek, not to show the comedy *The End of the Clairvoyant* made by Svitacek and Rohac, who had once assisted Alfred Radok.

This typical product of Czech humour follows the tradition which began in the olden days with the bark-scarab and washroom attendant dramas, continued in the sixties through some of the thesis films produced by the directors of the New Wave (for instance, Schmidt—Juracek: *Black and White Sylva*), and led to comedies such as Rychman's *Six Black Girls* (1969). Unlike those rather unsuccessful movies *The Clairvoyant* was one of the funniest things ever made in Czech cinema. It ruined the careers of Svitacek and Rohac so severely, that they did not manage to direct another film until 1965 when they made the musical *If a Thousand Clarinets*. Svitacek remained faithful to the genre of the medium length farce.

* He was re-hired soon after.

† The end—let us hope not the definite end—of this administrator of orders is particularly bitter. He hesitantly permitted the realization of the films of the New Wave. For this hesitation he was almost liquidated by the radicals during Dubcek's era, and survived only due to the interventions of people like Vratislav Blazek. After the invasion, he permitted (whether explicitly or quietly I don't know) the use of Barrandov Film laboratories for the development of footage shot by Czech cameramen during the days of the tanks. He was arrested in September of 1970 for "anti-socialist activities" and held in jail without trial until the summer of 1971. In June 1971, at the Cannes Film Festival, a group of internationally known film-makers drafted and signed a petition urging the Czechoslovak government to release the man who "has helped greatly in the development of the most brilliant generation of directors". Among those who signed were Dalton Trumbo, Luchino Visconti, Joseph Losey, Nagisa Oshima, Dusan Makavejev, Louis Malle and others. Nevertheless, in July 1971, Mr. Polednak, along with five other defendants, was sentenced to two years in jail; some of the co-defendants, for whom no international petitions had been signed, got twelve years. His crime: "endangering state secrets". The nature of the "endangering"—at least in the reports I saw—was not specified. Prague underground has it that Mr. Polednak endangered those secrets by being intelligent enough to remember them—most of the others who are in the know lack such a memory and present therefore no security risk. According to Radio Yerevan (see note to page 252) the mysterious crime of the Barrandov director is strongly reminiscent of the Pentagon Papers Affair: he sold the figures of attendance at Soviet films in Czechoslovakia to the "Tirana Times".

He successfully returned to it in 1969 with a "schizophrenic metaphore", *In the Train,* about a phenomenon called double-think. Miroslav Hornicek, the author of the ancient satirical *magnum opus* about the supervisor of the public toilets, plays a double part of a schizoid passenger. The film is, according to reports from Czechoslovakia, a worthy continuation of the spirit of *The End of the Clairvoyant.* According to the same reports, the new feature film by Svitacek's co-director Jano Rohac, *The Long White Road,*—his first since *If a Thousand Clarinets*—is also a worthy continuation of the *Clairvoyant*: it was finished and held up in the spring of 1971.

Any normally thinking mind would have seen *The End of the Clairvoyant* as a satire against the declining morale of the nationalized tradesmen. The Novotny clan interpreted it as an attack on the very foundations of nationalization. They used an old Stalinist trick based on the theoretically insufficiently defined distinction between so-called "constructive" and "destructive" criticism.* The hero of the movie owns a clairvoyant business: everything in the store is flawlessly elegant, the service is personalized and excellent, including oriental incense, mysterious dim lighting, and the clairvoyant's exquisite costume. Every customer receives a prediction of happiness, health and success. Then comes February of 1948, and the clairvoyant business is nationalized. The clairvoyant takes off the costume of the Indian magus, and works in a crumpled corduroy suit; the service is suddenly sloppy; the customers have to stand in line and after filling out a number of idiotic questionaires, are treated to a group prophecy. The predictions are now very brief and frequently pessimistic. However, after working hours, the Prophet hurries home, puts on his oriental robe and lights the incense. Then he receives private customers, who once again get first class private service, including the happiest predictions.

*In practice the difference is simple: constructive criticism deals with insignificant things related to the population as a whole rather than to the people's representatives. It attacks absenteeism, the malfunctioning of public services, or, at best, it might ridicule a self-important lower official, obsessed with his miniscule powers. On the other hand, to criticise anything significant is destructive. Some of the tabus were, for instance, the mess in the nation's economy, erroneous party resolutions, etc. It may also be expressed as criticism *en détail* as opposed to criticism *en gros.* Constructive criticism is however susceptible to a certain danger. It might be "en detail" and affect "insignificant things", as is certainly the case with the decline of the morale in the nationalized small businesses. If however it passes the level of the so-called "communal", that is artistically irrelevant, weak satire, and moves into the realm of art, which means that it acquires a somewhat more general or metaphorical significance, it might easily turn into "destructive" criticism. Such was exactly the case in *The End of the Clairvoyant.*

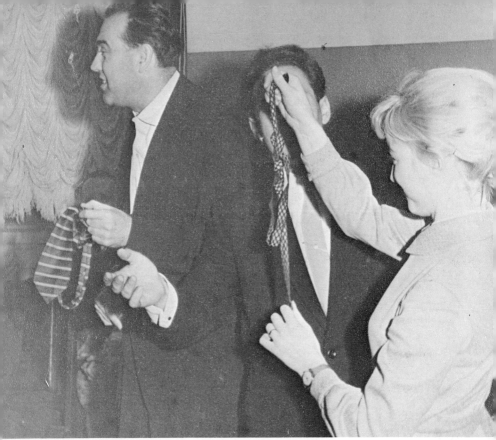

Vladimir Svitacek (End of a Clairvoyant) *starts a game of strip-poker in the Leningrad underground. He never told me how the game ended; possibly because the blond on the right is my wife.*

In one of the scenes the bored nationalized soothsayer looks out of the window, then he quickly reaches into a drawer for a pair of binoculars and stares through them at the terrace of the house across the street. There, basking in the sun, lies a beautiful girl in a tiny bikini (which may well have contributed to the banning of the film). It was as if the soothsayer had looked into the future. The girl was played by a student of the Film Academy, Vera Chytilova.

The School of Milos Forman

In the beginning was a black anecdote, which no one made up. In a small town in Eastern Bohemia, the Gestapo arrested a member of an anti-Nazi underground organization. He wasn't a professional conspirator, just an ordinary villager, who considered it his duty to do something against modern bestiality. After the Gestapo gave him a few good lectures on modern bestiality, he came up with what he thought to be a clever idea. The interrogators wanted to know the name of his contact in the underground network, and so he told them; however, the man he named had nothing to do with the organization. The villager acted according to his pre-Nazi ideas about the police. He assumed that a person who knows nothing can disclose nothing, and that the Gestapo will let him go because he will prove to be useless. The Gestapo did indeed arrest the unsuspecting and totally innocent victim. He was a Mr. Forman.

He did not disclose anything, but they did not let him go. In addition some racial flaws were discovered in the family, and so they arrested his wife as well. The man later died in Buchenwald, the wife in Auschwitz and their eight-year-old son Milos was cared for by a succession of kind uncles; one of them was a Mr. Svab in the Eastern Bohemian town of Nachod.

This uncle was a rather obese, middle-aged gentleman, who owned a grocery store, and as a hobby practised mountain climbing on the nearby sandstone rocks. I was a member of the same mountain-climbing club—not so much for the love of the sport, as for the love of a pretty mountain-climber— and I often stopped by the good uncle's store. A little black-haired boy used to sit on the barrels of sauerkraut (a terrible rogue according to his uncle) and watch the customers intently. I didn't pay much attention to him, and later I forgot him altogether. Years later, when Socialism came to Nachod, the good uncle abandoned his easy life and his mountain-climbing and, at a rather advanced age, became a miner. It was hard on him, but it helped his pretty daughter to a metamorphosis from a bourgeois progeny to a miner's girl, and eventually enabled her to study at the Dramatic Conservatory. The little boy, who used to sit on the barrels of sauerkraut, meanwhile studied script-writing at the Prague Film Academy.

67

Milos Forman

Nachod, my native town, where the kind Mr. sheltered the young Milos.

Sometimes I feel that this original black anecdote embodies all of Forman, his poetry and his philosophy. It contains the cruelty which so enraged some West German critics when they saw *The Firemen's Ball.* It expresses the melancholic loneliness of a small boy surrounded by the dreary world of a grocery store. It incorporates in a nutshell the old story of the cruel clash of youth with the adult world—one which Forman, luckily for the cinematographic art, will probably never be able to get rid of. "The critics expect," he said during the shooting of *The Firemen's Ball,* "that a new work is totally new. That's impossible. Throughout his life a man retells the same story over and over again."

When a man begins his life the way Forman did then it might really be impossible. Too many members of his generation entered the world the way he did, whether they lived in that particular corner of the world or elsewhere. The formanesque story cannot lose its actuality because the world takes care to carefully and constantly update it.

I had long forgotten the little boy from the shadow of the sauerkraut barrels and was working on my own loves. I was of the generation obsessed with film and jazz. Every day I went to the movies (my father was the director of one of the two Nachod cinemas, and I was admitted free, even to the competitor's

68

"I opened the door, and there stood the most famous Czech star, Jana Brejchova, smiling at me . . . . . I was completely overawed . . . ."

house). Every day I listened to the big swing band of Miloslav Zachoval in Cafe Port Artur, or blew the tenor saxophone in a student band called *Red Music,* (which got its name through misinterpretation of the name *Blue Music,* at that time an important professional swing group). The country was ruled by the Nazis, and the beautiful melancholic music— swing— connected us with that distant world of freedom and beauty, where fifteen-year-old Judy Garland sang in movies we were not allowed to see.

Nachod, with its student jazzbands and mountain-climbers, its timid young men and its well brought up young girls wary of their virginity became the subject of my first novel, whose catastrophic fate is described in the previous chapter. Another of the victims of that explosion was the then recently published first *Almanac of Jazz and Dance Music,* which carried my story *A Word I Shall Not Withdraw,* later published under the name of *Eine Kleine Jazzmusic.* The story originated alongside the novel: ideologically a completely innocent tragicomical tale about a student band which in spite of the Nazis gives a swing concert in a small town. The not quite Aryan trumpet player pays for that provocation with his life. By that time, however, it was my excommunicated name that forced the decision, and not the contents of my writing. *The Jazz Almanac* went into the shredder; a malicious printer saved a few copies, which then circulated through the Prague underground. And so one day someone rang

the bell; I opened the door, and there stood the most famous
Czech star, Jana Brejchova, smiling at me. I have preserved from
the earliest age an unweakened adoration of beautiful women;
and as I was—for better or for worse—reared by Hollywood
and the cult of stars, a beautiful woman who acts in movies will
turn me, despite all my life experiences, into a stuttering idiot. I
was completely overawed by Jana, and it took me a while to
realize that the black-haired fellow accompanying her was
talking to me. "...guess you don't remember me. I would really
like to make a movie of *The Cowards*. But as it is right now impossible, I would at least like to write a script of *A Word I Shall
Not Withdraw,* if you would allow me to do that."

What a question! The husband of that beautiful star I would
allow anything. His name was Milos and he was the now grown-
up little boy from the shadows of the sauerkraut barrels. At that
time he had already had some kind of a film career but his
greatest success was Jana. He graduated in 1955 from the script-
writing department of the Film Academy, but his ambitions and
interest lay higher than to be a supplier of raw products, which
film scripts certainly are. Not that he would not have wanted to
write—he did. He was one of the young men who made
pilgrimages to the small house on the Prague island of Kampa
where, on the second floor, Jan Werich chaired meetings of artists and where, on the first floor, lived in self-imposed seclusion
(as a protest against what was happening in the world) the great
modern Christian poet Vladimir Holan. At that time Milos
wrote poetry, and he scintillated with ideas for scripts—but he
wanted to shoot them himself.

His school certificate did not entitle him to do so, and he
became an assistant to Alfred Radok (in *Grandpa Motorcar*
he even played a small part) and took part in the experiment of
Laterna Magica. However, his obsession with art was the only
thing he had in common with the expressionistic and technically
daring wizard of effects, Radok. Milos saw the world differently.
Radok's explosive personality was certainly a good school, but it
prevented the full expression of another remarkable personality
at the same time. Therefore, the real Forman appeared for the
first time alongside another, much lesser director, in a film of
much smaller acclaim than the spectacular Laterna Magica. The
director's name was Ivo Novak, and the film was called *Puppies.*

70

It was a gentle and humorous story of young people, offering here and there a few glimpses into the real life of young people. After years of socialist-realistic fairy-tales this was a complete novelty, and the critics predicted a great future for Ivo Novak. He inexplicably failed and never became more than an average director. Nothing in his second film, *The Main Prize* (1958), resembled *The Puppies.* Whereas in the first film one could feel the touch of real life, the second one simply displayed the well-worn formula of the situation comedy in which a pauper wins the grand prize in a lottery. While in the first film Jana Brejchova practically forgot that she was an actress, in the second one the actors just performed the prescribed motions of well rehearsed puppets. The difference was incredible.

It isn't any longer. One of the old nuisances of film-making is that the result of what is basically a collective effort is credited wholly to the director. Very few people noted at that time that the theme of *The Puppies* was conceived by one Milos Forman, who also co-operated on the script and worked as an assistant director. His greatest achievement in the film was the seventeen-year-old heroine, whom he later successfully lassoed and led to the altar, at a time when she was already receiving more than 500 letters monthly from admirers, some from as far away as Mao's China.

This greatest star of post-war Czech film lived in lodgings, and after the wedding she moved into Milos' apartment. It was a single room divided by a locked door from some kind of an office. During silent moments spent over the drafts of the script for *Eine Kleine Jazzmusik,* we used to hear voices negotiating the debiting per contra of lumber. Instead of a bed, the room had a low home-made nest consisting of blankets and pillows, from which protruded the head of the greatest Czech film star sleeping after a night of shooting. Around noon the film star tumbled out of her boudoir and, while I discreetly turned away, retired in her pajamas to the bathroom. They shared it with the clerks who negotiated on the other side of the door. The bathroom door was secured by a rather flimsy latch. After the star had returned and dressed behind a screen, she would cook something on a gas stove. Sometimes it was even edible. At times, when she wasn't shooting, she had to go and type in the Studio offices.

And so we sat there in the room with a view at the Vltava

river, contriving a story on a nowadays world-acclaimed for-manesque theme about young people, who even during the most difficult times thought mainly about jazz and pretty girls, and mercilessly (and in our story tragically) clashed with those insisting that young people have mainly other things in mind. The script contained a number of typical Forman scenes; such as an argument between the young hero of the movie and his father about whether it is possible to fight the Nazis with songs; or a ruse which helps two members of the jazz band escape from a precarious situation in the German barracks. The two get away through the showers, where a German company is just taking a bath. The clever disguise which the two assumed—they strip-ped—rendered them indistinguishable from the members of the superior race. In those magical days when we were enchanted by our own fantasies, Milos dreamt that we could play the parts of the two youngsters ourselves. If it were not for what happened later, we would have probably been the world's first male nudies (at that point we still had the figures to do it) and Czech film would have had another first. It didn't happen because the Great Assembly of Dramaturgists did not rejoice over our script.

This Assembly was a body of monstrous proportions, and its unmanageable size prevented it from passing anything smaller than the proverbial telephone poles which, according to a well known Moscow underground joke, are in fact well-edited trees. Once the august body spent four hours pondering a single sentence in a certain script. In it a policeman, who had just participated in a bloody suppression of a strike, walks over to a fence and urinates. Questionable was the urination: doubts arose as to whether this aesthetic element should be considered an acceptable functional expression of the policeman's loathsomeness or if it wasn't after all overly naturalistic. The second opinion prevailed, the authoress was summoned and advised to substitute the abominably urinating cop with something more appropriate, for instance a drunken priest. But in the end the cop remained in the film. It appeared that the typist had made an error, and the sentence should have read: the policeman walks over to the fence and stands silent (in Czech *mlci*—he is silent; *moci*—he urinates).

To this Assembly we submitted our musical comedy from the Protectorate *The Band Won,* to which we added the epithet *antifascist* (in accordance with the better judgment of cleverer

72

friends). It helped nothing. The script came back with a fascicle of comments, and I felt like a character from a Hollywood muck-raking novel. Being young, inexperienced and helpless, we began to comply with the suggestions. We re-wrote the script and submitted a new version. Back it came. And so like a boomerang it travelled between the Assembly and ourselves, until the jazz band was replaced by a symphony orchestra, then a brass band, and finally disappeared altogether. Instead of Forman's humourous scenes, the work now boasted some classical pictures of the plentiful problems of workers' sabotage in Nazi factories—though, as I recall, even those were not strictly classical (like the one with the workers, resembling a gigantic centipede, who carried a just completed body of a bomber to the railway station, but the fuselage would not pass through the local Arc de Triomphe, erected in honour of the Fuhrer). Well, it was after the conference in Banska Bystrica.

At approximately that stage of development came a sudden reversal. One of the members of the Assembly, who seldom attended the numerous meetings and was therefore quite uninformed, demurred at the following puzzle: why is the script called *The Band Won* if there is no trace of a band in it, and why does the subtitle read *antifascist musical comedy,* when it is clearly a tragedy?

We naturally acknowledged the comment and the scenario once again turned into a boomerang. This time we cunningly skipped the brass band, and returned the symphony, which we quickly transformed into a jazzband. Then we cut the majestic sabotage scenes, justifying this by their exorbitant cost. Instead, we smuggled back the naked shower scene, this time however with the German soldiers wearing towels around their waists. I don't know whether this is a custom in any army, but it was in our script.

So, with the help of the Assembly, we managed to return the script to something like its original form. The world around us was also experiencing various changes; the counter-attack of the stalinist guard began to falter due to the breakdown in hinterland operations, and it slowly turned into a retreat. The whole campaign resembled the Ardennes operation. Two short years after the first submission of the script and with the most persistent commentators being happily absent, the Assembly finally okayed the film. I remember that evening as if it were yesterday. We were walking down the illuminated Wenceslas Square and could not believe reality.

Well, we didn't have to believe it for long. Someone hurried—undoubtedly with the best intentions—to Radio Prague, and the evening news reported: "The latest from Barrandov! A new film in the making: a musical comedy about a student band from the Protectorate based on a work by Josef Skvorecky." Damn it, I said to myself. They didn't really have to...so soon...and on the radio...

Sure enough—first thing in the morning the phone rang, "For Christ sake, come immediately to the Studios." And that's where I was given the good news. President Novotny, my old friend and critic, had listened to the radio that evening and was very angry. It did not even occur to him that a musical comedy from the time of the Protectorate could be something other than *The Cowards*. Neither Milos, nor myself, nor the dramaturgists of the production group were able to explain to anybody that the work in question was the innocent *Eine Kleine Jazzmusik*. When Milos fought his way to some highly placed party officials and finally managed to persuade them, it was too late. To explain the problem to the President was, at that time, still a feat belonging to the category of tight-rope walking without a safety net. Nobody found the courage. And so I returned to the translation of American literature (the mark of Cain still prevented me from attempting to publish further artifacts of my own), and Milos...

That was in 1961. Laterna Magica was affected by interventions from above and Milos, together with Jano Rohac *(End of the Clairvoyant),* lived off writing burlesque sketches under an assumed name for the Prague Alhambra, which was secretly frequented by Soviet tourists, who considered it the den of depravity.* He was offered the position of an assistant director in an idealized war fable called *There, Beyond the Forest* (1962), and depressed by all the calamities (which were topped by his

*In one of the shows written by Milos, the theatre experimented with strip-tease, but after a few performances the vigilant Mr. President once again intervened, and so they returned to dancing in bikini. The Soviet tourists "officially" considered even that to be an antisocialist depravity.

74

divorce from Jana) he accepted. To gain relief from the dreariness, he would visit his friends at the Semafor theatre, frequented at that time by many others. That was where he got an idea. "Suchy and Slitr, and all of us," he said in a subsequent interview, "admired Voskovec and Werich; but their early beginnings, particularly the legendary *Vest Pocket Revue* from 1927 we knew only from hearsay. It suffered the fate of all famous theatrical production—it disappeared into oblivion, changed into a legend, and no-one will ever know what it really looked like. I used to say to myself that Voskovec and Werich would have been happy to have their *Vest Pocket Revue* on film." So he went and, with the money made from the obscene burlesques, he bought a 16mm camera; then he approached Suchy and Slitr with an offer to make a documentary about the Semafor.

It happened. Semafor announced sham auditions for a female singer and crowds of unsuspecting misses flocked to be captured on the malicious sixteen. When the first few hundred yards of rushes of this privately made film were developed and projected, the screen revealed a documentary hitherto unequalled in Czechoslovakian cinema. It was a cruel record of embarrassing female self-love, conceit and dreams of fame. The machine—camera—revealed the grotesqueness of a life that has illusions of its own beauty. It functioned in this instance as Leo Tolstoy's famous eye, watching the performance of an opera, not in the context of the fictional action, but as an action of its own. It revealed the ordinary and banal. Later, when *The Audition* was shown to the public, same of the critics commented on the film's cruelty. Milos later wrote, "the cruelty which glares at you from the screen is present in the very nature of the audition... to film an audition and deprive it of that cruelty, would mean depriving it of its essence. The essence of the audition is still not the real battle. It is merely the induction procedure. And I know nothing crueller and more embarrassing then the induction procedure...even the greatest future hero goes through it naked like all the others."

Cruelty mercilessly joined with the grotesque. How can one avoid remembering the man whom the Gestapo first mistakenly arrested, and then, to make sure, beat him to death.

The private producer, Forman, showed the first rushes to the representative of the government studios, Vladimir Bor, who had earlier kindly but unsuccessfully defended *Eine Kleine Jazzmusik,* and was finally overruled by the President. It was a happy choice because Vladimir Bor, who was one of the founders of the *recese* movement*, had throughout the difficult times a feeling for things defying any norm. When he saw Milos' rushes, he immediately bought them with government money, had them blown up to thirty-five, and financially encouraged the director to complete the documentary short.

However, in the end, it wasn't a pure documentary: Milos is too much of a natural story-teller to be satisfied with something that does not contain at least a reflection of that oldest dynamic art form, the story. At the sham audition he noticed a dark-haired girl with a beautifully large mouth, who sang with one of the two hundred or more Prague rock groups (in English, although she didn't know the language—a practice common in such groups; he also picked an inconspicuous blond, then added to the documentary a subsequently manufactured simple plot. A department store sales-girl asks her boss for permission to leave work so that she can attend the audition. When he refuses, she skips work and goes to the audition, where she "bombs out". The dark-haired girl, toughened by the hard training given to her by the first guitar player of the amateur rock group, upon seeing the blond's failure, succumbs to an attack of self-criticism and although she is practically in front of the microphone, turns around and proudly leaves. She was one of the successes of Milos' first independent directorial endeavour. Soon after, she became his second wife and the mother of twins, Peter and

*The movement, although it was founded earlier, flourished particularly during the second world war. In its provocations it is ideologically related to dadaism, French pataphysics, surrealism and similar harassments of originally the bourgeois, later in the case of the *recesists,* the Nazis and finally all the rhinoceroses. From innocent jokes, such as all-day following of randomly selected pedestrians who eventually tried frantically to run away from the pursuers (the director Jiri Krejcik as a young man specialized in that), the recesists proceeded towards feats which are probably world records in the harassment of the mighty; sometime in 1942 two of them, with the help of home-made forged documents, penetrated into the winter recreational resort of the SS units in the Alps. They spent a week skiing with the embarrassed SS-men, pretending to be Czech employees of some secret department of special tasks. It is unnecessary to stress that they could have lost their necks. The whole story, supported by the originals of the forged documents and by documentary shots from the SS nest is contained in a book about the recesist movement, compiled by the same Vladimir Bor. Just before it was to be published in the spring of 1970, it was stopped by the Czechoslovakian censorship.

The Well-Paid Stroll: *an S + S jazz opera, later made by Forman into his only TV movie.*

Matey; she also became a successful Czech film star, with which I, if I may flatter myself, helped her a little.*

At the time when he was editing his foolish singers into one of the most fantastic sequences of Czech film, Milos brought me the manuscript of a novel written by the sculptor, Jaroslav Papousek, called *Peter and Paula*. He asked me to read it and give him my opinion, as he would like to shoot it. I read the book, and it was as Milos would have written it, if he were a writer. It resembled his style in all aspects: the hero was a grocery-store apprentice (the good uncle came to my mind), shyly in love with a high-school student. The illogical dialogues between the human pups and their inner monologues, reminded me of my own novel, *The Cowards,* from which Milos used the following sentences as an epigraph to the screen-play of *Peter and Paula:* "Suddenly it struck me that I should be thinking about Irena, if I loved her. So I started to think about her. At

*Milos brought his camera into the Semafor theatre once more in 1966 when he made a TV film based on a successful "jazz opera" called *The Well Paid Stroll,* written by Suchy and Slitr, who also starred in it.

77

Forman's greatest non-actor, Mr. Vostrcil, as Father in Peter and Paula: *a working class Czech version of Mr. Babbitt.*

first it didn't go so well, so I remembered how I recently at the pool caught a glimpse of her breasts, and all of a sudden I was doing fine."

The battle with the Barrandov dramaturgy began. The story of the grocer's apprentice contradicted everything demanded of films about the young by the socialist-realistic aesthetics. The boy got no satisfaction from his work; he was really supposed to be a kind of a watch-dog, because his job consisted mostly of preventing the customers from stealing. But when, in one of the best scenes of the film, he finally notices a shoplifting old lady, he does not find enough courage to intervene. He follows the old lady out of the store, and along the street all the way to the suburbs, where he finally lets her go. This naturally arouses the displeasure of his boss and of his father. The father's pompous preaching only further alienates the perplexing son, whom the old man tries to approach.

Once again then, the theme is the cruelty of the inconspicuous clashes between the young person and the adult world. This obsessive theme of Forman's was so powerfully expressed in the grocery attendant's drama, that one of the last remaining socialist-realistic critics, Trapl (who still dared to publicly defend the discredited canons), completely failed to see all the other, frequently very acceptable qualities of the film (e.g. Peter's friend, Cenda, a bricklayer's apprentice, likes his work very much because it makes him a real worker, not a variation of a house dick), and he condemned the film as decadent, pessimistic and reactionary. Some Soviet critics did the same. The Soviet Union is possibly the only country with a developed film industry where Forman's films were never publicly shown.

Kolin is a medieval town in Central Bohemia, famous for its brass band, founded at the end of the nineteenth entury by Frantisek Kmoch. This man was a kind of a Czech Philip Sousa; although not responsible for the deformation of the helicon into a more convoluted shape, he did compose a large number of popular marches, and when he died that band lived on, and survives to the present. The town organizes an annual brass band competition, which carries Kmoch's name. Milos's staff arrived in Kolin in the middle of one of these festivals, and the atmosphere of the brass band world enchanted them. It penetrated the definitive script of *Peter and Paula;* the conductor of the Kolin band, Mr. Vostrcil, got the part of Peter's father and another semi-documentary was made. It was called *If It Weren't for Those Bands;* later it was merged with *The Audition* and, after the premiere of *Peter and Paula* in 1963, shown as a feature film. The method was similar: into the footage of the documentary Milos edited a simple anecdote. Two friends, both of them trombone players in competing bands, have to choose between going to an important rehearsal or attending motorcycle races. The motorcycles win, and the conductors of the respective bands, after long sermons, fire both the delinquents. The only thing that really happens is that the boys switch bands. In the final scene the motorbikes are once again forgotten and the young men are happily blowing their trombones in the competing bands.

The well-known theme: the clash of the two mutually uncom-
prehending worlds of the old and the young. The well-known
method: a simple anecdote in the form of a documentary. All
received grander proportions in *Peter and Paula*. The elements
of style and method were for the first time united into a great
totality.

The danger inherent in the extraction of events from their
spacio-temporal context is generally recognized. We must first
fully understand the implications of realism, which was called
"socialist", to be able to comprehend the importance of neo-
realism and of *cinéma vérité* for the young Czech film-makers;
why it influenced them perhaps more then their Western
colleagues. It affected even Milos, but he was too much of a
story-teller to submit to the incalculable elements and the
passively registering camera. Of the *vérité* finally only the non-
actors remained in his films, and if we are to talk about direct
influences, then it might be proper to mention the almost forgotten film *Il Posto* by Ermanno Olmi, which Milos admired and
which is related to *Peter and Paula* both in motive and in feeling.
"I think we are somewhat confusing the terms," Milos wrote in
his directorial confession. "We speak of the tendency of *cinéma
vérité* as of a method: the point seems to be that the word
"vérité" means that in films lies should be challenged. This is
most important, and not the style and method. It had approximately the following development: years back they used to
say, 'That's just like in the movies' (meaning that it is unbelievable); then came, 'He filmed it' (in the sense of someone
fooling another); and now comes the third phase, when we want
the viewer to believe what he is being told from the screen."
    Evidently a rather unorthodox understanding of *cinéma vérité*,
but typical for the New Wave of Czech cinema. One of the oldest
questions is being considered here. "A writer's job is to tell the
truth," wrote Hemingway, and none will understand that
banality so well as people who, because they were denied the
freedom of artistic expression for most of their lives, do not find
it banal.

The directors of the Ur-Wave were of course also concerned
with truth. Unlike them, the New Wave soon realized that the

truth also is—and in the final analysis, is foremost—a technical problem. Naturally *what*—but from there came *how*.

Many people in Czechoslovakia thought that Forman was overcoming this fundamental problem of form through improvisation "on location". The directness of dialogues, including the fumbling search for words evident in the non-actors, would seemingly support such an assumption. In fact Milos is probably the slowest and most careful screen-play writer of all the directors. *Peter and Paula* took him a year, and the script for *Firemen's Ball* eighteen months. His first American film, *Taking Off,* took just as long. Despite that, Milos' films seemed to uphold the finding of William Faulkner: "The moving-picture work of my own which seemed best to me was done by the actors and the writer throwing the script away and inventing the scene in actual rehearsal, just before the camera turned." The reality of Milos' films is somewhere in between: "Every creative work is fundamentally an improvisation. Even when we write screen-plays we imagine every situation from all angles, we try to make up this or that...ideas come and go without any particular preconceived order, and the resulting scene is therefore the final product of the continuous improvisation of ideas. The consistent adherence to the screen-play during the shooting (if the film is to be in the style of *cinéma vérité*) is an expression of conceit on the part of the authors, who imagine that they managed to create characters with all the specifications of their personalities, character, thought, with all the unpredictable variables...However, improvisation alone is not able to make the film, it may at best improve it; therefore, it is necessary to have a script of such quality, that even if nobody manages to come up with anything else, the work will have meaning and a certain standard."

The *vérité* element in Forman's films lies predominantly in the use of non-actors. "There are basically two types of non-actors," says Milos. "Those who are only able to be themselves—for instance the Mother in *Peter and Paula*—and others who can act, but these have to be at least one degree more intelligent than the characters which they are playing. This is the case with Peter and his father...they aren't really playing themselves, they are doing a deadly straight parody. They reach a ceiling, determined by their own intelligence, while actors are able to spiritually live a role above their own ceiling.... It is very advantageous to combine a good actor—it must be a really good actor—with a non-actor. It helps both of them. On

Loves of a Blond. *I was to get the part of the soldier in the center, but Milos found me too "intelligent" for it and gave it to Vladimir Mensik.*

the one hand, (the actor) gets from the non-actors that undefinable ability to express himself without affectation. He in turn inoculates them with the very important feeling for rhythm and the expression of a point, which the professional actor possesses...the value of non-actors lies primarily in their inimitable originality. They have one other tremendous advantage: if I write a bad dialogue or a whole scene, that is if I write it naively, or even untruthfully, an actor is able to provide it with the illusion of truthfulness, and thus cover up my mistake. The better the actor, the easier it is to conceal my stupidity. In the performance of a non-actor, who remains constantly himself, my naivety protrudes like wires out of a broken umbrella. The non-actor is a kind of seismograph. Every stupidity which I commit is to him an earthquake, which causes him to lose his footing."

Naturally using non-actors also has its disadvantages. They not only function as a seismograph of the expressiveness of the dialogue, but also of many other things. Early in the shooting of *Firemen's Ball,* Milos noticed that the performance of the man portraying the fireman who steals the headcheese from the raffle was growing day to day worse: as if the person were changing from a talented non-

82

actor to the worst amateur hack. It appeared that the gentleman's wife always rehearsed with him the scene which was to be shot the next day, and very authoritatively directed him. Consequently, Milos took the scripts away from his non-actors, and acquainted them with the contents of the scenes and dialogue according to the Faulkner method: "just before the camera turned".

A major problem is to find suitable non-actors. Eighty percent of the candidates will not do. Once, during an Autumn day in 1964, I myself wouldn't do. In the room where debates about debiting per contra could be heard, Forman's team, Milos, Ivan Passer and Jaroslav Papousek, met with three men: two of them were clerks, Ivan Kheil and Jiri Hruby, and one was a writer—myself. The situation was explained to us: three middle-aged reservists at a dance are trying to pick up some girls sitting at the next table. Since they are a little afraid, they encourage one another. One of them has a wedding band, which he drops on the floor. Milos described the embarrassing situation graphically and then added: "Well, gents, now act!"

I choked up, and couldn't think of a single thing. I managed to utter a few hysterical cries, and then I simply listened to Messrs. Kheil and Hruby, who argued so well, that they almost ended up realistically bloodying each others noses. Later, as we were going for dinner through the misty streets of Prague's Old Town, Milos told me: "You know, you are too intelligent for that part." According to his own theory, I should have been just the man for the part. However, Milos—in keeping with another principle of his—finally gave it to an excellent professional actor, Vladimir Mensik. To tell someone that he is too intelligent to be an actor is a very nice way of letting him know that he should stay with screen-play writing. Milos is a very considerate person. The fact that he so gently threw me out made possible the greatest scene of *Loves of a Blond* (1965).

The Blond helped Milos to get out into the world. Those who envied him maliciously claimed that he used a well tested formula: a young girl with love problems. But even such masters as Edgar Allan Poe, certainly one of the fathers of modern art, used the formula quite unashamedly, because they knew it to be one of the most moving formulas in life. After all, as Chaplin says, "who on principle avoids cliché, faces the danger of becoming a bore." Milos wrote: "One morning I met a young girl, sadly standing with her carpet bag in front of a Prague railway station. She travelled from some village to Prague to visit a boy. She had his address, but she couldn't find him, since the address was false." Here in a nutshell were the *Loves*. The important thing, Milos stresses, is the basic situation. It is easy to develop a story from it, which "I then try to tell so that it pleases me. It must also please and move those for whom it is meant." "To tell an entertaining story" in the age of sophistication, probably does not resound too ambitiously. But Milos goes on to say: "I think that all that which is noble, and which has remained in art and literature since ancient times...and which is also significant for strong contemporary works of art, has always concerned itself with injuries and injustices perpetrated against the individual. That is because we always perceive the work of art as individuals. There, at the bottom of all those great works, are the injustices, which no social order will eliminate. Namely, that one is clever and the other stupid, one is able and the other is incompetent, one is beautiful while the other is ugly, another might be honest, and yet another dishonest, and all of them are in some way ambitious. And it indeed does not matter that we are arriving at eternal themes."

It may be that at this point we are quite far removed from contemporary sophistication, but we are close to the tramp in a bowler hat. I personally will always prefer the tramp. Milos in his films approached the desired state where his work speaks both to the man in the street, and to the intellectual. I see this as an indisputable sign of an art, which is by no means minor.

This sensitive person drew upon himself from the very beginning of his career the hatred of people who, irrespective of what they are saying, always demand that art be the servant of politics, and not its partner and companion, or, in case of great art, even its teacher. *The Audition* was accused of anti-humanitarian callousness. *Peter and Paula*, of choosing from among the millions of theoretically happy young socialists the atypical story of a decadent grocer's apprentice. *Loves of a Blond*, according to many, adversely affected the morale of the young, because in one scene it revealed to them the state secret, that during love-making people usually undress. At that time Milos received scores of anonymous letters. In one of them the writer threatened to kill him and "all those other kikes, when

Jana Brejchova's sister, Hana, in Loves of a Blond. *"I am bored with beauty, really,"
said Milos in an interview. "I find more beauty in unrepeatable faces."*

we'll once again start doing things the right way." By the
majestic plural this radical did not mean the Nazis but those
"marxists" who, during Dubcek's era secretly, and after the
Invasion publicly, gathered around the antisemite Jodas (a
single typing error would make the name into an interesting
nomen-omen), and who now seem to be conspiring against the
"revisionist" Husak. Then came *The Firemen's Ball.*

Until that time nobody thought of Forman as a social critic.
Suddenly came a story whose philosophical core is an expression
of cruelty of inter-human relations: ruthlessness of man to man,
dullness and callousness, which survive even in socialism and
are sometimes simply transformed into new shapes. A dying old
man is to be given a commemorative pick-axe at the firemen's
ball, because the firemen have discovered that he has cancer.
They speak about it with complete nonchalance. A group of
pitiful beauties is uninhibitedly ogled by a bunch of lewd middle-aged men. A grandfather whose house burns down, is

85

Two unrepeatable faces: the one on the left is Vera Kresadlova's in Audition, *the second is that of an anonymous Greenwich Village teenager in* Taking Off.

displayed on stage during the ball in his long underwear, and an enterprising waiter utilizes the gathering of the crowd at the fire to increase his beverage sales. The charity raffle is pilfered by the people, and when the cancer-afflicted old man (who was all evening prevented from going to relieve himself, because the firemen aren't sure when they will perform the presentation) finally goes to receive his pick-axe, it is discovered that someone had stolen it.

A startling picture of society. It disgusted in a strangely similar way the American writer Phillip Bonosky, the Moscow critic Bolshakov, the reviewer for the West German *Der Spiegel* and the famed humanitarian* Carlo Ponti, who reportedly first

*Western film tycoonery seems to be swarming with humanists. When Milos offered his first American script to Paramount they refused it, attacking Milos on the very same terms leveled against him by the philosophers from Mosfilm, from the Novotnyite apparatus and from the CP of the USA. The script, they said, ridiculed ordinary people. Jay Cocks, writing in another organ of the international humanists, *Time*, described the method of *Taking Off* (the movie made from the refused script by the less humane Universal) as "simplistic misanthropy". Well, let us suppose that Milos is a misanthrope: if any of the contemporary film-makers has a right to be one, would it not be the boy whose parents were, on the strength of a very simplistic radical theory, done away with by the rather sophisticated cremating equipment in a little Polish village? So maybe he really is a misanthrope, and maybe the way the Czech directors make films is simplistic: unlike some of their Western colleagues, such as Godard and others, they certainly do not seem to care much for the sophisticated concepts of "the people" to whom "all power" should be given. However, they have been taught not only their theoretical lessons, and so, perhaps they can be forgiven for having outgrown both 18th century romanticism and the children's disease of slogans made up from undefined terms. Milos, like the rest of them, probably does not have much understanding for "the people"; he only happens to have some understanding of the people. That is perhaps why, in *Taking Off*, he was able to make all "those beautiful, flawed, lovely faces singing those sad songs" (*Newsweek* magazine) speak for a thousand political treatises.

*Milos shooting his first American film,*Taking Off. *The man lying beside him on the floor is his excellent cameraman, Miroslav Ondricek.*

87

Firemen's Ball: *Should Frank have returned the stolen headcheese, or shouldn't he have?* — *The greatest political metaphor in Czech cinema.*

protested against the selection of types for the beauty contest (he wanted prettier girls) and in the end found the film anti-humanitarian. Consequently he refused to distribute it. In all these condemnations one could hear, as the film critic, A. J. Liehm, pointed out, the echoing of the words of the long departed Czarist critic F. Vigel, written about an author, who "invented some kind of an unreal Russia, in it a mythical town, into which he gathered all the evils, which you would hardly find in all of real Russia". The critic had Gogol, and his play *Government Inspector* in mind; Count Tolstoy-American, in accordance with Vigel, then suggested "sending the author shackled to Siberia".

When President Novotny saw the film at a regular private screening, he, according to his son's alleged words, "climbed the walls". Due to his intervention (the second one in Milos' career), the film was for a long time not distributed. The President of course disliked other aspects of the film than those that irritated Mr. Bonosky and the West Germans: namely the scene which, in the Czech context, is the most brilliant example of allegory—so magnificently inconspicuous, that a foreigner would miss it.

There is a power failure, and in the ensuing darkness people pilfer the raffle prizes. The Fire Chief becomes exasperated: he

88

Milos's American crowd in Taking Off: *"I really don't think people are so different (in the U.S.) that they should cry or laugh at different things."*

orders the lights turned off again, beckons the people to return what they have stolen, and promises not to search for the culprits. The lights go off and soon come on again—to reveal a single person putting a stolen item back on the table: the Assistant Fire Chief is returning a headcheese. A quick meeting is called, during which the firemen split up into two camps. One side maintains that Frank, once he had stolen, should not have returned anything, because he only embarrassed the fire-brigade. Others object that Frank was right in returning the headcheese because, in doing so, he confessed his crime and thus contributed to the honest image of the firemen. It is all a hilariously naturalistic argument of village bumpkins over a stolen headcheese. And it is all a metaphor, well understood by all in Czechoslovakia. The President was the head of the Party faction, which for a long time refused to admit the truth about the frameup of Slansky and his co-defendants.

The President was not the only one to climb the walls as a result of *Firemen's Ball*. The voluntary fire-fighters also hit the ceiling, and Novotny found in them some unexpected allies for one of his last campaigns against the artists. The devoted members of the fire-brigades univocally related the philosophical metaphor to their unphilosophical corporation. They declared

89

Firemen's Ball: *"I find more beauty in unrepeatable faces."*

that if that is how the film-makers see it, they in turn will not fight fires. In a country where, with the exception of large cities, fire-fighting depends almost exclusively on volunteers, this could have meant a catastrophe. As a result, Forman's team had to embark on a strange tour of the country, explaining to the indignant fire-fighters that they had had no ill intentions.

Suddenly the dormant sparks of political upheaval erupted into a fast-spreading fire. Novotny fell, and Dubcek came to power. We met once again with Milos and decided that the time had come to do what the deposed President thought we wanted to do when he intervened against *Eine Kleine Jazzmusik*. We decided to shoot *The Cowards*.

Milos, however, already had a contract with Paramount to write and shoot a film about American youth. So we only drafted a synopsis and decided that while Milos was in the United States making his film, I would write the first draft of the script. Upon his return we would complete the screen-play and shoot it in the summer of 1969 in the town where the good grocer uncle once gave Milos shelter.

That was in the spring of 1968, and in August the tanks arrived. We seem to have had little luck in our co-operation. All the same I am happy to have met Milos, and both his beautiful wives; to have been bound to him by friendship, the most precious thing in life, and I nostagically recall how he rejected me at the auditions for *Loves of a Blond,* in a way that really didn't hurt.

That is how it was with my friend Milos Forman. I am not a film aesthetician to attempt any kind of an exhaustive recapitulation. One important aspect of his work, was I believe best described by the surrealist Vratislav Effenberger:

Cynicism for the sake of cynicism, wrote Rene Crevel, is cynicism against truth...but Milos Forman's cynicism is not directed against truth. Forman managed to preserve the type of humour, which is vicious, dangerous, concealed and explosive. He dared to do something for which he should not be forgotten, if he will find his way to a more acceptable climate: he hit the petty Czech citizen. He aimed at cowardice, apathy, football fanaticism, brutality, avidity, goodnatured emptyheadedness, parochialism, tap room philosophy, and egotism, and he hit the bull's eye: he struck exactly those centers of spiritual wretchedness, from which spring essentially all kinds of Fascisms and Stalinisms...in (his) active understanding of reality, in this feeling for contemporary forms of aggressive humour, and for the critical functions of absurdity, in the fanatical anger, which in his case can only be a function of some new inner light and freshness, that is where Forman's work meets the most advanced functions of modern art.

Reminiscing about Milos, one of his characteristics comes to my mind: he knew how to preserve his integrity even in situations where he risked everything. Rather than assist on films with which he disagreed artistically, he left his safe job and freelanced. In a socialist society this is a complicated ploy. Rather than begin a film with an incomplete screenplay, he ignored the possibility that the producer might wish to find a readier man. Rather than give in to the taste of a famous foreign moneybag, he gambled that he might have to somehow repay him eighty thousand dollars which, for a citizen of a socialist country, is a task about as simple as walking around the world on the meridian. Rather than accede to the dramaturgical ideas of a large American corporation, he risked an even greater dollar debt in a situation which for him, as a Czech, was extremely uncertain.* I remember how once during the shooting of *Firemen's Ball* he gave me an American screen-play, and asked me to read it and give him my opinion—at that time he did not yet speak English well. I told him what I thought of the script, and Milos returned it. That precious screen-play was brought by a gentleman who took first a transcontinental, and then a transatlantic flight straight from Hollywood. When he could not reach Milos in Prague, he chartered a plane and flew after him to Spindleruv Mlyn in the Giant Mountains, where the *Ball* was being made. Milos refused it. The gentleman boarded the chartered plane, then the transatlantic and finally the transcontinental plane, and once back in Hollywood, he entrusted the property into more reliable and willing hands. Remembering it, I must always think of the little boy from the shadow of the sauerkraut barrels. Somehow he never did become anyone else.

Milos is the only director of the New Wave who created something that might be called a school. All his films up till now are the result of excellent team-work, and both his colleagues have already made their own films. When someone becomes very successful, others begin to prove that he actually plagiarized. When Passer, after making the medium length study of football fanaticism *Dull Afternoon* (1964) made the poetic, refined and musical *Intimate Lighting* (1965) with Papousek, but without Forman, it was said that he outformaned Forman. When Papousek, after the thematically refreshing, but directorially unmanaged, *The Most Beautiful Age* (1969) came up with the cruel philosophical farce, *Ecco Homo Homolka* (1970)—having written and directed both the films himself—the thing to ponder was whether Forman really equals Passer plus Papousek, or whether Passer and Papousek are only Forman's epigones. Fortunately, their friendship was never in the least affected by these strange ponderances.

The truth seems to be rather simple. Although Forman would never say this about himself, he is the primary source, the original vision. A long time before the empty-headed sage offered his hardheaded son banal pearls of wisdom in *Peter and Paula,* Forman thought of the situation of a pompous father and his stubborn son for *Eine Kleine Jazzmusik.* Already at that time he had filled it with

*"How I Came to America to Make a Film and Wound up Owing Paramount $140,000," Milos Forman *Taking Off,* Signet, 1971.

Bored with feminine beauty, Milos chose this particular unrepeatable face to become that of his second wife: Vera in Passer's Intimate Lighting.

Ivan Passer in America

the characteristic contrast between life and the petrified ideas about life, with those unusual cadences that later sprang from the mouths of his non-actors. Already he was inventing the conversations about nothing for "human pups"; in *Eine Kleine Jazzmusik,* Suzi Braun, the swing singer was to have them with the fellows from the student band, though in the end they took place between the blond and the piano player. Incidentally, this blond was played by Hana Brejchova (the younger sister of his first wife), who was supposed to star as Suzi Braun at the age of fourteen, and who later appeared as the naked model in Papousek's *The Most Beautiful Age.*

Essentially, however, the work of Forman's team is teamwork. "It was only later," says Papousek, "that I began to formulate my own aesthetic position regarding cinema. I never had the feeling, incidentally, that the boys [Forman and Passer] were expert film makers while I was only a sculptor who got in the way. Nor did I feel that they contributed more than I. Each of us was an equal among equals."

The three friends resemble somewhat the mystery of the Trinity on a rather secular level. Forman's original vision was, I would say, enriched and deepened by the sensitivity of his congenial friends. Collective creation, which is one of the specific properties of

93

the art of film, was ideally realized in the co-operation of the trio. When the three directors parted, each of them emphasized in their own works their contribution and their particular subject: their specific nuance of the school.

It seems to me that Ivan Passer is the philosopher of the trio. He is also the laziest—although Milos is also a very staunch advocate of hypnology. Often during the work on *Eine Kleine Jazzmusik,* I thought he was thinking hard, and then I discovered that he was sleeping. But Ivan is the Oblomov of the three. "I dread the idea," he wrote, "of making a film every year. I am convinced that after three years I would be no longer capable of making one."

As a philosopher he is somewhat existential. "I am not interested in the story, but in the state of being," he said, about *Intimate Lighting.* "To find the meaning in life, means to find the ultimate task of which a person is capable. It means that he must find his own upper limit, which will always destroy him a little, but which will force him to use the best properties that he possesses. . . . The hero of *Intimate Lighting* is a person who probably understood it. I would say that he is a modern hero."

Intimate Lighting is a study of all of that. A cello virtuoso arrives after ten years to visit an old friend who teaches at a small town music school. He brings with him his beautiful fiancee (played by Forman's second wife, Vera); both friends get drunk together, remember the old times, raid the refrigerator, and play in a quartet—in short, nothing unusual happens. This is an exact expression of Passer's aesthetics: "I don't like ambitious films, which end in a compromise. I like those little films, which are as if by accident important. Those which you suspect of being more important than they at first glance appear to be." Elsewhere he says: "A man might live through momentous events, or important encounters, which influence his life. But it doesn't happen too often. We are rather influenced by everyday banal situations. These situations cannot be uninteresting, that is unworthy of interest, because after all the human life is made up of them. I think that. . .the physics of elementary particles provides answers to questions regarding the stars."

Unrepeatable or not, Ivan does not look bored by the beauty of Karen Black, while directing her in Born to Win, *his first U.S. movie.*

No, Ivan certainly does not look bored: Born to Win

Jaroslav Papousek directing

Herein lies the principle charm of that inconspicuous film, that won for Passer the New York Critics' Prize in 1970.

This is to date the high point of a career which, in several aspects, resembled Milos'. Wrong racial background—troubles during the war. Son of wealthy parents—troubles after the war. Thrown out of high school, he worked as an unskilled laborer, bricklayer, caster, learned tool-making, and after a severe case of hepatitis became a clerk. When he recovered, he travelled for two years as a circus hand. Through a happy coincidence he was accepted to the Film Academy, but two years later when his class background was discovered, he was thrown out again. But he stayed with film: first as Helge's assistant on *The Great Seclusion,* with Brynych on *Skid,* with Jasny on *The Pilgrimage to the Virgin* and *That Cat,* as well as working with Alfred Radok in the Laterna Magica. Finally he became assistant director to Milos Forman, whom he had known

96

since the age of thirteen when they were at a boarding school together; later they collaborated on the writing of Forman's screen-plays. Taking all of this into account we should understand another idea from Ivan's directorial account: "A peculiar contradiction exists between the maturity of a person as an individual and the infantility of a person as a social creature. In every gang, in every club...the person behaves a little below his dignity. In every pilgrimage, in every festival, in every uniform, and—with your permission—in every consistent realisation of philosophical ideas, I suspect a greater or smaller dose of infantility."

The third member of the triumvirate, Jaroslav Papousek, was originally a piano tuner, then he completed a degree in sculpting at the Academy of Fine Arts, and made a living from caricatures and cartoons. He wrote *Peter and Paula,* met Forman, and finally became a director. The film, *The Most Beautiful Age,* had a magnificent screen-play—one Prague structuralist counted over two hundred gags in it—but as a film it wasn't very successful. The reasons were partly *vis maior.* Along with the spirit of Forman's films, Papousek took over some of his actors, the blond and Peter's father, as well as the Old Fireman with cancer. This kind old gentleman had one of the lead parts in *The Most Beautiful Age,* but unfortunately died of a stroke when the Russian tanks arrived in Prague. At the time the film was only half finished. The screen-play had to be quickly and drastically rewritten, and although the result is still certainly worth seeing, it occasionally goes beyond the point where the peculiar charm of a non-actor's expression turns into diletantism, accompanied by an aftertaste of something unsuccessful.

However, in *Ecce Home Homolka* Popousek outlined his contribution to the works of the trio, in the disguise of a folksy farce. The film begins with a Sunday afternoon petit-bourgeois idyll of Mr. Homolka's family: Grandpa, Grandma, the son the daughter-in-law, and the twins, (Peter and Matthew Forman in their second film appearance) are getting set to enjoy a picnic in a forest full of vacationers. Suddenly they hear a woman desperately calling for help from the nearby bushes. The Homolkas act quickly and energetically. They pack up their sausages and beer, and gallop out of the forest. They *don't want to get involved with anything like that.*

That is what the film is all about. "Other people" are for

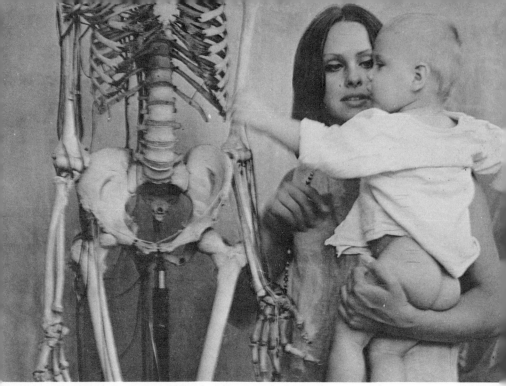

The symbolism of this still looks to me almost medieval: but it's just Vera in Papousek's The Most Beautiful Age.

Ecce Homo Homolka: *a petit-bourgeois idyll seen through the sardonic eyes of Papousek. The new Barrandov bosses reportedly liked it, except for the cross on the wall.*

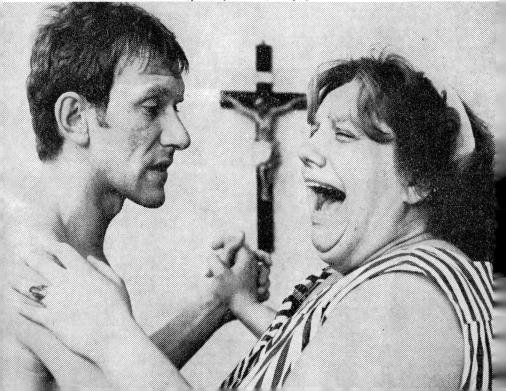

Homolka's family "they"; something almost generically different. The Homolkas live encased in their ultra-humble world, self-sufficient in their stupidity, conceited in their ignorance, profound in their emptiness, continuously revelling in their never-ending batra-chomyomachia. They are ideal objects for dictators and manipulators. We cannot but identify a continuation of the satire on man, which was the subject of *Firemen's Ball.* Papousek, who is the most industrious of the three (a resolute enemy of hypnology and a slave-driver), seems to be the socially critical whip of the school, trend, team, or whatever you want to call the phenomenon, which through the harmonious efforts of a story-telling observer of life, a philosopher, and a satirist, gave the New Wave its most remarkable characteristics.

Vera Chytilova

The first of the two ladies of the New Wave is, in my mind, associated with disaster. It all started somewhat in the manner of my meeting with Milos Forman. The doorbell rang, and at the door stood another beauty—this time a stranger. She stunned me; I didn't stammer, as in the case of Jana Brejchova (she wasn't a film star), but instead I completely misjudged her age, and took her for a young unsuspecting kitten. That afternoon, while sitting on the terrace of the Film Club Cafe, I managed to give a sterling performance of the father part from *Peter and Paula.* Had Forman seen it, he would have undoubtedly given me the role.

The kitten that sat facing me was thirty-one. By way of introduction she told me that for her admission examination to the Film Academy she wrote a screen play based on my story *The Racial Question.* This naturally pleased me, since at that time I was under constant attack in the papers. Then she asked me if I could help her with her thesis film. The script was written by her colleague Pavel Juracek, with whom she supposedly argued because she wanted the film to be more philosophical.

The thing was called *The Ceiling,* but I unfortunately liked Vera more than her script, and did not supply any philosophy. It was after all she, not I, who was the philosopher; in the end I had a very courteous argument with her, as I found the screenplay to be a rather tedious moral tale, considerably tributary to

Vera Chytilova

socialist-realistic "philosophy", which evaluated human efforts according to the governmental tariff of "social usefulness". In the screen-play a pretty medical student takes a part-time job modelling at fashion shows, and gets herself a stylish lover. Then she drops out of medicine and begins to alternate between her lover's bed and the shallow world of the fashion shows. Finally, disgusted by all of it, she boards a train, where she meets simple country people. Cleansed by this Rousseauvian communion, she decides to start a new life by returning to the study of human maladies. The kitsch bore an obvious ideological resemblance to the then fashionable "return to the people for cathartic purposes", as it was represented for instance in Jiri Fried's celebrated novel *Time Squeeze,* which I found particularly repulsive. The whole theme was nothing but a formally sophisticated re-birth of the reactionary baker, Mr. Seagull, under the influence of the miners (in the previously mentioned film *Seagull Is Late,* 1950) and this in turn was just a "progressive" modification of an identical theme which once had been a favourite of some of the worst Catholic writers. Both themes had a villager corrupted by the city, both contained a train ride to some village in the mountains, in both there appeared those full-blooded simple folk, as healing as the spring of life. The only difference was in the reactionary treatment given to the material by the Catholic writers, as exemplified by the introduction of the good parish priest, a character omitted from the "progressive" version, or replaced by some ponderous village communist.

Notwithstanding all that, I have always had a soft spot for

fashion models, and so I refused to belittle their eminently beneficial work. Vera in the end stubbornly made the film, but instead of the injection of even the wisest philosophy, she did something much more clever. Although the schematic morality remained, the director blunted it by completely shifting the emphasis to form: and very formalistic form at that. It was possibly the first formalistic film of the New Wave, discounting Vlacil's *The Dove* (1960), but that was protected against any criticism by the acceptable peace symbolism. *Ceiling* was a pure succession of beautiful objects—from the actress who played the model to the nature shots, rendered by the precise camera work into a twilight display of light and shadow. Vera later declared that "beauty is the means and not the end", but she quickly added: "If we were to forget that, we might say: if formalism, then beautiful."

The film bore noticeable traces of *cinéma-vérité*. It did not make much use of a hidden camera, but it utilized a concealed microphone planted in the models' dressing-room, where Vera herself would start conversations with the changing girls. The shots of the fashion show were thus accompanied by a phantasmagorial unrehearsed cackle of girlish noises, with the director's characteristic voice, identifiable by her peculiar pronunciation of "r" sounds, outstanding. She pronounced those sounds as the English do, which to a Czech ear is delightfully comical.

Vera made her second film, also a medium-length feature, *A Bag of Fleas* (1962), in my home town Nachod, which is famous for its role in the Czech labour movement. Some of its numerous cotton-mills still use the English milling machines bought at the turn of the century. The cotton industry always preferred women; after the war the factories built large dormitories and filled them with girls. At one time there were young females living there from all over the world. Besides Czech and Slovak citizens and girls from Poland, which is only three miles away, one could see, promenading on the square, Greek beauties from families that fled their country after the defeat of the Communist guerillas, Korean girls learning the trade, some Chinese and, I believe, even a few curious American students who worked there on summer jobs. This abundance had a shady side to it: the ratio of girls to boys in my home town changed since the days of my youth to 5 to 1 to the advantage (or rather disadvantage) of girls—a situation typical for several Czech textile towns and also, if you recall, the starting point of *Loves of a Blond*. *A Bag of*

Fleas is about the clash between what the adults call working morale and the natural needs of sixteen-year-old females, needs which are hard to satisfy in a feminized milieu. So the heroine of the film skips work because of her precious boyfriend; she is consequently summoned before the Works Committee, and severely chastised.

The film was staged from beginning to end; but through the improvisation of the given dialogue, particularly in the scenes with the worker-officials, Vera achieved an immediateness resembling Forman's films. The accent on form and the *l'art pour l'art* beauty temporarily receded; content became prominent—and that is where Vera's disasters started.

As it was, the film employed strictly non-actors—the real foremen and officials of the Nachod cotton-mills. The camera showed them realistically, that is unflatteringly; one of them was even introduced while performing the function of a self-appointed controller of morality at a dance in a local restaurant, where the youth indulged in "eccentric western dances"*. The non-actors, some of whom had political influence, spoke out against the showing of the film, and it took a full year of negotiations before *A Bag of Fleas* reached the cinemas.

Meanwhile Vera worked on a new movie, which proved to be very important in her future development. In it the *vérité* style (consequently abandoned by Vera) penetrated the formalistic style of the symbolic, stylized, generalized "philosophical" statement—and that subsequently led to approaching the work as an independent *objet d'art* in its own right. The film was called *About Something Else* (1963) and it really consisted of two juxtaposed films, capturing side by side two independent and unrelated lives of two thirty one year old women: A world famous gymnast, and an insignificant housewife. One of them sacrifices everything to a given goal: the Olympic gold medal. She neglects all that a woman, as a woman, should have—children, a happy family life—and ends up in a crisis. The other one sacrifices everything to her family. She neglects

*The dance in question was a variant of rock'n'roll, and the interesting point is how peculiar were the ideas about decent dancing, as reflected in the activities of the controller. Dancing with the bodies of the partners not touching, or dancing individually, each on his own, as it was occasionally showed in the newsreel shots from the "decadent West" was considered immoral. Consequently one could sometimes see voluntary protectors of morality, forcing the bands to play tangos, and making the young couples on the dance floor slither around glued to each other breast to breast and belly to belly.

everything that a woman should attain as a human being—the desire to become something, to achieve something, to assert oneself in society, not only at home—and also reaches a crisis. Both lives, seemingly diametrically opposed, lead towards the bitter feeling of *vanitas vanitatum*—although Vera herself said about the film, that it is "a drama of the eternal struggle for immortality amidst the finality of human powers". But after all, Vera is a philosopher.

In *About Something Else,* Vera's most prominent artistic trait became evident: her almost militant feminism. Sometimes I feel that Vera is first a woman, and only after that a human being—a characteristic which became clear in *Daisies* (1966).

However, before she started to shoot *Daisies,* we met once more for a joint effort which, in the end, again failed. It was at a time when Novotny's cultural department continued its Holy War against jazz and pop music by waging an artful attack against popular singers. A reflection of that war was evident in *A Bag of Fleas,* but in real life it was carried much further—all the way to several public trials.

At the first one, a group of "hooligans" was ceremonially convicted for secretly indulging in the perverse western dance of rock'n'roll in the hall of the Manes Club, which they had properly rented. They each served several months in jail for their anti-socialist activities. The leader of the group, if I remember correctly, was sent up for a year. Within a short time these perverse dances were performed publicly with the Young Communist League organizing the events, but that was all right, because as the Marx-acknowledged Hesiodos says—*panta rei*—everything develops.

I got involved in the Holy War on the side of the pop musicians with an article, "Who Takes Baths in Champagne?" I gained popularity with the singers, burdened my already overdrawn account at the Cultural Department, and aroused once again Vera's interest. The war culminated in the banning of the three most popular singers from public performance. The three singers, Eva Pilarova, Waldemar Matuska, and Karel Gott, were accused of some rather spectacular infamies: while on a trip in Karlsbad, Eva and Waldemar supposedly urinated from the balcony of the Hotel Pupp on the heads of some workers' delegation, while Karel Gott provided musical accompaniment by singing the favourite melody "The Bubbling Stream". Ad-

103

Eva Pilarova: *according to the novotnyite Cultural Dept. urinated on a workers' delegation.*

Waldemar Matuska: *according to the same source directed traffic, clad in a pair of socks.*

ditional misdeeds were revealed during interrogation: Waldemar, clad only in a pair of socks, was supposed to have directed traffic at an intersection and thus caused a traffic jam, while Eva was seen somewhere playing poker for "Tuzex" coupons*. It did not help the "perverts" that Eva had an iron-clad alibi for the urinary night (she was not in Karlsbad), and that the poker she was supposed to be playing was the game of *Monopoly,* (unknown to the informer) brought by the bass player **Ludek Hulan** from a trip to Switzerland (and the "Tuzex coupons" were really the paper money that comes with the game). The Cultural Department outdid Vyshinsky, and didn't even bother extracting a confession from the accused. A similar penalty was handed out to another excellent jazz singer, Eva Olmerova (whose case was worse because in her youth she spent a year in the house of correction); in a state of inebriation she reportedly fell off stage into the audience at the Alhambra night club, probably also onto a delegation—here most likely a foreign one.

At that point I considered writing a novel about all of that. It was to be called *There Must Be Something Wrong,* a quotation from *A Minor Bird* by Robert Frost. I saw Vera at a meeting of

*Special money obtainable in exchange for dollars, pounds, West German marks, and other hard currency. In special Tuzex stores one can get otherwise inaccessible Western products for the coupons (including Coke and Swedish cars). One can also buy girls with them called in the Prague slang "Tuzex girls".

Karel Gott: *"The Golden Voice from Prague"*, sang *"The Bubbling Stream"* to the urination.

the Preparatory Committee of the Czechoslovakian Participation at Montreal Expo, where Vera managed to embarrass the well-known minister Kahuda by suggesting that diabolical screaming and grinding of teeth should emanate from the Czechoslovakian Pavilion in order to bring out the contrasting heavenly beauty of the interior. During intermission I told her about the intended novel and recited Frost's poem:

I have wished a bird would fly away,
And not sing by my house all day;

Have clapped my hands at him from the door
When it seemed as if I could bear no more.

The fault must partly have been in me.
The bird was not to blame for his key.

And of course there must be something wrong
In wanting to silence any song.*

Vera evidently liked the poem better than the novel—in it the singer battling the administrative interference was in the end

*From *The Poetry Of Robert Frost* edited by Edward Connery Lathem. Copyright 1928, (c) 1969 by Holt, Rinehart and Winston, Inc. Copyright (c) 1956 by Robert Frost. Reprinted by permission of Holt, Rinehart and Winston, Inc., New York.

Eva Olmerova, *the greatest Czech scat-singer: fell from a night-club stage on a Soviet delegation.*

supposed to really lose her voice after an operation on her vocal cords. A few days later Vera once again knocked on my door—accompanied by the sociologist of the pop-music milieu Milan Schulz—and we started to concoct something according to Frost. One of the two suppressed singers, either Eva Pilarova or Eva Olmerova, was to star in the movie. At the studios they naturally threw out both us and the screen-play. One thing, nevertheless, is worth noticing. Once during a working session I told Vera about the principle of the blues—the three-verse structure, where the second verse is usually a varied repetition of the first; this gives the time to make up the third verse—and Vera, the formalist, became all ears. Under her somewhat autocratic leadership the screenplay took on a tripartite form—the second part being a varied repetition of the first; to one of our meetings Vera dragged the famous modernistic composer of serious music, Jan Klusak, and forced the already highly overtaxed musician to promise some very special score for our film. Vera,

es: *"If the world ruins everything, let us also ruin everything!" says Marie to Marie at the beginning . . .*

who in the typical philosophical manner goes from the generalized to the specific, described her vision of that musical accompaniment as a "symphonic blues". If I understood her correctly, it was supposed to be some kind of a three-part symphony built on the structural principle of the blues verse (not on their harmonic formula), which, I think, Klusak, who does not like jazz, failed to understand. But the script was refused, anyway, so Vera cast Klusak as one of the leads in *Daisies*, thus co-discovering for the New Wave a very expressive actor. (He subsequently appeared in Nemec's *The Party and the Guests, The Martyrs of Love,* and many other films.)

The feminist Vera possesses something of the provocative aggressiveness of the suffragettes. Our unsuccessful attempt at the film blues did not diminish her energies; first she pressured into co-operation the absurdist writer, actor and psychologist Ivan Vyskocil (also the co-founder of the "Little Theatres" movement), and when he resisted her too strongly, she found

107

another woman, Ester Krumbachova, who is, I am afraid, as far as feminism is concerned, an exact opposite of Vera. That is how began the fruitful co-operation, which has so far culminated in the movie *We Eat the Fruit of the Trees of Paradise* (1970). Around that time Vera married the best Czech cameraman, Jaroslav Kucera, and immediately put him to work. The result was possibly the most brilliant camera achievement in the history of Czech film. The newly wed directress finished the shooting in a considerably advanced state of rotundity, that possibly enhanced the tone of a certain mocking acrimony, with which the film treats the majority of male characters.

According to Vera's words, *Daisies* was supposed to be "a bizarre comedy with shades of satire and sarcasm oriented towards both the protagonists". It certainly was a bizarre comedy, but I am not sure whether the satirical quill really aimed at the two impish main characters. Also, I am not sure that the film really is "a parable on the destructive force of nihilism and senseless provocation", but it certainly is an excellent, rich, boldly and mischieviously made film. It begins with a montage: a nuclear explosion, tanks destroying houses. I suspect that the authoresses added the grandiose introduction* as a counter-measure against probable later criticism (their intuitions were warranted). Then two girls in bathing suits appear, sitting at the side of a swimming pool; they make robot-like motions with their hands (the process of formal stylization advanced a step further). Both have the same name—Marie—and except for appearance, they are totally interchangeable. This is how they speak: "We know nothing." "Nobody understands us." "The world ruins everything." "If the world ruins everything, let us also ruin everything." And they do. The subsequent action consists of a chain of scenes; some of them are about elderly gentlemen, who treat the pair in fashionable restaurants and night clubs, expecting rewards for their kindness. Each time, however, the girls only gorge themselves with expensive delicacies, then they take the elderly gentlemen to the station, make them board the train, and run away. One of the two arouses a younger Don Juan by stripping in front of him, and then refuses his advances (the Don Juan was played by Jan Klusak). They cause a disturbance in a

*It bears strong resemblances to Jires' thesis film *The Hall of Lost Footsteps,* which is a short built completely around the contrast of the horrors of war and the beauty of young love.

108

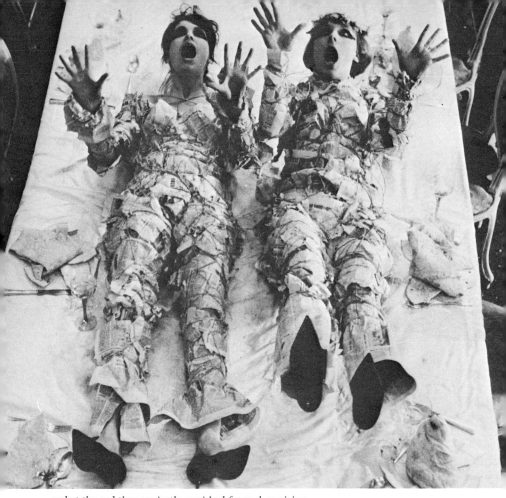

. . . and at the end they are justly punished for such cynicism.

night club, by dancing a violent version of the Charleston. They provoke wherever they go by reacting always contrary to what is expected. The spectacle culminates when the girls manage to stuff
themselves into a food elevator in a hotel and get into a banquet
hall, obviously prepared for some official overindulgence. They
begin by eating and end in a cream-cake battle. At this point comes
the final joke; it is *de facto* self-ridicule aimed against the moralistic
end of Vera's first film *Ceiling,* about the reformed model. The girls
realize what they have done, and instantly reform. In a dream scene,
the girls, whose effect is enhanced by decelerated camera action,
dressed in clothes made out of newspaper (symbol of "proper convictions"), sweep up the mess in a deadly tempo, arranging the
ruined remnants of the hors d'oeuvres and cakes on the soiled table-
cloths.

It was an instant catastrophe. A deputy of the National Assembly, a Mr. Pruzinec (the name is a beautiful onomatopoetic nomen-

109

We Eat the Fruit of the Trees of Paradise: *an objet d'art.*

omen, and could be translated as Mr. Jack-in-the-Box) rose and protested against the wastage of food, "at a time when our farmers with great difficulties are trying to overcome the problems of our agricultural production". Pruzinec ended with a pathetic call to the Minister of Agriculture, and to the Minister of the Interior, to take measures against the film and its directress.

Pruzinec's unbelievable interpellation circulated through Prague in a number of copies, and when it was read from the stage of the Paravan Theatre, the audience took it for a successful skit written by the manager of the Theatre, the satirist J. R. Pick. The film was held and shown for the purposes of damnation to selected "workers"; but they rather liked it, so it was finally released. The force of public opinion was by that time so strong that not even the President could stop the development, let alone Deputy Pruzinec, who quickly retreated into his box.

Vera made another short film before *Daisies, Snack-Bar "World"*, a part of the New Wave's omnibus film *Pearls in the Abyss* (1965). Her feministic hand reached for a story with a bridal motif, and she created, along with Menzel, the most visual part of this five story feature. After *Daisies* she embarked, together with her husband and Ester Krumbachova, on *We Eat the Fruit of the Trees of Paradise* (1970).

It was shown, and generally misunderstood (the fashionable appeal of the Czech New Wave having subsided), at the 1970 Cannes

110

We Eat the Fruit of the Trees of Paradise: *God dogmatically forbids, the Devil rationally tempts . . .*

Festival, but constitutes, I would say, a Kantian opus in the work of the philosopher, Vera: an extremely complicated work, built around the structure of a crime novel, framed by dramatic quotations from the second chapter of Genesis, about God who dogmatically forbids people to eat from the tree of knowledge and about the Devil who rationally tempts them to do so. The quotations are transformed into cantata, and complex musical as well as colour compositions significantly transcend the whole film. I remembered Jan Klusak, whom she had persuaded once to create a symphonic blues, and also the old experiments with the "coloured piano" made by the Czech Poetists of the Twenties. In this case the composer Zdenek Liska accommodated Vera: his music structures the parables and underlines each exchange. The film is really an opera, the symbolical plot being facilitated by the colour symbolism (Ester Krumbachova was originally a painter); everything fits into a bizarre and astounding unity, and is miles removed from the early flirtations with the *cinéma vérité.* It is an independent *objet d'art,* "a reality equal to any other created in the world", as it was described by the structuralist Jan Kucera, (not to be confused with Vera's husband Jaroslav). The emphasis is conspicuously on beauty, although the ambitions remain philosophical; and if anything is formalism, then it is this. But, it is as madame directress always required it to be, a beautiful formalism.

The last time I saw Vera, she was very strictly criticizing the for-

111

mal mistakes of *Crime in the Girls' School,* and the director, Jiri Menzel, blushed like an apprehended schoolboy. She had started as a student of architecture (that might be where the architectural qualities of her best films came from), then she worked as a draughtsman (viz. her sense of form), then she turned into a model (emphasis on beauty and feminism), finally she got a small part in *The Emperor's Baker,* and the film world swallowed her. First she worked as a clap-stick girl, then as an assistant, and finally she was accepted by the Film Academy. She went on to become one of the leading, and indeed truly revolutionary, personalities of the New Wave. She is the first important Czech directress; of her predecessors, Thea Cervenkova, an early pioneer, never made a film worth mentioning; and Zet Molas, alias Zdena Smolova, shared Vera's avant-garde creed but lacked her talent, and ended as a pro-Nazi informer. In a true feminist tradition Vera combined intensive intellectual effort with a feminine feeling for beauty and form. I believe that in her last film she escaped the danger of mere eclecticism, of which she is accused by Vratislav Effenberger. Besides, she has been accused of appropriation and imitation from the very beginning, and not only by orthodox surrealists. "Of course, if you do things the old way," Vera answered them once, "no one will accuse you of being an epigon, of copying those who did it that way long before you. But just you dare to try it another way!"

According to newspaper reports, Vera is currently working with the writer Iva Hercikova (script writer for Schorm's *Five Girls to Deal With*), on a screen-play about Bozena Nemcova, a classical Czech authoress, who was a contemporary and admirer of Charles Dickens. It is not, as it might seem, an escape into the past, so well known from the recent history of Czech cinema, because it points towards a combination of Vera's traditional feminism with the most sympathetic feature of her philosophical statement: "The artist may, and indeed must express only what he knows and what concerns him, because he thinks it should be changed. We want to create a new social morality and in the same breath we—artists—lie. Lying in art should be outlawed....What more could we lose as artists, if we lost truth?"

Bozena Nemcova was a very lonely nineteenth-century female rebel; despite the Victorian morality of her time, she had several known lovers, and dedicated her life not only to the fight for

112

women's rights, but also to the rights of her humiliated country. In an unhappy marriage (which was forced upon her by her parents), exploited by her publisher, she vegetated, surrounded by a hypocritically patriotic society, until she finally died at the age of forty-two of tuberculosis, before she was able to carry out her plan of emigrating to the United States. In the hands of Vera Chytilova, a philosopher and revolutionary of form, it could be a story "of something else", rather than a depiction of the fate of one unhappy nineteenth-century, woman writer.

Jan Nemec and Ester Krumbachova

Jan Nemec is the *enfant terrible* of the New Wave. Practically all the members of the movement had what were euphemistically called "problems". As we saw, they enraged the President himself, and Deputies raised hell over them. The troubles of Jan Nemec, however, reached new heights.

Nemec is an irritable hothead. Although, unlike Forman and Passer, he had not until recently had first-hand experiences with the terror, cruelty, cynical apathy and injustice of the world, he reacted against them in perhaps all of his films with the greatest intensity. "There exists one everlasting conflict," he said, "the hopeless struggle between intelligence and stupidity, between the individual and the totality, and one eternal problem: the fundamental unwillingness of people, or of humanity as a whole, to deal with problems which concern them." Elsewhere he remembers: "I resent one thing: that I was not allowed to shoot as my thesis film a screenplay based on Arnost Lustig's story ' The Street of Lost Brothers '. It was about elderly parents who believe in the return of their missing son, because his death in a concentration camp was never confirmed. I had a detailed screen-play, an idea how to make it . . . but one of the well-known creators—then a professor at the Film Academy—objected that it was undignified to make a film about deranged members of the bourgeoise, who are incapable of joining in the building of socialism." This rather frequent form of parlour perversity evidently substituted for the shock of direct experience, and forced Nemec to take an intensive interest in problems which concern even those who are not directly affected.

While at the Academy—where he was considered the worst

113

Jan Nemec

student—he selected as the subject for his third-year film a story of the Polish non-conformist, and probably the most prominent literary talent of the Polish "thaw", Marek Hlasko, called *The Most Sacred Words of Our Life,* and for the first time he clashed with the authority. He knew Hlasko's story from a manuscript translation—the book in which it was to appear was later confiscated by Czechoslovakian censorship—but the professors found the thing indecent, and allowed him to make it only after an intervention by Vaclav Krska. The entire story is a conversation between lovers lying naked in bed. Nemec started to shoot in the school studios and, surprisingly, all the students wanted to come and watch the worst student at work; probably for the first time since *Extasy,* naked people were being filmed in Prague. When Nemec finished shooting, somebody stole the negative and so no one, with the possible exception of the thief, ever saw the result.

Vaclav Krska had the greatest effect on him at the Academy. Nemec considers Krska's *Moon Above the River* to be an avant-garde film of its time. It is a story about feelings, full of emotions and desires, and as Nemec says, for the first time in Czech cinema it reveals the personality of the director. In that sense, to Nemec, Krska is a predecessor of Antonioni, and he may be right. Krska had the misfortune of producing his best works at a time when virtually no Czech films were being sent to festivals abroad.

That is probably the only misfortune that Nemec did not have.

114

Diamonds of the Night. *"Ominous powers that awaken in a person when he becomes a member of a crowd": from hunters of hares into hunters of Jews.*

His thesis film, *The Morsel* (1960), received the Silver Rose at the Festival of Student Films in Amsterdam. The theme came once again from Arnost Lustig, who also co-operated with Nemec on the latter's first feature, *The Diamonds of the Night* (1964). Earlier, Nemec worked as an assistant with Krska and Fric. A compilation film which he made during military service was a poetic confrontation of the spring of 1963 and the last days of the Second World War. He named it *Memory of Our Day* (1963), and won the Army Film Prize for it.

Diamonds of the Night (1964), based on Lustig's fiction *Darkness Casts No Shadow,* tells the story of two youngsters trying to escape, in the last days of the war, from a "death march".* They are running through a forest, hungry and exhausted, but manage to beg a piece of bread from a peasant woman; in the end they accidentally encounter a group of old men, long past military age, who had gone out hunting; now, instead of hunting animals, they begin to hunt the two people.

So much for the story. Nemec, however, did not film the story; he filmed the mental states of the two boys—their hallucinations, day

*At the end of the war, in an attempt to delete traces of the crimes committed in concentration camps, the retreating Nazis evacuated prisoners from some of the camps and moved them further into Germany. The prisoners, all of them in extremely poor physical condition, were forced to walk long distances without food or water. Those who were too weak to continue the "death march" were usually shot by the SS guards.

115

dreams and nightmares, their notions and ideas. He simply tried to express their inner world during the attempted escape from death. That is the essence of the originality of the film, which was welcomed by the European film critics as the beginning of a new style. In fact, it is reminiscent of a single predecessor, Bunuel's *Andalusian Dog,* in which the director tried to film dreams. Nemec's work is noted for its bold editing, mixing reality with visions, delusions and dreams. In the final sequence, which shows the transformation of the old German men from rabbit hunters to head hunters, the film changes into a metaphor about the ominous psychological powers that awaken in a person when he becomes a member of a crowd. Those apparently normal German grandfathers become murderous beasts, while the fleeing boys become the hunted game. *Diamonds* received the Grand Prix at Mannheim in 1964, and the Critics' Prize at Pesaro in 1965.

That year, Nemec took part in the omnibus film *Pearls in the Abyss* for which he made *The Impostors.* It is a story with absolutely no action: two old men in hospital are exchanging tall stories about their past. One used to be a famous opera singer, the other a racing driver. Nothing happens—the two just talk and talk. The only action is a pictorial epilogue: the barber, who is shaving both the old fellows as they lie dead in the morgue, tells the hospital attendant that the two were absolute zeros, who kept boasting of imaginary careers.

To film something so totally devoid of action presents a problem. Nemec solved it basically by editing. He shot only two very long close-ups of the faces of the talking old men—which he alternated by rhythmical cutting, so that he achieved an unreal nightmarish effect. He might have been simply testing the method which he used in his second most famous film to date, *Report on the Party and the Guests* (1966), where faces play the most important part.

With this film began his short, but very important, co-operation with Ester Krumbachova, as well as my friendship with both of them.

Truly, I don't know how old Ester is. Once I impolitely asked her and she answered, "Well, I'm certainly not as youthful as you are."

". . . I'm certainly not as youthful as you are." One of Ester's lies during the shooting of Report . . .

116

She is an uncommonly beautiful woman; I first saw her in the Viola café, where Ivan Vyskocil tried to persuade her to appear on the stage of his literary cabaret, because he had heard that she wrote stories. Readings were fashionable at that time and a number of writers, including myself, turned into entertainers once a week. Ester, a perfumed elegant lady in a costume made by the best Prague couturier, shook from premature stage-fright, and the performance never materialized. Instead we began to visit her regularly with my wife (who knew her from my TV musical *The Banjo Show,* for which Ester had designed the costumes) in her apartment in Krc, where the fragrance of Ester's perfumes mingled with those that her tomcat Pete exuded into an ill-definable olfactory cocktail. She found Pete on a rain-soaked street, took him home, and because she couldn't bear the thought of somebody hurting him he is still a full-fledged male, and in the accustomed manner of tomcats he lures the ever-absent females. The eau-de-Cologne and sandalwood only partly neutralize the penetrating odour with which Pete impregrates Ester's carpets.

Everything in her apartment is aesthetic, elegant and pleasant, and in the middle of it all sits Ester in a low-cut dress speaking to Lindsay Anderson about her father, who was (according to her account) an unbelievable mixture of a Gypsy and Hungarian with a Slovak, and a dandy of the old school, complete with gardenia, monocle and walking stick, and a serious advocate of *quieta non movere* to boot.

Ester's own life was rougher—even before she started to make Czech films. As a young girl she joined the anti-Nazi underground and spent some time in a Gestapo prison. After the war she attended the Academy of Applied Arts and became a costume designer, first in theatre and then in film. Her rise was not very smooth, and was interrupted by several falls caused by Ester's excessive outspokenness. At one time she worked as the proverbial female brick-layer on border-region construction projects. Finally she established herself in the Barrandov studios, where she designed costumes for a large number of films.

Being an unusually strong personality, Ester affected many a good Czech film with her finery and millinery more than is usually presumed. Film is after all a visual art and the way the actors are dressed may sometimes speak while the director is silent. I remember Ester's passionate elaborations on the concept of costumes for

118

One of Madame Krumbachova's hats. Though this one was not "a triumph of the art of costume design in a certain, rather negative sense," it is a fine specimen.

such unusual films as were Kachyna's *The Coach to Vienna* or Jasny's *All Those Good Countrymen,* in which the costumes always intelligently helped to create the characters. Sometimes even against the will of the character, because Ester is, like Vera Chytilova, (whose English 'r' Ester splendidly imitates—in Vera's absence, that is), one hundred percent *woman,* but unlike Vera she is not a feminist. Once, for instance, two directors were desperately trying to figure out why a well-known film star (also, frequently and with lusty hatred, parodied by Ester) looked somehow undefinably abominable in the most important scenes of their super-spectacle. My wife discovered the cause but did not tell the directors. In those particular scenes, the star was wearing a hat designed by Madame Krumbachova. It was a triumph of the art of costume design in a certain, rather negative, sense.

She actually met Honza (the Czech diminutive for Jan) Nemec through costumes—she designed his *Diamonds of the Night*—and although Nemec is far more youthful than I, a great love developed; also an exemplary, although often explosive, co-operation. Nemec was always a great writer of screen plays. He produced them almost as fast as the watchful overseers threw them back at him. (They managed to throw back a goodly number of them, among others a script based on Kafka's *Metamorphosis* and one on Dostoyevski's *Wet Snow*). Before this Ester had started to write philosophical short stories and gentle sketches about cats. In the screen-play of *Report...*, Nemec's violent resentment of social ills merged with

119

The Banjo Show: *Madame Krumbachova's sexy costumes (worn here by the Incognito Quartette).*

Ester's elegant venomousness and her sense of design to produce one of the most important movies of the New Wave; at this point Nemec achieved a completely original, theoretically justifiable style, which stands in direct contrast to the style of Milos Forman. Anyway, the New Wave was never a movement that would follow a clearly defined programme (with the exception of its obvious humanism) but simply an example of what an intelligently managed socialist cinematography could achieve.

"I believe, that a movement striving to achieve the most accurate external copy of life," says Nemec, "is only one of the developmental stages. It will certainly enrich the film language, but I maintain that the trend should be towards stylization. It is necessary for the author to create in a film his own world, which is totally independent of reality as it at that particular moment appears. The world of a composer is created of tones and chords, the painter's world is made of colours and lines, but when we consider film, we may talk of very few authors who managed to create their own film world. We may certainly speak of Chaplin and Bresson, and Bunuel. Why do I consider it so important? If I were to aim in my films predominantly at an external similarity with the world, I would waste a lot of energy and divert the viewers attention from the crux of the matter with which I am dealing. The viewer then necessarily asks, how life-like the work really is, whether it resembles life the way he experiences it, whether it duplicates it exactly, or only approximately. However, it is evident from the very first shot, that external similarity is of no relevance, then the audience is forced to give up its favourite comparisons, and has to concentrate on the meaning and the author's intentions. So, for instance, with Chaplin you cannot tell where and when his adventures take place. You recognize fundamental elements: a city, morning, rich man, beggar.... And in a world, which is only the world of Charlie Chaplin, you may follow his bitterly ironic testimony."

It is probably good to be acquainted with such thoughts of the director, if one is to fully understand films such as *The Report on the Party and the Guests,* or the *Martyrs of Love.* In the *Report...* seven guests are walking to a garden party. Suddenly, while walking through a forest, they are surrounded by a band of men, who begin to interrogate them. When one of the guests objects, he is attacked by the ominous gang and knocked to the ground. Unexpectedly, the Host appears and explains everything: the interrogation was only a joke organized by other guests, also invited to the party, and led by the Host's adoptive son. Everybody is reconciled, and each guest takes his place at the prepared tables, located in a beautiful secluded spot near a pond. During the feast the Host ventures his opinions, the guests speak and twaddle, and some of them gradually adapt their own opinions to those of the Host. He constantly reassures them of his only wish, which is that they should feel happy with him. Eventually all of the guests, with one exception, assure the Host of their happiness. The dissenter gets up unnoticed and disappears. When his absence is discovered the Host permits his adoptive son to head a group of guests to look for the fugitive, bring him back, and also "make him happy". The whole company rise and leave, accompanied by monstrous dogs, to pursue the victim. The screen darkens; we can only hear the barking, and then the angry growling of the huge police dogs as they capture their prey.

It is evidently a parable about the process which takes place in all modern societies—the adoption of a dominant ideology—and about the destruction of those who do not adopt it. Nemec tried to express the parable by the linkage of verbal and facial reactions of the characters. The characters posed the main problem—and *Report...* was to a great extent a communal endeavour of the Prague intellectuals. Most of those who participated were non-

121

Report on the Party and the Guests: *the Host (Ivan Vyskocil). "Not intended to resemble Vladimir Ilyitch . . ."*

actors, and usually friends of Jan and Ester: I appeared in the film as the Gourmand completely oblivious to the surroundings; my wife played a Coquette; Evald Schorm had the part of the Man Who Escapes from the Party; the psychologist Jiri Nemec was the Yesman; the writer Ivan Vyskocil played the Host; Helena Pejskova, a dancer, played the Sexy Girl; her sister, Irena, a medical student, the Homely One; the part of the Unhappy Bridegroom was given to the photographer Milon Novotny, while the puppeteer Jana Pracharova played a Hare-brained Woman, and the composer Jan Klusak became the Host's Adoptive Son. The pop writer Karel Mares was the Protesting Guest knocked down in the forest, and there were many others. We were all carefully (and maliciously) selected according to appearance, as each character was to appear only in situations typical for the particular character and speak in clichés characteristic of the type. The entire film was a composition of minute details, a kind of a movable pointilism, in which people keep talking and talking—yet the resulting mood of the film is a strange deafness, an appalling apathy, and a peculiar alienation. The appearances of the characters are usually contrasted

Report on the Party and the Guests:

The Coquette (my wife). "Faces carefully (and maliciously) selected . . ."
The Host's Adoptive Son (Jan Klusak).
The Sexy Girl (Helena Pejskova from the Ballet of the National Theatre).
The Guest Who Refused to Be Happy (Evald Schorm).

123

The Protesting Guest (Karel Mares): "Many scenes were arranged according to well-known photos..."

against their personalities: so, for instance, Jiri Nemec, who looks like a very decent person, finally proves himself to be the most active ally of evil, because he always manages to condone it, while giving the impression of sincerely disagreeing with it.

The final effect was of a nightmare, a strange combination of an unreal framework with realistic details of speech and action. The influence of the designer, Ester, was evident from the strong "pictorial" conception of the film. Many scenes were arranged according to well-known photos or paintings. Thus the opening of the film reminds one of the impressionistic "*déjeuner sur l'herbe*". The fight between the objecting guest with the host's son Karel resembles news shots from Vietnam and elsewhere. The guests, eagerly listening to the host, bring to mind the photographs of Nazi officials listening to the Fuhrer; finally, the arrangement and setting of the

Report on the Party:*"The influence of the designer Ester was evident from the strong 'pictorial' conception of the film."*
Top: *the Coquette, the Sexy Girl and the Hare-Brained Woman.*
Bottom: *the Guest Who Refused to Be Happy, the Foul-Mouthed Guest (Pavel Bosek) and the Protesting Guest.*

124

tables, with the flowers and candelabras, is composed after the banquets given on the occasion of the Nobel Prize announcements. Everything is a mirage, and yet you feel that it is also reality.

I recall nostalgically the days in Teptin, where the film was made. Ester, with the expression of a martyr (she belongs to that kind of creator who suffers while she works), ran from table to table in her short dress (a creation by Podolska—comparable to Dior in the western world), adjusting the baroque candelabras and, with her fragrant fingers, arranging the withered rose in the crystal vases, while we pretended to be enjoying the stale food on the gilded plates (for economical purposes the food was changed once every three days although it was summertime; not even Mr. Jack-in-the-Box would have a cause for criticism). More often, and with considerably less nostalgia, I remember how we once sat with Honza in the Barrandov projection room, watching the rushes of Mr. Vyskocil, and Honza suddenly paled and said, "Jesus! On the screen he looks like Lenin!" And I suddenly realized that this was exactly what gave the scene a kind of flavour of impending horror, whose source, until then, I could not put my finger on. Ivan Vyskocil really looked like a carbon copy of Vladimir Illich. "Shit," I said, "I think you're in for it!"

He was. Mr. President hit the ceiling, and stayed there throughout the screening. A deadly white Honza, with a somewhat wilted Ester, visited me one evening to inquire about the details of my own disaster with *The Cowards:* what terms were used against me, what methods, and whether I really spent some time in the cooler—a rumour which was mistakenly circulated throughout Prague.

Nothing so radical happened, either to me or later to Honza and Ester; the premiere was only delayed until the President cooled off, which had become almost customary with the films of the New Wave. This time it took him an unusually long time, and before he recovered, the busy-bees Honza and Ester whipped up another delight for the personal pleasure of the head of state, *The Martyrs of Love*. This time it was not an attack on a political climate, or its methods, but it was guilty of something almost as obnoxious: it was incomprehensible.

Jan Nemec at work on my wife and Karel Mares in Report on the Party and the Guests.

Report . . . *the Gourmand (myself) among Ester's candelabra.*

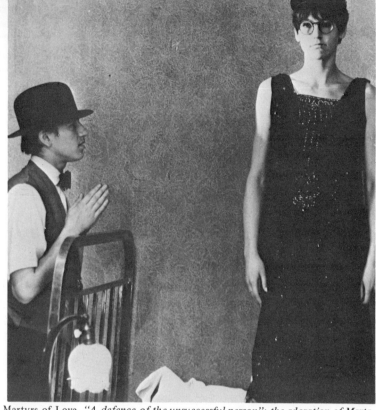

Martyrs of Love. *"A defence of the unsuccessful person": the adoration of Marta (Kubisova) by the shy operator.*

Mr. President was also famous for his distaste for everything that he could not understand; Majakovsky probably wasn't one of his favourite poets. When the Odeon publishing house, where I worked for some time as an editor, printed for its friends New Year's greetings with clever calligraphy by Jasa David, the director (who used to be the personal secretary to Klement Gottwald) proudly presented them to the President. The handsome statesman climbed to his accustomed place; the caligraphies were confiscated by the censor; and the director had to pay their production cost from his own pocket, upon a direct order by the President.*

Learning from such experiences, Nemec decided to follow the

*This was one of the rare instances when the President displayed something resembling black humour. Another case was reported in relation to the demotion of the Minister of Education, Mr. Cisar, in 1966 or '67. Cisar's daughter, a student at Charles University, was arrested during the May Day student demonstrations. The severely embarrassed minister was summoned to the Prague Castle, and the President asked him where he wished to be sent as an ambassador. "To Paris," replied the minister. The President chuckled maliciously and decided, "You will go to the Paris of the East!" And he sent him to Bucharest, which is how that city was referred to in Czechoslovakia before World War Two. It is difficult to decide whether this is true or whether it is just another Czech story. The fact remains that Miss Cisarova served her time in prison, and her father really did go to Bucharest.

example of Majakovsky, and launched a preventive war in support of exclusive art. He handled it rather sophistically: "I am convinced," he wrote, "that a certain kind of exclusiveness will fulfil its positive role in the evolution of the desired harmony...by evoking on the part of the creators the desire to make more communicative and accessible films." His quick reply to the frequent hypocritical objections referring to the unfeasibility of art films (the "exclusive" Czech films made more money abroad than ten folksy films at home) was somewhat demagogical: "The question is, whether a film is really a film—as Chaplin, Bresson, and others say—only if the auditorium is full."

The resistance to the incomprehensible *Martyrs of Love* was an inexplicable mistake. In the three stories, united by the common theme of shy lovers, there is about as much incomprehensibility as in the poems of Sergei Yesenin—and as much beauty. The authors of the stories said about them:

These aren't pictures of or from life, but three stylized love - adventures. Rather than attempting to show the world as it is, these are fables or songs, The first story, called "The Temptations of an Operator",is intended as a silent comedy; it has practically no dialogue, and it aims to be funny with a bit of sadness. If somebody gets put off by the somewhat gloomy character of its milieu, let him kindly remember the places in Chaplin's comedies—the huts, dives, hovels, and dumps—which as everybody recognizes do not serve to nauseate life, but rather are a backdrop for the spirit of the work; the work itself being almost exclusively a defence of a withdrawn and unsuccessful person. This should also be the meaning of the three stories: the grotesque confession of the operator, Nastenka's sentimental dream, and the wonderful nocturnal adventures of Rudolf the orphan.

That is indeed what the film is like. I think we can apply to it Saint Exupery's words: "The important things we can see only through our heart: eyes cannot perceive them." Once again the author's affinity towards Bunuel comes out: if in the *Diamonds of the Night* Nemec filmed nightmares, here he captured daydreams, just as Bunuel once filmed dreams. The film again boasts excellent design, with the stress on visual effect. Again it contains a succession

129

of pictorial compositions, with the actors' faces being selected with great care in order to create atmosphere, character, symbol and parable. It is once again a predominantly lyrical film, affecting the innermost centres of the viewer, his feeling and emotions, and not his reason. The particular emphasis on emotions and mood, and the lyrical approach make Nemec's work an organic part of the great tradition of Czech art; it it were necessary to determine the Czech contribution to world art, its major offerings would be found in the realm of poetic and lyrical presentation of reality.

After *The Martyrs of Love,* Honza's and Ester's collaboration ended, as did their marriage soon after. I suspect them of going through that bourgeois formality only because of Ester's apartment; they were far too romantic as lovers to need an official document for their love. Soon after the disaster with *The Party and the Guests,* Ester's nosy neighbours warned the appropriate authorities that the idle (i.e. free-lancing), coquettish, perfumed, divorcee Ester was occupying a one-bedroom apartment all by herself, in addition to having a frequent over-night male visitor, a fact which caused moral indignation. Both problems, that of occupying excessive living quarters and that of immorality, were resolved by a short official ceremony at the Old Town City Hall, and the neighbours, for a change, began to complain about mewing cats. They were referring to Pete and his companion, Snail, which was a kitten whose heartrending cries Ester heard one night at Slapy, where she and Honza bought a cottage. She ventured into the forest and, by successfully imitating feline sounds, managed to lure the abandoned creature into her kind embrace.

In that particular cottage, we spent the New Year's eve of 1967. Honza was currently experiencing new "difficulties", having made a film in Holland without the approval of the Czech national film authority. In any event, the film *Mother and Son* (1967) could not have been very popular with the President, despite the grand prix from Oberhausen. It dealt with the birth of fascist sentimentality: an ex-convict murders a plainclothsman, who once tortured him. The grief-stricken policeman's mother sits at the grave and shoots at the pigeons who defecate on her son's tomb stone. Although still deeply in trouble, Honza was already contemplating a film about the so-called Strahov events*,

*He indeed made it in the spring of 1968.

130

during which the police brutally attacked the striking students, and chased them all the way into the dormitories. The result was a number of students injured, and one crippled for life. The event did not lack the absurd touch. There were constant power failures in the dormitories, which made it rather difficult to study. The students took to the streets chanting, "Give us light!", which the overtaxed police brains, stupefied by the constantly discussed ideas about the ambiguity of art, interpreted as subversive slogans demanding the freedom of press and import of foreign literature. So they reached for the billy clubs.

It was an idyllic, snowy night at Honza's and Ester's cottage in Central Bohemia. In nearby Prague, the President was trying to save his skin by plotting with the conservative generals. By this time he was only President; the position of First Secretary of the Party had been taken over by someone called Dubcek. Ester cooked a traditional lentil soup; we baked sizzling hot-dogs impaled on her knitting needles in the fireplace; Ester's beautiful eyes glistened; she wept. Ester is thoroughly feminine, and New Year's Eve is a sentimental time. Ester loves the Bible. She took it from below the darkened television set, inserted a finger into it as if she were probing a wound, and the pink fingernail pointed at a verse: "And the four angels were loosed, which were prepared for an hour, and a day, and a month, and a year, for to slay the third part of men. And the number of the army of the horsemen were two hundred thousand: and I heard the number of them. And thus I saw the horses in the vision, and them that sat on them, having breast-plates of fire, and of jacinth, and brimstone: and the heads of the horses were the heads of lions; and out of their mouths issued fire and smoke and brimstone."

It was not exactly an encouraging superstition in the early morning hours of the first day of the year of our Lord, 1968.

After that I saw Ester very infrequently. I remember meeting her after she returned from abroad, where she had been attending some coproduction negotiations. With her typical healthy hatred, she described the course of a party, and in the same fashion in which she once imitated the English 'r' of Vera Chytilova, she parodied the fantastic conversational leaps of Western socialites, who would in one breath deliver a cool compassionate speech about the tragedy of a distant nation and, after another sip of

Ester

Scotch, describe, with humourless humour, some bedroom gossip. Ester presented the West, or at least the circles into which an interesting foreigner is introduced, as a domain inhabited by neurotic idiots, and she did it very convincingly. Through the window of her apartment, we could see long lines of shabbily dressed citizens of a counter-revolutionary nation waiting in front of the butchershop and dairy. The beige lady harmonized beautifully with the dusky Prague setting, and I realized that Ester loves our ill-fated country more than all its official lovers.

I met her for the last time in January of 1969, a few days before Jan Palach's suicide*. Together we attended a friendly meeting with the workers of the largest Prague metal-works, where the ex-president, Novotny, used to have his fifth column. A huge poster hung at the gate, resembling the shock-workers' posters of the fifties: an oversized face of a man in a flat cap, with a tear in his eye. When we came closer we noticed it was a bloody tear with the date 21,8,1968 in it. We taped the discussion and the factory paper reprinted it. In September of 1970, *Rude Pravo* wrote about the meeting, that on that occasion right-wing opportunists met with their friends, the reactionary writers. That was the last time I saw Ester.

*A student of Charles University who immolated himself in protest against the Soviet occupation of the country.

The Murder of Engineer Devil – *"gently ridiculing the amorous dreaminess of gentle women. Vladimir Mensik (who stole my part in Loves of a Blond) and Jirina Bohdalova.*

I didn't even get to see her directorial debut. Honza had collaborated on the screen-play, but that terminated after the separation. We printed the script in the magazine *Plamen* which was banned soon afterwards. Judging by the scenario, the film should bear no traces of Chytilova's feminism. It is a phantasmic, dream-like story, gently ridiculing the amorous dreaminess of gentle women. A story not of this world, full of magic, miracles, and of very original humour: the protagonist falls in love with an engineer called Devil, who in the end turns out to be a real devil, who once in a while turns into a kind of an abominable snowman. The whole thing cannot be described in traditional and rational terms. It contains a touch of surrealism, with its delight in sentimental campy kitsch. Once again everything is conceived very visually, with an overwhelming display of colours, shapes, costumes, objects, hair, etc. All told, *The Murder of Engineer Devil* (1970) is a portrait of Ester's soul, which is just as feminine as Vera's.

The part of the dark-haired object of the operator's erotic dreams in the *Martyrs of Love* was played by an attractive Czech pop-singer Marta Kubisova. In the spring of 1968, Nemec made with her a series of short films for television later released as *A Necklace of Melancholy,* a work of great artistic purity combining the beauty of Prague's baroque architecture with the beauty of Marta's face, and with the aesthetics of modern rock. After the arrival of the tanks, Marta daringly recorded several of the best protest songs, and became the idol of Czechoslovakia. During a reception at the Prague Castle, she kissed the First Secretary Dubcek, who at that time was no longer greeted by his former friends. As a result she was prohibited from appearing in public, banned from television,

133

Marta in A Necklace of Melancholy. *She kissed the same man as Mr. Brezhnev did — yet she had to go while he stayed. Was it because . . .*

radio, and records.* Later, Nemec married her. They live at the cottage where Ester's pink finger found the Apocalypse; Marta is expecting a child, and both of them are supposed to be living on their home-grown vegetables.† They are living in much the same way as, on the other side of the world, does Allen Ginsberg, who was also banned under President Novotny after he was elected King of May by the students of Charles University.

*In connection with this a malicious anecdote circulated around Prague: "Do you know why Brezhnev so seldom appears on TV? It's because he kissed Dubcek in Cierna (the place of the final pre-invasion negotiations between the Czechs and the Soviets).

† In late 1970, Marta suffered a miscarriage and nearly died. The singing trio of which she had been the star, *The Golden Kids,* ceased to exist. First the other two members, Helena Vondrackova and Vaclav Neckar, reportedly refused to break with Marta after they had been shown the notorious pornographic photographs (see footnote on page 238); they claimed that Marta's private life was *her* private life, and that anyway the photo was not authentic (which it was not). Later Vaclav Neckar (the young railway apprentice, Milos Hrma, from *Closely Watched Trains*) was reportedly banned from television by the former president's former in-law Jan Zelenka, now general manager of Prague TV, for having refused to cut his long hair. He is now used mainly for export to the East. Vondrackova, was forced to give concerts in the USSR where, according to eyewitness reports, she shocked the Party puritans by appearing on the stage bra-less. Early in 1971, she was sent by the State Concert Agency on a one year tour abroad. The rationale behind this decision is again understandable: the absence of the extremely popular Helena will facilitate the process of forgetting the better old days on the part of the young audiences; on the other hand, under the present conditions, Helena herself certainly welcomes a long trip abroad. And, last but not least, her sweet beauty may create a favourable image of her native country, and identify it with the Czech government in the minds of the very forgetful Western audiences. This is an old trick: the handsome, somersaulting officers of the Red Army Ensemble thrilled the Toronto society ladies in their minks and miniskirts, not so long ago, so that they refused to accept leaflets distributed by Latvian immigrants in front of Maple Leaf Gardens. The business was good in spite of the efforts of the immigrants, as the Canadian promoter of the event wrote in the papers with satisfaction, and all was right with the (Canadian) world.

. . . all animals are equal, but some are more equal than others?

Before the arrival of the tanks, I met with Honza over two projects. The first was to be a film version of my novel *The End of the Nylon Age,* written in 1950, confiscated by the censor in 1957, and finally published in 1967. It describes the course of a carnival, given in 1949 by the American Institute in Prague, and is full of dreamy debutantes, gilded youth and frustrated young men and women of the time of the great social turning point. It also shows the snobs of the international cocktail circuit observing the agony of a particular society. An ephemeral dance before the Fall of the Great Axe. Honza was attracted to it by its atmosphere of the lost world, and by

135

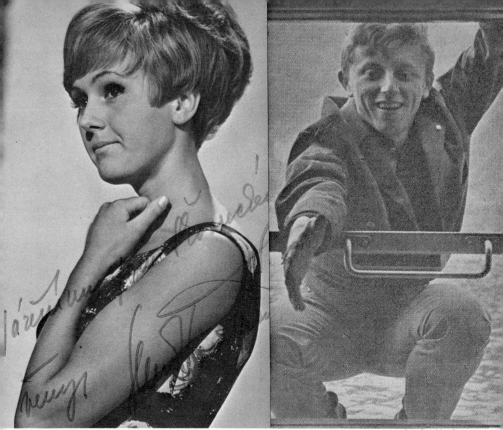

Helenka Vondrackova: a pop-singer for export.   *Vaclav Neckar*

its background musical motifs containing melodies of Glen Miller, Count Basie, and Chick Webb. Everything went smoothly; the new president either wasn't interested in film, or he was friendly, and the only "problems" that we encountered came from the United States. The swing melodies which Honza wanted to use to create an atmosphere were all copyrighted, and the rights would have cost more than the rest of the production. We left the negotiations up to the agencies and started on the second project, which was offered to Nemec by an American producer.

It was to be a documentary about the Czechoslovakia of 1968, and Honza made it in a very erudite fashion. It showed prisons whose only inhabitants, after the political prisoners had been released, were criminals; it showed churches in which the liberated clergymen once again held services; it was about the Prague hippies and their friendship with foreign flower children, who during that summer journeyed to Prague from all over Europe; it was also about a folk festival, where Dubcek and Smrkovsky danced with the people; and about the general happiness, which spontaneously affected the masses: a point counterpoint of time which was rather pleasantly out of joint. I wrote the commentary, we edited it on the

136

19th of August, 1968, at the laboratories in Vodickova Street. On the twentieth I left for a vacation in France.

I saw the film in Paris in October. It had changed and was then called *Oratorio for Prague* (1968). Tanks smashed into the idyllic counterpoints. Next to the dancing Smrkovsky, lay a boy shot by a machine-gun. Next to a priest raising a chalice, stood two boys with a bloodied flag. Next to Dubcek waving to the crowds, a Soviet political officer waved his revolver at the crowds from a tank turret. One of the cameramen who had made the film was, at that time, lying in a hospital with his jaw shot off.

I met with Honza in a hotel in the Latin Quarter; he seemed to be deranged. We got desperately drunk on pastis, and Honza left for a film festival in West Germany, where the progressive German students booed the *Oratorio for Prague*. The film contains a shot of Czech people who, for the first time since 1948, were permitted to decorate the graves of the American soldiers who had died on Czechoslovakian soil while driving out the fathers of the booing youths.

Later on I spoke to Nemec in Prague. He had returned from the Soviet headquarters where he demanded to see the *White Book on Counter-Revolution in Czechoslovakia* because someone had told him that he was mentioned in it. The Soviet officers willingly showed it to him, and when the choleric Honza, who got mad over the appropriate paragraph in the text, accused the officer of spreading lies, the latter was quite embarrassed. Just as embarrassed as the boys in the tanks had been, when nobody welcomed them, although they had been told they would be showered with flowers.

Still later, Honza supposedly asked for permission to make a film about Lenin. I don't know the outcome of his supplication, but I doubt that he will be making it in the forseeable future. It is a shame. Lenin is nowadays, depending on one's inclinations, either God or Satan. I would say that, in Nemec's film, he would probably turn out to be the man who, towards the end of his life, warned the Party about Stalin.

Evald Schorm

Besides an attractive exterior, cleverness and stubborn will, Vera Chytilova is well known for her hysterical fits. The most famous

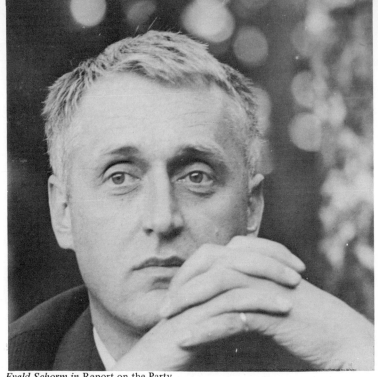
Evald Schorm in Report on the Party

one was during an acting class while she was still at the Academy. Under the guidance of an expert, the student directors were supposed to perform a love scene. At first glance, the two were a nice pair: the slim, dark-haired gypsy-eyed Vera, and a tall blond Scandinavian type, who could have served Alfred Rosenberg as an example of the best of the Nordic race. But when the professor beckoned them to begin their scene, the gentleman took a few elephantine strides and stepped on Vera's foot. The fit followed: the actor was showered with an overabundance of English 'r's and Vera was assigned a more erudite Jiri Menzel.

However, neither philosophers nor opera singers are usually renowned for their flexibility of limb and, although Evald Schorm is quite justifiably considered a philosopher of the New Wave, it is less well known that he began his career as an opera singer. He was a member of that peculiar product of late stalinism—the army opera. I don't know where the army got the idea to start its own opera ensemble, when not even Russia ever had anything like it. However, Russia never had a General Cepicka either, who profitably married the president's daughter, and then went on to prove his reliability by actively participating in the torture of Slansky and Co. In order to gain popularity among his soldiers, the lawyer-turned-general improved the quality of the mess hall chow to that of the succulent repasts of the international hotels: all of this at a time when the civilians were living on rations. They threw him out shortly after he

138

ordered the officers to wear sabres as a part of their uniform; the sabres were too long and the officers kept tripping over them. He failed to accomplish his greatest dream, which was to dress all troops in ceremonial uniforms. The bright red, baby blue, turquoise green and pious purple breeches would differentiate the various sections of the army.

The opera was probably a product of the terpsichorean fantasy of a parlour-room General, and I am desperately trying to imagine the six-footer Evald attired in turquoise breeches and singing an aria from *La Traviata* to a platoon of bombardiers.

When the opera went the way of the cashiered general (who became the head of the Patent Office), the washed-up maestro tried to get into the Film Academy. He was accepted but embarked on his film career with peculiar scepticism: "I have failed in several professions, and I doubt that I will succeed in film. Yet, directors are often recruited from among failures. Kozintsev expressed it once beautifully when he said that anybody is a director who does not prove that he is not."

Overly sensitive and slightly superstitious people defend themselves against their own fear of the world's cruelty by assuming the identity of a simpleton. "Pepicek, Pepicek, I'm coming to a bad end!" With this petrified sentence delivered in the pitiful tone of a lamenting village pauper I connect Evald Schorm. He always and everywhere repeated it: in my apartment when we wrote the screenplay to *End of a Priest;* in the studio when he tried to make himself invisible behind the camera; in the hotel room which we shared in Pocepice, where the film was made; and on location, in the morning while he was taking an overdose of sedatives in order to remain calm. "Oh no! Not me! How can they want instruction from me? I don't know anything!"

Naturally it was self-stylization, a subconscious defence. I know it well. It is an insurance against that final failure which awaits almost all of us, when we are removed from the list of those who still have something to say. So that when the time comes, we will be able to say, "But gentlemen, I kept telling you, I am an idiot." Or, if this should be more in your style, "How could you idiots understand a genius like me?" In either case you end up shooting yourself, just like Hemingway.

An artist needs such self-stylization: it serves him as a protective thick skin, which is something William Faulkner knew so well. "The

139

world is terrifying," says Evald Schorm, "and yet it is beautiful, and that's how it is with everything; things exist so close together, that between love and cruelty, between one thing and another there is but a tiny, negligible distance."

With Christian humbleness he began to make documentaries and semi-documentaries from the milieu recommended to the attention of the artists several years earlier: *Blok 15,* about the construction of a high dam; *Ground to Ground* about miners in the Ostrava coal mines; *Trees and People,* showing the work of lumberers in the mountains. Years earlier "masters" of literature and direction gave that world a quick glance, then stuffed it into the appropriate formula, and received the State Prize in appreciation of their mastery. "This theory of mastery," said Schorm, "caused so much damage in all spheres, that it makes me afraid: mastery has become a catch phrase; any nonsense, if it pretends to be masterful, allegedly turns into a work of art. For example, if a bad film employs only trained Distinguished Artists,* it will be great."

His own documentaries were not made in the "quick glance" style. They provided him with a profound and authentic knowledge of the worker's life, prevented him from going down the usual road towards naturalism or comedies of the "folksy" kind. His vision is too democratic to allow him to see workers "as grotesques or as pastoral decorations", as they were seen, according to Evelyn Waugh's assessment, not only by artists of past centuries, but also by a number of socialist realists. Schorm says the following about naturalism: "I don't believe in the future of empiricism, because then the greatest writers would have been cops and lawyers. I find that the key to everything lies in great perceptiveness and an open, approachable soul, which is able to re-live also things that happened to other people."

To other people. After the documentaries about the life of the working class, he made a poetic documentary, *To Live One's Life* (1963), about the photographer Josef Sudek; a film about loyalty to an idea, and about sacrificing one's life to art. Sudek is a typical Prague character: a one-armed (he lost his arm in World War I), hunched old man, whom you can see dragging a gigantic plate camera on a tripod up the steep streets of the Old Town.

*The title of Distinguished Artist was invented in the Soviet Union, and is usually bestowed upon excellent senior artists, or upon those who serve fearlessly in the field of ideology.

Evald's To Live One's Life: *Mr. Josef Sudek . . .*

However behind the cliché of a "typical Prague character" hides one of the few true artists of photography. The skill with which he managed to capture the magical beauty of the medieval city with his old fashioned camera was never equalled by anyone—painters not excepted.

Schorm was attracted to Sudek by the photographer's obsession with art, since that happens to be Schorm's own personal vice. "I would say to myself...you lose a book, you lose a life," he likes to quote Jerzy Andrzejewski (*Ashes and Diamonds*). "Life? Isn't that too much? Maybe not. Don't think that such ideas are forced upon a writer by weakness, by hysterical exaltation or by shortsightedness. When a person...loses what he really loves from the bottom of his soul, then he cannot suppress the idea, that he is also losing a part of his own life, that inside him some kind of an inner light is irreversibly dying out, that an indispensable tone is being silenced forever...."

It was becoming more and more evident that the New Wave was joined by a true philosopher. His documentary work culminated in two films: one about birth, *Why?* (1964), the other about extinction, *Reflections* (1965). The subject of *Why?* was the catastrophic drop in the birth-rate in Czechoslovakia. After the legalization of abortions, it became a rarity to see a pregnant woman entering a hospital to give birth, and the sociological statistics indicated darkly that the nation was heading towards

141

Courage for Every Day: *"resembles the tirades from Osborne's* Look Back in Anger".

dissolution. This sociological affair became, in Schorm's hands, a meditation about motherhood and the meaning of life. The same question brought him to the hospital for the incurably sick in *Reflections.* Here he created a film-symposium, inspired by the poetry of Vladimir Holan (who used to listen to the poems of Milos Forman), a poetic danse-macabre, a totally black creation, entirely pessimistic, mercilessly capturing the desperate desire of the moribund to live; it also showed how the proximity of death awakens long forgotten moral and philosophical questions. Of all the Czech film-makers, only Schorm could have made such a film, because, despite his great admiration for Bunuel, he is an intrinsically Christian artist. "As far as my future is concerned," he wrote, "my heart sinks when I think about it. These are pathetic words, but I am a pathetic person."

His first feature film, *Courage for Every Day* (1964), is indeed

. . . and Prague photographed by his plate camera.

143

pathetic in a certain sense. It captures the working-class reality fifteen years after the revolution. Schorm doesn't present it as a socialist-realistic fairy-tale, but neither does he sceptically shrug his shoulders over it, in keeping with the *ex post* critics of the revolution: "This of course is *not* how we imagined it!" The film is a frontal attack against the betrayal of ideals, and the fact that the President and his advisors labelled this truly revolutionary work of art as a slander against the revolution, is just another Czechoslovakian paradox. Euphemistically, *Courage for Every Day* had the usual "problems". First it couldn't be shown, then the film critics (who now openly opposed the President's taste) awarded it a prize—but Schorm was forbidden to receive it. After ten months of wrangling, he finally got it but, for a change, the film was banned from participation in any foreign festival. When it finally appeared in French and Italian cinemas, the local critics understood what the socialist president was unable to comprehend. "Schorm passionately and without prejudice attacks the problem of the human consequences of what is usually summarized under the term 'stalinism'," wrote the Italian Communist paper *L'Unita*; and Schorm received the Critics' Prize at the Pesaro festival.

It was a story of a man in his thirties, who in the early nineteen fifties became an enthusiastic shock-worker. He was a true socialist, disregarding all personal interest and motivated only by the idea of working for the good of the people. As such he was praised, decorated and honoured. But times changed. Many of the "eager socialists" of the early fifties advanced to become officials, bureaucrats and directors. When the post-revolutionary visions of the pork-eating workers' glistening faces disappeared, and the ideas of proletarian brotherhood and love went the way of all premature utopias, the traces of idealism vanished from the factories. Workers have good eyes. They noticed that the loudest advocates of unselfish work frequently received lucrative positions as a reward for their unselfishness, which they then protected selfishly.

The film's hero, shock-worker Jarda Lukas, becomes, amidst this inconspicuously changing world, a somewhat comical remnant of the past. He gets into a spiritual crisis complicated by a breakdown in his relationship with his girl, and slowly awakens: he discovers that reality is not identical with his vision. However, and this is typical for Schorm's moral attitudes, he does not become a cynic, as was

144

the case with so many others: he does not take advantage of his medals or his outstanding character references in order to join the ranks of the satiated prophets of equality, who criss-cross the country in their luxurious Tatra 603 limousines—that peculiar symbol of "the more equal among equals", manufactured especially for "government representatives" and totally inaccessible to "ordinary" people.* Instead, in one of the film's final scenes, he delivers an angry speech to workers sitting in a tavern. The intensity of his oration resembles the tirades of Jimmy Porter in Osborne's *Look Back in Anger*—but it aims at much more clearly defined goals. He accuses them of betraying the revolution. However, by now the workers don't give a damn about the old slogans; they work in order to be paid, to feed their families. They far too frequently go by a new unofficial slogan: "Who doesn't steal from the state, steals from his family." Jaroslav throws it all into their faces: he maintains that they have exchanged the zeal of the revolutionary for an abundance of beer and soccer. But nobody in the tavern listens to his raging philippic. At that moment he is a truly comical but, at the same time, pathetically sterling character of the past. The workers have more interesting things to discuss over their mugs—the recent soccer match for instance.

The subsequent "difficulties" of this ideologically pure work are fully understandable, if we realize that the author sinned against one of the fundamental taboos of socialist realism, namely the rule: "of the workers nothing but the best"—with ominous suggestions of a devious governmental method rooted in antiquity *(panem et circenses)*. The work bore the trademarks of Schorm's style with negligible traces of *cinéma-vérité,* and no signs of the formanesque smile at reality. The film used only professional actors, and not even the most malicious critic could find in it any formalism, be it beautiful like Vera's or otherwise. It displays an austere, structural direction, which is economical and stylistically pure, which does not depict but creates. The general concensus of the Czech critics was expressed by one of the sharpest theoreticians of Czech cinema, Jaroslav Bocek, who said, "We are dealing with the profoundest talent of the generation."

Evald's second feature film *The Return of the Prodigal Son* bears

*Czech humour interprets the 603 as follows: Tatra 603 is a car which accomodates six people, who do zero and collect three thousand crowns monthly. At a time when *Courage for Every Day* was being made, the average monthly salary was approximately 1400 crowns.

The Return of the Prodigal Son: *"What is normal?"* *(Jana Brejchova with Jan Kacer)*.

all the markings of his style, polished to excellence by greater directorial experience. From the statement of betrayal of the revolution, Schorm advances to the psychological and philosophical analysis of the causes of this betrayal. The Osbornian hysteria of the working-class hero from *Courage for Every Day* is replaced by subdued questions with which a suicidal intellectual confronts himself and others.

Outwardly this man is a happily married, successful, young architect: he attempts suicide, but is saved and treated in a mental institution. From there, after an uncertain love affair with the wife of his doctor, he returns to his own wife and starts working again. At a party given to celebrate his return, the director of the company "rewards" him with a "philosophical" speech about life, which makes the young architect rudely and without explanation leave the room, faint, and subsequently return to the institution. The reasons leading to his suicide are not disclosed; we can only assume them from the discussions between Jan, the architect, and his doctor. The theme is: What is normal, and what isn't? Jan tells the doctor about his conviction that a person should act in accordance with what he considers right, irrespective of whether it will damage his career or complicate his life. The doctor asks him whether he, himself, is capable of acting in accordance with such maxims, and Jan admits he isn't. "But is that normal?" he asks.

And another question: "I would like to know, if I would be capable of not betraying, under torture. You've never actually thought about it, have you?" he asks the doctor. "If they tore out your nails and burned your skin? I have often thought about it. You say that you've never thought about it. Which one of us in normal?"

This is obviously a great and topical Central European theme (naturally not only Central European, but hardly Canadian), and causes the audiences to hold their breath. In contrast to such, in a sense, absolute questions the director's sophistic "philosophy" sounds all the more provocative. "You categorically reject any compromise," exclaims that sage, "but look here, isn't that the easiest approach to life? I am really convinced that the rejection of any kind of compromise stems from fear, uncertainty, and from suspicion of the value of the cause for whose benefit the compromise is to be made. It is obviously always important to consider why we are compromising, and further, not all compromises are alike. There are certain things which overreach the private realm...certain great and pure ideals...." At this point Jan leaves the party without uttering a word. The director booms after him through the hall, "which are worth pursuing, and which require of us...even compromises. I am simply convinced that a great, supra-personal cause somehow sanctifies the compromise...."

But is that normal? Jan does not ask the question at this particular point, but it is suggested by the confrontations of this profound film. The company director's speech once again awakens in a Central European viewer associations and echos, which resound throughout the recent and not so recent history. There is no clearcut answer to these questions—however, if people cease to ask them, or are forbidden to ask them, everything is possible and and the less pleasant possibilities have a much greater chance of occurring.

That is why everything in the film is in half-tones—from the camera to the dialogue. There is a kind of bewitching magic of absolutely serious art about it, the cathartic effect of a classical tragedy.

Schorm's method became even clearer after *The Return of the*

147

Prodigal Son: to give questions and provoke by thought, and not by formal exclusiveness. It is important to provoke, to be a pike among the lazy carps in a pond. "I believe that in life one should assume the most radical position. As it is written in the Bible: yes, yes—no, no. Quiet agreement and compromise produce dreadful results. Things either have to be run to a head, or left alone, but once a person begins to reconcile himself with something, the outcome is usually bad." His third feature, *Five Girls to Deal With* (1967), again posed a provocative question: How are we? Why are we that way?

It is a story about five teenagers, and about the strains that exist in their apparently close friendship. The heroine, a gentle and sensitive girl, is the daughter of an important local functionary in a large town, who is the head of the housing bureau. The family obviously belongs to the "new class": and the father, from the position of the director of housing, was privately able to solve the public housing shortage. They live in a beautiful villa, originally built and owned by someone else. The other four girls clearly come from other circles; one of them is a proletarian, and her family's flat is a far cry from the official's house. Measured by the canons of orthodox socialist realism, the basic situation of the film is profoundly sarcastic: in the old melodramas of the fifties, it would be the girl from the villa who would be moody, malicious and evil, while her poorer girl friends would display good-natured kindness. Here we see the gentle and sensitive daughter of an influential official, trying to please her socially less lucky companions by feeding them potato salad and lemonade from the family fridge, while her parents are absent. The girls whom life preferred less are malicious and evil. Their basic feeling towards the "lucky" Natasha is envy. They hurt her in all kinds of minor ways, so that Natasha finally seeks spiritual protection in an innocent love relationship with the son of the castle custodian. Her friends are jealous of it and destroy it by means of a nasty intrigue. Natasha first romantically considers suicide, and wants to jump in the river, but when she sees the cold current she is overcome by a natural, child-like fear. She thinks everything over and slowly changes her mind. Ultimately, she comprehends the Great Social Truth: if they attack you, you have to fight back, and in this fight anything goes. She stops being the good girl who wanted to please her friends because she desired their friendship. She complains about them to

148

her influential father, tells him what they did to her and asks him to visit the school principal and demand that they be punished. She wins, and perhaps she has just taken the first step towards becoming a malicious, moody and evil member of the new ruling class.

Schorm emphasized the urgency of the message by adding a new element to his work: throughout the framework of the story runs, as a romantic parallel, Karl Maria von Weber's tale of "Der Freischutz", and it serves as a pathetically mocking moral commentary. The drama of the five girls takes place in Liberec, a large provincial industrial city with a repertory opera company. In such cities, the opera still retains the romantic function which it used to have in the nineteenth century. Night after night, the gallery swarms with adolescent girls, all in love with the first tenor. Four of the *Five Girls* are also permanent visitors of the gallery while Natasha sits in her parents' box. Taking advantage of her father's connections, Natasha arranges that the girls meet their idol in her parents' house. Instead of gratitude, she receives only further envy. The opera which the goggle-eyed girls watch night after night is the romantic drama of "Freischutz". Its final chorus:

> Let us lift our eyes towards Heaven, and let us solidly build on the Eternal One's direction: he, who is pure of heart and without sin can childishly rely on the mildness of the Father!

makes, in the content of the action, a derisively ironical point. Schorm made prolific and original use of his own operatic background. While enriching his up till now straightforward method with a special kind of symbol and allegory, he triumphed also in another way: he proved that even the oldest elements of art—plot, tendency, morality—have their place in the most modern art—if it is, of course, art.

A single guest in *Report on the Party and the Guests* refuses to submit to the game of happiness, which the Host with menacing kindness orders his guests to play. He is the only one who does not compromise, who "brings his situation to a head", and leaves followed by the kind Host's police dogs. I was originally supposed to play this silent idealist (it is a silent part, so I might have managed, despite my intelligence), but then Honza gave the part to Schorm, and it proved to be a correct and logical decision. Honza

End of a Priest: *Evald instructs Vlastimil Brodsky (the Priest) and Jana Brejchova (the Village Mary Magdalene) how to struggle . . .*

indemnified me with the small part of a gourmand, who in one scene is passionately embraced by the sexy girl (Helena Pejskova—but the scene unfortunately fell victim to the editor's scissors). Despite the fact that I missed my second big chance in the movies, I don't regret it, because during the shooting of the *Report . . .* I told Evald the story of the fake priest.

It later became the subject of our joint effort, the film *End of a Priest.* For two years we worked on the screen-play, then during the President's last attack against the intellectuals in the fall of 1967, it was "held up", but in the spring of the year of ungrace 1968, it finally went into production.

It was in fact a realisation of an older promise that Evald and I once gave to Jana Brejchova, and her husband, the actor Vlastimil Brodsky (her second husband after Milos), that I would write a comedy for them, which Evald would direct. For a long time I couldn't come up with anything, until Evald took a liking to my story of the false priest. I had read it in the papers sometime in the

150

... and this is how they struggled — with John Lords (Vaclav Kotva) — in the film.

fifties: an adventurer passed as a priest for about eight months in a mountain village in Eastern Bohemia. He lived entirely off the generosity of the unsuspecting parishioners, who were happy to have a Father, at a time when a disproportionally large number of priests worked at digging of ditches and in the uranium mines.

We would meet, and I saw nothing more than a comical story, of which I am a fairly accomplished weaver. Evald kept lamenting "Oh no! Not me! What can I come up with! Just you write it yourself, Pepicek!" So I wrote, reinforcing myself with Bols vanilla liqueur, which I would offer to Evald, and he carried on, "Oh my God, Pepicek, don't give me any of that stuff! I'll get drunk! I'll turn into an alcoholic! I'm coming to a bad end, even without booze!" Then, after emitting a most heart-rending lament, and in between two glasses of the vanilla liqueur, he gave my somewhat barren story a twist, which filled it suddenly with meaningful overtones. As was the case with anything touched by Evald's blessed hand, it finally turned into a philosophical parable about the world we were

151

End of a Priest: *the parable of the Wedding*   *The parable of the Cured Incurable (Josefa*
Zdena Skvorecka and Jaroslav Satoransky).   *Pechlatova and Vlastimil Brodsky).*

both interested in, because it was our home, and its foolishness and
injustices hurt us. A parable about the world after the revolution.

Once upon a time and once upon a place, in a village, there lived
a priest, who was really a runaway sexton, and a school-master; a
man of the concrete, and of the abstract—the priest who likes people
en détail, and the school-master who likes them *en gros.* "Men are
good," says the school-master in the scene of the Temptation on the
Mountain. "They just have a few faults." The Priest replies, "Men
are evil. They just have a few good qualities." The two mock-heroic
characters represent thereby two principles of vital dialectics. At
that time we believed that in their interaction and love-hate relationship lay the concept of the village.

Under the large peasant hand of the ex-opera singer, the story
began to gain counterpoint; we implanted in it the ancient legend of
Jesus and Mary Magdalene, the prostitute who loved him, the symbol of the she-ass, the parable of the wedding and the adulteress to
be stoned by those who are without sin. Everything changed into a
platonic idea of a Czech village, permeated by the reality of secret
police as if by thorns, and framed by the pattern of a chaplinesque

End of a Priest: *the Actors and the Gendarmes.* "*Everything changed into a
platonic idea of a Czech village, permeated by the reality of secret police as if by
thorns*".

End of a Priest: *the village Vanity Fair.*

The parable of the Reformed Sinner.   *The Temptation on the Mountain (Jan Libicek as the Teacher, Vlastimil Brodsky as the Priest).*

farce. Upon the school-master's instructions, the priest is stopped while driving from one village to another, between masses,* and forced to take a breathalyzer test. He fails to convince the police that he has not partaken of alcohol, but rather of the Blood of our Saviour. The police chief has no understanding for the metaphysical variants of chemistry. The Priest has drawn attention to himself. Another catastrophe appears on the horizon: two bishops, one black and the other white, who for the lack of any other common language, dispute in Latin. The white one is showing the black one the desolate parishes of the "once upon a time— once upon a place" country—and in the most desolate of them all they discover a priest—who doesn't know Latin. At that moment the secret police arrive, interested in further details about the man who confuses blood with alcohol. It all results in a classical

*The motorization of the clergy became a peculiar characteristic of that almost clergyless country. It was not unusual to meet a black-helmeted man on a motorcycle tearing down some country road, pursuing with the speed of a Hell's Angel his holy calling: to manage three or four masses in a single day in three or four different mountain villages.

"Under the large peasant hand of the ex-opera singer the story began to gain counterpoint": Evald, my wife and myself during the shooting of End of a Priest *in Pocepice.*

154

Mack Sennet chase scene. Finally, we see the priest moving hand over hand along a roof-beam of the dome; from the right side approaches, in similar fashion, the school-master, whose conscience stirred him to repentance when he realized that it was the priest, and not the cop who is his real ally. From the left side carefully edges the policeman. The three of them hang there next to each other on the beam. Then the priest, turning his eyes towards Heaven and crying out in a smallish voice, "My Lord, why have I forsaken three?" lets go and falls towards his death—God knows, maybe the death of a martyr.

But we must have used an incomprehensible code. At the Cannes Festival, the film passed without much attention, and the positive American reviews later considered it to be a fairly successful, if somewhat malicious, joke. The female reviewer of a very influential New York weekly thought that the school-master, who kept repeating the wildest Party clichés, was actually quoting Chekov.

It was made in the village of Pocepice; night after night Evald lamented and moaned in the hotel room, and then doped himself to sleep—everything was suffused with phantasmic, almost medieval, coincidences. The village was discovered, independently of me, by Evald's excellent cameraman, Jaromir Sofr. It was a beautiful, typical village with a baroque cupola crowning a charming small church; during the first shooting day, one of the extras, a local old lady, came up to me and showed me an ancient photograph of a handsome young priest, who turned out to be my uncle. Unwittingly, I had returned to Pocepice, which fifty years earlier had been his first parish. Storks kept circling above the camera; the bird family has lived in this corner of the world since the time of the Crusades. Pocepice inherited the stork in its coat of arms from its feudal lords. It holds a sealed letter in its beak. In the twelfth century, the master of Pocepice set out with Richard the Lionhearted to free the Holy Lands, and was captured by the infidels. One day, while still among the infidels, a friendly stork ran up to him—and the knight recognized in the bird one of the members of the Pocepice family who, in his bird-like freedom and without the authorities' approval, spent the winters in the sunny south. The knight tied a letter to the bird's neck, which the bird delivered to the Lady in Pocepice, and subsequently the Lord was ransomed.

The local Father read and approved our screen-play, but then he almost chased the stage hands out of the temple because they ate

156

roll-mops on the altar steps and discussed, in improper language, the short skirts of Jana Brejchova. Apparently the church finally had to be re-consecrated, and the pious old grandmothers, who naturally didn't understand the film (just like the President's dramaturgical overseers, with whom it wasn't so natural), wrote to the bishop of Prague. This otherwise intelligent priest had to write a pastoral letter, which forbade any future use of churches for the purposes of film-making. Gueye Cheick, the African student who so brilliantly performed the part of the Latin-speaking black bishop, was killed in a car accident, during the last day of shooting.

As I listened to my own dialogue being spoken by the actors facing the cameras, I was gripped by fear. The ancient war traumas, and those from the fifties, were suddenly returning to claim their rights, and I began to have the uncomfortable feeling of being a prophet. Five miles away from Pocepice, in the neighbouring Sedlcany, I discovered the graves of my ancestors. Josef Skvorecky died there a hundred years ago, and rests under a leaning tombstone in the shadow of a medieval church. The Central Committees of the various Parties were exchanging angry niceties and then they met at Cierna. The students in Prague assembled daily at the Old Town Square, and the nerves of the population were stretched taut. Mr. Libicek, in the part of the school-master, was telling Mr. Brodsky, who played the priest, "I am all for dialogue, Father, but it isn't very possible that you should have the lead in it. Considering my position in the village, this would seriously endanger its life."

The final scenes of the film were completed on the 20th of August, 1968, the day after I finished mixing the dialogues for Nemec's optimistic documentary. In one of the last sequences, the chief policeman gives the signal to begin the raid of the village with the suspicious priest. I saw the finished film in January of 1969. These were days which began with terrible depressions. Once while walking with a friend along Wenceslas Square, I met the painter Emanuel Famira, who was a leading member of the Jodas ultra-Stalinist group. He knew my friend and gave us a pleasant smile, "You are still here? Well, you aren't running away this time. We'll get you all! Not one of you is getting away. We'll close the borders and it's 'Goodbye Charlie'!" Suddenly, I once again felt the putrid vapours of the anonymous letters which Milos received after *Loves of a Blond*. I went to the Film Club, and survived the day with the help of Miltown and alcohol. Time went by; each day began in a

157

Five Girls to Deal With: *"measured by the canons of orthodox socialist-realism, the basic situation of the film is profoundly sarcastic"*.

darker depression, and dragged on, goaded by alcohol, toward the unnatural euphoria of the evening resounding with Evald's lamenting, "Death is reaching out for us, Pepicek! All of us are coming to a bad end!" The gentle hand of Jana Brejchova, the star who once, in better days, used to stick her ruffled hair from the nest on the floor, filled my glass. The ghost of my poor old mother-in-law visited me, and feared for the savings books.

Before the arrival of the tanks we had another plan: to write a film where the two pairs of comedians would appear side by side, each of which—in their own generation—shaped the young people's poesy and attitudes towards life. We wanted to make a film with Voskovec and Werich, and Suchy and Slitr. Eva Pilarova, the symbol of the ideal girl of the sixties, was to join them in a kind of pentagon. The subject was a tiny motif from the detective story, *Murder for Good Luck,* by my friend, Jan Zabrana, a poet and translator of Isaac Babel and Ginsberg. We had written a synopsis once before with Milos Forman, but at that time the dramaturgy did not grasp the idea.

The beginnings were promising: in the house at Kampa, the kind Mr. Werich promised to appear with pleasure in a musical detective story if Mr. Schorm directed it. Mr. George Voskovec, who was by now a distinguished film and Broadway actor, wrote from New York that if there were work for him at the Barrandov Studios he would be happy to come. Jiri Suchy was far too great an admirer of the older duo to refuse, and Jirka Slitr was my old friend from the jazz country of the Eastern Bohemian foothills.

The tanks arrived, then they hid in the forests and the garrison towns, and the director of Mosfilm who came after them spent his time buying writing pads and felt pens (unknown in Russia) all over Prague. I kept hoping, while I wandered through America —the country which I loved as a boy, but where I arrived too late. Then at Christmas of 1969 Jirka Slitr died of gas poisoning. So now, even if a miracle should occur, we couldn't do it. We will never be able to do it.

In the spring of 1970, Schorm completed another feature called *Seventh Day, Eighth Night.* The screen-play was written by Zdenek Mahler, Radok's original dramaturgist from the Laterna Magica and the nephew of the famous composer. Zdenek Mahler wrote in his play *The Mill* that "every idea when realized is terrible". The film was a study of fear. "The greatest malefactor of modern life,"

Jana with her daughter Terezka – at about the time when "her gentle hand used to fill my glass".

says one of the moribunds in Evald's *Reflections,* "is fear. Fear is a natural gift, but the excessive fear which we find in modern society annihilates a person, hurts him and, simply speaking, is cruel."

Seventh Day, Eighth Night has not had its premiere yet. Together with three other finished films, (and about twelve unfinished ones) it was seized in the spring of 1970, when the Barrandov management changed. However it was not destroyed—and this is where the situation differs from the fifties—but only deposited in the famous Barrandov vault for eventual later showing. I cannot avoid remembering a story told to me by a very important Czech painter—a pre-war Party member. Once, while in Moscow, he was permitted to visit galleries closed to the public. There hang in constant (hopefully not eternal) darkness, thousands of modern paintings. They did not destroy them as Hitler's Reichsmaler-führer Adolf Ziegler, who evaluated the works of *die entartete Kunst* by kicking holes through them with his well-polished jack-boot, would have done. The ancient Russian paradoxical irreverent reverence towards spiritual accomplishments contains a mystical foreboding that despite all the simplifications of the great revolutions, things in the end remain complex; that *reductio ad quotationem* is a temporary thing, and that the revolution will eventually have to deal with all its consequences if it is to remain the *spiritus agens* of progress.

While this book is being written, Evald is completing a film for Vojtech Jasny about the relation between dog and man, and is

160

Jiri Menzel in Capricious Summer

apparently preparing a film version of Janacek's opera *The Step-Daughter.* Evidently an escape to youthful loves. I am reading from his year-old directorial confession: "Everybody would like to rely on some form of revenge, everybody would like to believe in it. However the field of liberty and freedom lies possibly beyond the borders of expediency. The notion of Liberty may be related to the feeling of futility, and to the knowledge that whatever a person does has no meaning, but despite that he does it fully and with pleasure."

Jiri Menzel

I am convinced that the reason Jiri Menzel did such a superb job with Hrabal's *Closely Watched Trains* lies in the fact that he himself is essentially Milos Hrma, the shy apprentice who unsuccessfully tries to make love to the pretty conductress Masa. I am not trying to say that the Oscar winner still doesn't have a way with women, certainly not. "Every time he feels tired, he puts his head on a girl's

161

Kill Kitten Klan in Six Black Girls: *"The new faces were prettier but it was not our old Klan dominated by that contemptuous beauty, Mrs. Kresadlova-Formanova".*

shoulder, and now that he is who he is, the girls are always there to put his head on." According to Alan Levy, this is what Jiri Slitr said about Menzel, and as the latter directed two girl-filled shows at the Semafor for Slitr, it is certainly based on first-hand knowledge. There are, however, libertines who even after fifty years of amorous adventures can still respond to moonlight. Hemingway belonged to this breed; I suspect that he married four times only because he fell in love four times, and didn't quite know how to solve the problem otherwise.

In a certain sense, Menzel is also a member of that family, although he does not solve his erotic dilemmas in such a radical way. He will always remain the schoolboy who turned hot and cold when the strict Madame Directress Chytilova chastised him for the mistakes in *The Crime in the Girls' School,* and who even after several years of friendship never addressed me other than "Sir".

We conceived the farce of *The Crime in the Girls' School** during the spring of 1965 in the garden of the Brevnov monastery in Prague. In the garden stands one of Prague's most beautiful baroque shrines, *a basilica minor,* consecrated to St. Margaret. It is

*The film released under this title consisted of three separate stories. Only the one about the Kill Kitten Klan was directed by Menzel.

Kill Kitten Klan in The Crime in the Girls' School: *Misses (from the left) Savonarola, Judas, the Imperial Dragoness, Jackie Ripper, Dracula. Miss Herodes is missing from the photo.*

built on the remnants of a romanesque church dating back possibly to St. Wenceslas' time, that is to the tenth century, which in turn was built on an old pagan burial ground that could have been ten thousand years old. On that prehistoric site we dreamt up the trivial story of a girls' gang called the "Kill Kitten Klan".

We based it on a story from my book *The Mournful Demeanor of Lieutenant Blueberry,* a tale about the mysterious disappearance of a math teacher, about signs of a struggle in his cabinet, and about suspected murder; all of which is in the end explained by the teacher's absent-mindedness. Nevertheless, there was a crime, but of an entirely different nature: the seduction of the detective's daughter, a student of the graduating class, by the chemistry teacher. The original version did not contain the "Ronald Searle" style gang; this was conceived by our joint dirty fantasies. At that cloistered garden, in the presence of ancient traditions, we got the right idea: we correctly assumed, that the true charm of the film would lie in the combination of feminine beauty with death—exactly according to Poe's ancient philosophy of poetic composition. Following the example of another KKK, the "Kill Kitten Klan"* was to have its Imperial Dragonness: in that connection I forced Menzel

*The Math teacher was named Kote, which in English means Kitten.

163

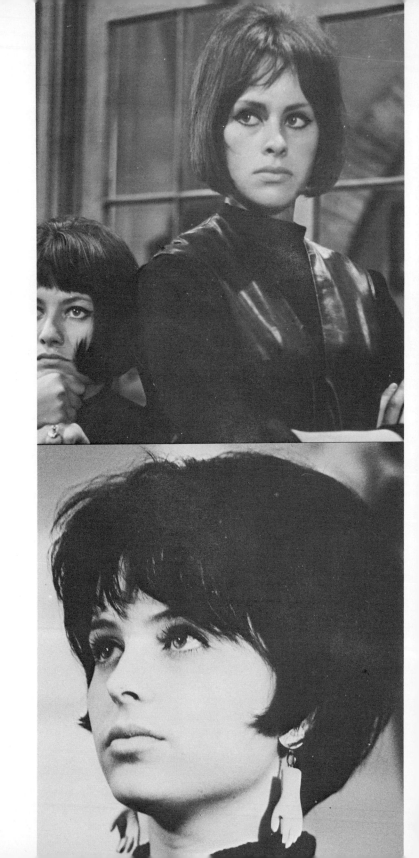

Petr and Matej Forman in The Crime in the Girls' School *(with Miss Judas).*

(who didn't really need much forcing) into a decision he later did not regret, to give the part to Vera Kresadlova, Forman's new wife. She is as the saying goes "a great girl", a very unassuming female; outwardly however, she presents an almost ideal personification of contemptuous feminine beauty: a true Imperial Dragonness. The fact that she is slightly bow-legged only enhances the image. Then we made up roles for her and Milos' twins, the one-year-old Petr and Matej. (This was their first part; since then they have become stars in Papousek's *Ecce Homo Homolka.)* We had yet another idea. All six members of the Klan were given phantasmic names: Miss Judas, Miss Herodes, Miss Babinska, (something like Miss Jackie Ripper), Miss Lomikarova (in an English film this could be Miss Dracula), and Miss Koniasova (Miss Savonarola).

The charming brunette who played Miss Jackie Ripper enriched the film with her own gag, which was not in the screen-play. Not even Mr. Director could have come up with it. In one of the scenes

Imperial Dragoness I. (Vera *in* The Crime in the Girls' School).

Imperial Dragoness II. (a sweetened up version in Six Black Girls).

165

Madonna with Twins: Vera, Petr and Matej Forman (not even she knows who is who).

the members of the Kill Kitten Klan are interrogated by staff members. When all of them are turned away, Miss Jackie Ripper sticks out her tongue at the Head-mistress. It was astounding, and after the premiere the Barrandov specialists asked Menzel through what trick he had achieved it. Well, it was not a trick. The delightful mouth of the black-haired girl concealed the tongue of a full-grown ant-eater. She could literally touch her forehead with it.

During the tongue scene, a friend of mine, whom I recommended to Menzel for the part of a lecher and *Playboy* reader* because I knew he would be suitable for the role, became very interested in Miss Jackie Ripper. I saw him giving her a long line behind some props, and then he badgered the production manager for her phone number. Three days later, when he came to the studio to finish his scenes, I asked him, "How are things with Miss Jackie Ripper?" He cautiously looked around and then disgustedly declared, "Nothing doing, man. I think the Director's after her."

*The English teacher confiscates the magazine during the interrogation, but since he has never been to any English-speaking country he translates the name as Play, boy! and assesses it for the benefit of the assembled teaching staff as a magazine for the sporting youth.

Maybe he was. About twice I saw them together at the movies. I could not help remembering Menzel's own description of his novice years, when instead of going to the movies he would rather go to the theatre. In his bitter experience, the cinema was a place where couples held hands, but whenever he tried to hold his date's hand she would not allow it. Our famous compatriot, Dr. Freud, comes to mind, too, although at that time I did not know that soon Menzel would be playing the part of a psychoanalyst in *Closely Watched Trains*.

He told me about his novice years on the memorable day when he finally became the proud owner of an object which is certain to heighten male sex-appeal. He bought an East German automobile "Trabant", manufactured predominantly from plastics, run by a power plant which is used in the U. S. to propel motorized wheel-chairs.* With some misgivings I consented to join him on the maiden voyage that was to take us to Jirka Slitr's cottage in Zdar nad Sazavou.

Zdar is about forty miles outside of Prague, and we covered the distance in less than five hours. On the way there we didn't really talk much. I was holding onto the plastic door-handle, ready to jump if Menzel left the road and drove into the river; Mr. Director tried to change gears every hundred yards or so and, whenever he succeeded, we advanced a little further. Five hours and seven fines later we arrived at Slitr's cottage, where we cheered up over wine and new songs, which Jirka sang for us to his own piano accompaniment (they were from the show *The Devil from Vinohrady* which Menzel was to direct in the near future at the Semafor), and around six in the evening we set out on the return trip. We arrived at Prague just before midnight. The traffic wasn't so heavy, and Menzel used me as his psychoanalyst.

It was one of the nicest nights I have ever experienced, and I am grateful for it. There was a warm wind and above the gently rolling hills of Central Bohemia hung a giant operatic moon. Nothing brings men closer together than talking about women; not in the sense of enumerating bedroom victories, but rather the romantic defeats.

Later, in the studio, I found him even younger and more boyish than before. During shooting he lost weight and turned green. The

*After the success of the *Closely Watched Trains* he became so affluent that he exchanged the self-propelling buggie for a Swedish SAAB, and smashed himself and it up a week later south of Prague. They were both put together again, but the rumour has it that the SAAB later ended its worldly days under the caterpillars of a tank.

167

last day he resembled a corpse; his chlorophyll cheeks permeated by a posthumous yellow. The cleaning lady advised me to take him to a doctor, as she was sure he had stomach ulcers. Her late husband had them and looked just like that.

He did not have ulcers but rather creative pains, maybe multiplied by other sufferings. He regained his natural colour only after the strict Madame Directress Vera criticised him for *The Crime*....At that time he first assumed the colour of a freshly boiled lobster and then paled into the normal grey of the white race. I liked the film, although Vera didn't, and I was not the only one. When Menzel showed the film to a group of famous directors in Paris, they were much kinder to him then the perfectionist Vera.

Miss Jackie Ripper married the assistant director, and Menzel the gentleman gave her the part of the conductress, Masa, in *Closely Watched Trains. The Trains* is certainly his *magnum opus,* at least to date, although the anecdote, *The Crime in the Girls' School,* is not too bad at all. *The Grand Prix,* Menzel's contribution to the omnibus *Pearls in the Abyss,* is probably the most filmic of all Hrabal's filmed stories; *The Capricious Summer* continued, in a more than dignified manner, the Czech lyrical tradition, while *Crime in the Night-Club* was one of the best attended films of the post-invasion year, and is still running.

Pearls in the Abyss (1965) was in a certain sense the Manifesto of the New Wave. With the exception of Milos Forman, who was at the time working on *Loves of a Blond,* all the major representatives of the movement took part in the film. Vera Chytilova contributed a phantasmagoria about a suburban wedding called *Snack-Bar World;* Ivan Passer made a study of the "football soul" in *The Dull Afternoon;* Jan Nemec added the dialogue of two dying braggarts, *The Impostors;* Evald Schorm remained faithful to his document-artistic background in *The House of Happiness* about a real-life primitive painter, while Jaromil Jires' contribution was a love story of a young labourer and a saucy Gypsy girl called *Romance.* Juraj Herz shot a weird tale, *Salvage of Cruelties.* Passer's and Herz's stories were left out of the omnibus, which was in any case too long, and were shown separately.

Menzel selected Hrabal's story *The Death of Mr. Baltisberger*,* which was inspired by the tragic death of a young West German motorcycle racer during the Czechoslovakian Grand Prix in the

---

*The story was clandestinely circulated under this title in the early fifties. Later Hrabal renamed it to *The Death of Mr. Baltazar,* and in the film it is called *Grand Prix.*

early fifties. In both the story and the film, the race is seen through the mythologizing eyes of a few motorcycle fans; it is really a chain of folkloric narrations with the motorcycle race turning into a legend. This is fairly easy in literature, and Hrabal is a master of that genre, but it is more difficult to accomplish in film, because of its rather uncinematic quality. Menzel's solution had the touch of a genius—and it was purely cinematic. He selected a section of the circuit, where the race led down a hill towering against the horizon, and placed it in the centre of the frame. Then he filmed it with a telephoto lens and fast-action camera. Fantastic silhouettes appear on the horizon and slowly descend along the winding road down the hill in a perpetual front shot. The machines and riders in crashhelmets move in a somewhat ghastly but very elegant, slow ritualized dance—in the rhythm of Bach's B-minor Fugue. The resulting effect lies somewhere between a poem, a *danse macabre,* and a legend. The Angels of Death are coming to claim Hans Baltisberger.

Closely Watched Trains is so good that even the merciless Madame Directress Chytilova should not make Menzel blush. Upon reception of the Oscar for it, he very humbly attributed most of the credit for the film's success to the novelist Bohous Hrabal, which is something that directors don't usually do. In this particular case Menzel actually deserves more credit than directors usually do. Under his courteous supervision Sir Hrabal arranged the novel's complicated time relations into a synoptical order, and then Menzel's keen eye selected an incomparable cast. *Closely Watched Trains* is, from an ideological point of view, the culmination of the anti-heroic trend, which began so catastrophically with *The Cowards*. In the latter, the author took the liberty to suggest that, even in times of revolutions, young men, besides being preoccupied with the sacred matters of the nation, also give some thought to the well-guarded sanctuaries of their girls. Hrabal developed this heretical idea to its logical conclusion, when within the framework of a trivial sabotage story, he elaborated upon the horrors of *ejaculatio praecox*. The heroic death* of Milos Hrma, who blows up the Nazi munitions train, is

*The sentimental Menzel made two endings, one of which was optimistic. The explosion blows Milos high up into the air and he lands on top of a blossoming cherry tree, whose fragrant embrace saves him. The callous and foul-mouthed Hrabal talked him out of this one. Carlo Ponti, who wanted to distribute the film in the West under the emasculated title of *A Difficult Love,* fortunately did not see that version or the history of the Czech-American Janosik could have repeated itself.

Closely Watched Trains: *the Judas kiss of Miss Jackie Ripper.*

preceded by the hero's unsuccessful suicide attempt, which is Milos' reaction to his premature emissions. In the Soviet Union the film was found to be an insult to the anti-Nazi resistance movement and, because of the Oscar, Menzel was accused of plotting with the Hollywood Zionists. This is, however, understandable as it is well known that in the Soviet Union children are brought by a stork.

The audiences, the critics and Jiri Menzel all liked *The Crime in a Girls' School,* and because, as Ivan Passer says, "a man should make movies that he himself would like to go and see," we started to write a sequel. It was called *Crime in the Library of Manuscripts,* and it was a comical horror about a diabolical twelfth-century psalter in a university library, and about the disappearance of a scholar, the only person able to read the secret script and medieval Latin of the book. He was kidnapped by the good old Kill Kitten Klan, whose members had heard that the Psalter contained the recipe for a love potion. Since in the present days of feminine erotic dictatorship men are generally sexually dissipated, the poor girls under the leadership of the Imperial Dragoness wanted to help themselves to an artificially potent lover. They tried the love potion on the asthenic scholar with such success that they fell madly and

Capricious Summer: *the disproportion between the "grand" literary style and the "tiny" contents.*

immediately in love with him. I am not sure whether the Women's Liberation Front would enjoy the film.

We had a problem: the original cast of the Kill Kitten Klan was almost completely out of commission. Miss Herodes got married and was expecting a baby in Denmark. Jackie Ripper was in Prague, but was also expecting. Miss Judas, who appeared briefly in... *Trains,* succumbed to the tragic Czech passion of gluttony and gained too much weight. Miss Savonarola meanwhile became too famous and refused to appear as one of the group. We had to postpone the project and instead, Menzel began shooting *The Capricious Summer.* He took a liking to another idea I had called *Crime in a Night-club,* and then the five friendly powers arrived. *Crime in the Library of Manuscripts* was made by Ladislav Rychman in 1969 under the name *Six Black Girls* by which he meant *Six Brunettes.* My strong objections against the change of the title went unheeded. The original Kill Kitten Klan was by that time totally decimated by further pregnancies, weight acquisitions and emigrations, and so Rychman recast it completely. The new faces might have been prettier, but it was not our old Klan, dominated by that contemptuous beauty, Mrs. Kresadlova-Formanova.

Capricious Summer was not too successful at the New York Festival, and it never should have been sent there in the first place. Its strength lies in the literary original of Vladislav Vancura, which is based on a single, but poetically effective, trick. The story is about nothing: three ageing burghers spend their days at a swimming pool,

171

Menzel learning to rope-walk in Capricious Summer. *Menzel rope-walking in* Crime in the Night Club

and at night admire a columbine performing with a tight-rope walker.* They carry on endless and totally idiotic conversations; but the conversations are written in a baroque metaphorical language which might have been appropriate if they were dealing with topics of eternal relevance. The verbal humour springs from the disproportion between the "grand" literary style and the "tiny" contents. It is a strictly literary affair which, from a cinematic point of view, couldn't be significantly improved by telephoto lenses or Kodacolor.

Menzel's treatment was flawless and reverent and, with the assistance of an excellent cast, he exploited the text to its full potential. Among the film-makers Menzel must be the most ardent servant of modern Czech literature and, were Vancura still alive, Menzel would probably address him as "Your Highness". In dealing with the author of *Marketa Lazarova* this would be quite appropriate.

My ideas about *Crime in a Night-Club* were a combination of Chaplin, W. C. Fields and Jean Harlow, and were fully shared by Menzel. I started with Jean Harlow and helped the distrustful youngster to another decision which he once again did not regret: I had him give a screen test for the lead singing part to Eva Pilarova,

*Mr. Director himself played the part of the tight-rope walker. He is very popular as an actor and has appeared in several Czech films, for instance *The Ceiling, The Accused, If a Thousand Clarinets, Courage for Every Day, Nobody Shall Be Laughing, Hotel for Foreigners, The Return of the Prodigal Son, Closely Watched Trains;* he repeated the part of a tight-rope walker in *Crime in a Night-Club.*

172

Menzel directing Eva Pilarova and Jitka Zelenohorska, with myself kibitzing in Crime in the Night Club

the Queen of Czech pop music and a phenomenal singer, who was said to be one of the greatest thespian anti-talents of our time.* Novotny's cultural department continually harassed her. Not long ago, the Prague Metropolitan Court sentenced both her and her boyfriend, Pavel Sedlacek, to prison terms for buying 60 American dollars on the black market, and giving Sedlacek 2,900 crowns (which is about $414 at the official rate or $58 at the real rate of exchange) to "illegally purchase an automobile in West Berlin". She received a one-year suspended sentence and Sedlacek eighteen months unconditional. The fact that, by that time, the state had already earned about $190,000 from exporting her records did not help her in the least. A glorious trial took place, embellished by an impressive claque of janitors and cleaning-ladies, who were in fact police informers and who ventured their profound assessments as Eva left the court-room in tears: "And for such whores we toil!" Whether condemned or publicly disgraced, I will never cease to admire her; to write a film for her was always one of my dreams. She confessed to me the insurpassable difficulties she encountered in the musical *Cancan,* where she was not only supposed to act, but also to dance. Nevertheless, I had faith in her and it inspired me. Being well acquainted with Eva's vocal cadences, I managed to incorporate them into the dialogue; consequently I must claim

*Menzel had earlier used her in *The Crime in the Girls' School,* but there only as the invisible singer to the musical accompaniment. Her scat singing increased the atmosphere of the grotesque tension in the most mysterious scenes with the Imperial Dragoness, Mrs. Forman.

Some individualities of the state's elite in Crime in the Night Club. *The heel holding the hat is Mr. Valenta, the station master of the* Closely Watched Trains.

a little credit for the fact that from the moment Director Menzel saw and heard her screen-test, he not only started to call her "lady Eva", but every day before she left the studio he kissed her hand, as if he were a Pole. He arranged to have several beautiful skin-tight evening gowns made for her, designed from pictures of Jean Harlow, and Slitr with Suchy composed for the picture some of the best songs she was ever to sing.

Naturally I was also writing the movie for Suchy and Slitr. They had, for many years, been incessantly plagued by Novotny's boys, as, after all, was everything that was alive in Czech culture, and that the people liked. Once they "arranged" for the Semafor group to move from the theatre where they had found shelter, because the tenants in the house "suddenly" started to complain about the noise after 10 p.m. The group was forced to shift for more than a year from one small place to another, both in and out of Metropolitan Prague. With a persistence well worth a better cause, Novotny's boys accused them of spreading decadent moods among the youth, until they could no longer get away with it; the will of the people was too strong and the sombre characters from the Secretariat were

Pavel Sedlacek, who accepted 2.900 crowns and went for 18 months to the cooler.

The incomparable Eva "Fitz" Pilar who embezzled $60 belonging to the State.

finally forced to acknowledge the existence of Semafor.* To create even the humblest vehicle for the art of Suchy and Slitr also belonged to my day dreams.

Unfortunately, things did not work out as well during the shooting as we had imagined. Eva did indeed star both vocally and physically, and Suchy and Slitr were as irresistible in the filmed songs as they were on the Semafor stage. The court-room scene, in which Slitr through brilliant argumentation got himself condemned to death, was an excellent example of his acting abilities which were to some extent related to the art of Stan Laurel. However, the

*Recently, the same sombre characters, no longer posing as Novotny's boys but now under the banner of the "true leninists", resumed their Holy War against the people's will. After the tragic death of Jiri Slitr on Christmas 1969 they deprived Jiri Suchy of his post of director of the Semafor theatre which he had founded—ostensibly because of his signature on the 2000 Word Manifesto, something he refused to apologise for. In the summer of 1971 Suchy was foolish (and courageous) enough to ask permission to cast Marta Kubisova, the singer who was the first to be ostracised after the coming of the tanks, in his new musical. Soon afterwards this gentle and humane artist, who in the last fifteen years gave the nation more intelligent entertainment than anyone else, was reportedly banned from Czechoslovak Radio.

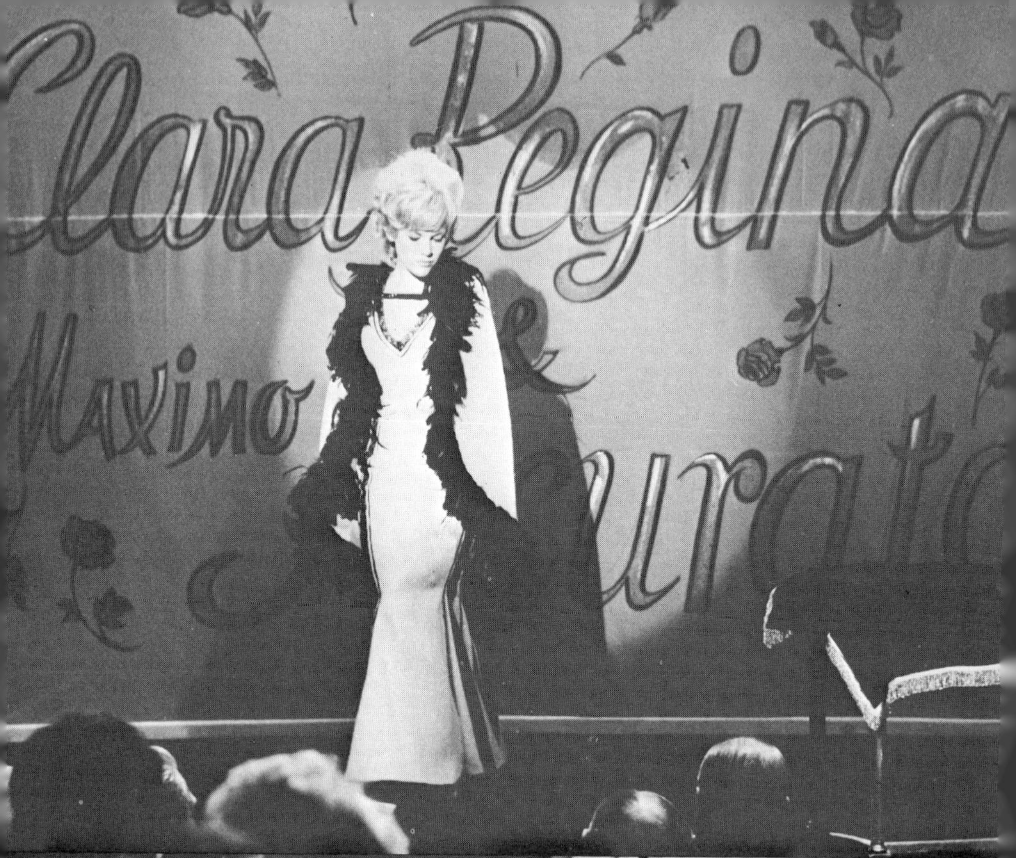
Clara Regina

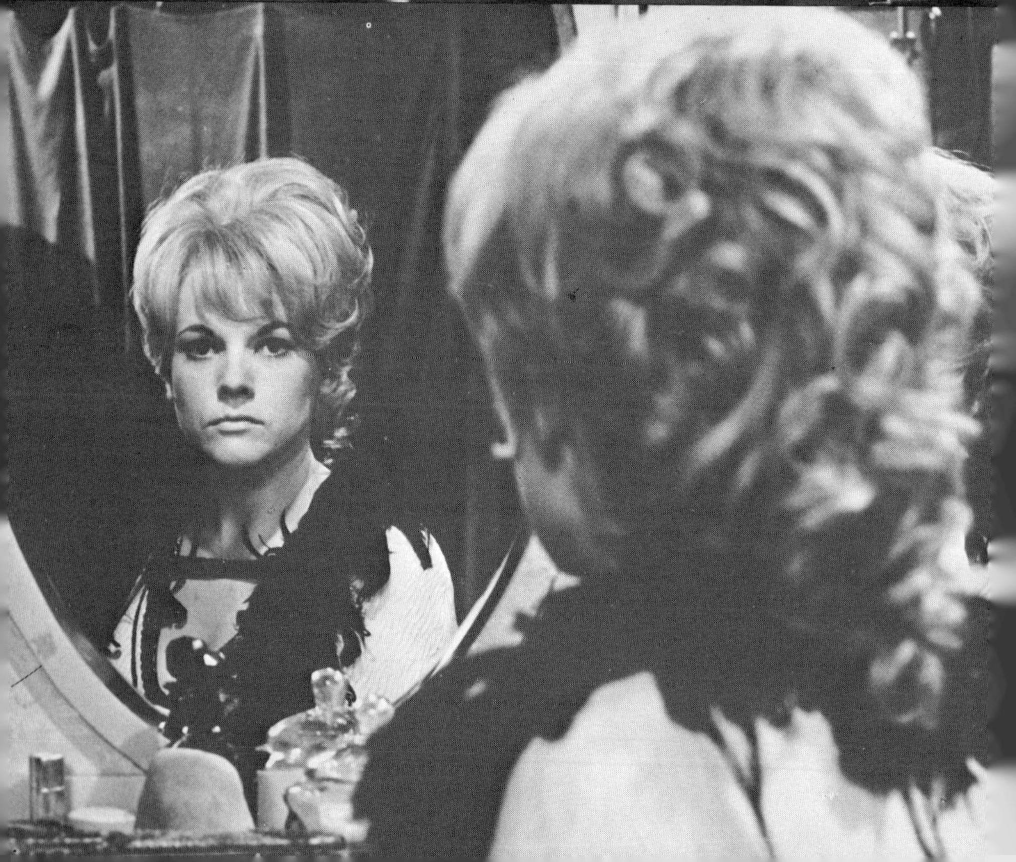

The Gallows Song: "Let's go across the barbed wire where the meadows end in the far-away land . . ." Jirka Suchy and Jirka Slitr in the final scene of The Crime in the Night Club.

Barrandov technical arrangements failed absurdly. For instance, they could not get a sufficiently springy trampoline: the trick which was to enable the Minister of the Interior to fall out of a third floor window, bounce off the trampoline and enter a second floor window, failed. The whole action had to be transferred one floor lower and consequently the logical sequence of events was disrupted. Furthermore we discovered that Jirka Suchy, notwithstanding his other excellent artistic qualities, lacked Chaplin's pantomimic abilities, and so most of the fancy number with a jack-in-the-box in the shape of a life-size policeman had to be cut. During the shooting Jiri Menzel turned alternately green, white and purple. The film was half finished; we were still missing an end and I, for the life of me, couldn't come up with it.

Then history provided us with one.

Crime in the Night-Club is the story of a singer, Clara Regina,

Eva in the Night Club: *Menzel arranged to have beautiful skin-tight evening gowns made for her, designed from pictures of Jean Harlow.*

This is the face that launched a thousand bureaucrats on a girl-hunt: Eva deciding to sing "just for the Minister of Interior".

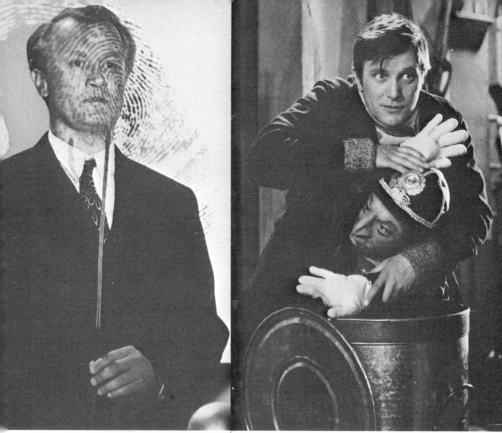

Jirka Slitr almost implicates the Minister of the Interior into the murder.

Jirka Suchy struggles with the Jack-in-the-box (not to be confused with the deputy).

who is endowed with a very jealous husband, a trampoline artist. The action takes place in an unidentified country at an unidentified time. The country's Minister of Interior falls in love with the singer. Night after night, he sits in his private box in the night-club and, night after night, he sends roses to the singer with a note that says, "May I hope that you will sing just for me?" Night after night, the singer keeps the roses and replies to the Minister that "hope he may".

One evening the Minister adds to the roses a pearl necklace, which is promptly stolen by the juggler, who was one of the singer's old suitors. Suspicion falls on the simple-minded porter, played by Jiri Suchy. Being accused of theft, he retains a lawyer, Jiri Slitr. For the lawyer this is his first case; he had studied law for a quarter of a century and managed to graduate only after his high-school friends became professors at the Law School. What follows is a somewhat

The Crime in the Night Club: Minister of the Interior (Vlastimil Brodsky) with his body-guards.

Jiri Suchy and the late Jiri Slitr: "Their songs helped to form the emotional world of the young generation of the 1960's in a truly revolutionary fashion".

179

complicated detective story. The Minister's personal murderer is sent to the night-club to murder the juggler, because the pearls were false and the juggler has therefore turned into a potentially dangerous witness. However, when the personal murderer climbs into the juggler's dressing-room, he finds the juggler dead. And so forth. To everybody's surprise, the dull-witted lawyer presents such a brilliant defense, that he almost implicates the Minister in the juggler's murder. Unfortunately, the cunning Prosecutor interprets his arguments just as logically, makes them point at another criminal, and accuses the lawyer and his client of the murder. The decision now depends on the testimony of the singer, who is evidently in favour of the victimized duo. At that point, the Prosecutor reverts to demagogy and puts the case to the jury with the following question, "Do you believe the Minister—or this damsel from the underworld?" Naturally the damsel cannot withstand such competition and the lawyer with his client is sentenced to hang.

During the trial, however, the singer falls in love with the lawyer, and now wants to save him. She consents to the Minister's old wish and "sings just for him" in his bedroom. As a reward, the Minister pardons both the condemned and sends a special foot-messenger with the reprieve to the prison. He also immediately dispatches his personal murderer to take appropriate care of the foot-messenger.

Both the condemned men are standing under the gallows awaiting the messenger's arrival. When the executioner inquires about their last wish they ask to sing a song—and they sing a long, endless song about "the country on the other side of the barbed wire, where the meadows are fragrant and green". They sing and sing until they lose their voices and continue in a whisper—the foot-messenger slowly approaches the gallows—the personal murderer rapidly approaches the messenger—and this is where the film ends. Alan Levy wrote, with reference to the end, that it is "the perfect political metaphor for present-day Czechoslovakia: still singing with a noose around its neck, and the end just a little in doubt."

We were sitting in Forman's Paris apartment near Bois de Boulogne, when the radio announced that Jiri Menzel had resigned from the jury of the 1968 Locarno Film Festival in protest against the Grand Prize nomination of a film made in one of the countries which declared that they knew the wishes of Czechoslovakian people better than the people themselves, and contributed at the

180

same time to the Orwellian dictionary by calling an armed intervention *brotherly assistance*. The horror, which throughout that autumn
had filled my Paris stay, grabbed at my throat, and I said to myself
that when I once again meet Jirka in Prague it will be me who will
be calling him "Sir!"

"Mummy don't drink so much from the fat uncle!" Matthew Forman suddenly addressed his mother. "Don't drink from what,
Matty?" asked Vera. "From the fat uncle," repeated Matty, pointing towards the pot-bellied gallon bottle of wine on the table, while
simultaneously looking at me. I understood the uncomplimentary,
but very fitting comparison. Children don't know the concept of
"rudeness", just as they don't understand the deadly and maybe
ridiculous arguments of the adult world. Despite the seriousness of
the moment Vera giggled and then said she was sorry. I also smiled,
and I was sorry that I was not Matthew's age, or that I was not
dead.

Vera then played in Menzel's last film, *Skylarks on a String*
(1969) based on Hrabal's book of short stories *Pabitele*.

The few who saw the film maintain that it is the best work Menzel
has ever done. *Skylarks on a String* was, in the spring of 1970,
locked in the Barrandov vault for an indefinite period, together with
Schorm's *Seventh Day, Eighth Night,* and some others.

The Others

The Forman—Passer—Papousek team, Vera Chytilova, Jan
Nemec, and Ester Krumbachova, Evald Schorm and Jiri Menzel
are the best known and most characteristic representatives of the
New Wave. No movement, however, is adequately described by an
enumeration of its major personalities, and the Czech New Wave is
no exception. The group of young people who moved the Barrandov mountain* was larger than the world might imagine, and it included artists who are unknown to the world, due either to
unusually bad luck, or because they worked for a long time as
"mere" screenplay writers, before they began directing.

*The non-Czech name of the mountain where the Studios are located comes from a
French paleontologist, Joachim Barrande (1799-1883), who there discovered rich
deposits of trilobites, large extinct Silurian arthropods characterized by a three-lobed
body, which were one of the oldest highly organized creatures on Earth. The annual
Barrandov prize, the Prague equivalent to the Oscar, is called the Golden Trilobite.

Jaromil Jires

If we consider Milos Forman the most characteristic representative of the New Wave, then Jaromil Jires is certainly the most
unlucky of the group. Yet it was his thesis film, *The Hall of the Lost
Footsteps**, completed in 1958 and distributed shortly afterwards,
that first indicated to the public that something completely new was
happening at Barrandov; his first feature *The Cry* was released in
February of 1964, two months after Chytilova's *About Something
Else,* and six months prior to Forman's *Peter and Paula.* While the
others successfully made their way through the intricate web of
dramaturgical snares, Jires and his projects became trapped in them
for five years. Except for his contribution on the omnibus *Pearls in
the Abyss* and a short documentary about the 19th-century Czech
journalist, K. H. Borovsky, he did not return to the cinema until
after the Invasion with *The Joke* (1969). The surrealistic pictorial
poem *Valerie and the Week of Wonders* appeared in the spring of
1970.

The Hall of the Lost Footsteps was a harbinger of something entirely new; it was a political film aimed at the apathy with which a
majority of people accept great military and political catastrophes,
and learn to live with the atom bomb under their pillow. "I respect
Camus' *La Peste*," wrote Jires at that time, "because it states that

---

**Jires first studied camera and only later switched to direction, so that he photo-
graphed the film himself.*

182

evil lies within the people who due to cowardice either don't react to evil at all, or react nonsensically." As a political issue the *Hall* was of course no novelty by 1958; Czech film had already produced Helge's *School of Fathers* and Jasny's *September Nights,* with the ominous clouds rapidly gathering above *The Third Wish* and *Hic Sunt Leones.* But all these films were made in the traditional realistic style of a straightforward narrative. *The Hall of the Lost Footsteps,* on the other hand, was an experimental vision combining colour and black and white film, shocking the viewer by radical cuts, and placing, side by side, the emaciated prisoners of a concentration camp and pretentious love chases through blooming meadows.

Consider the paradox: Jires who entered the scene with a strongly developed sense of formal experimentation and the feeling for the small gentle pleasures of life, as he proved in *The Cry,* wasted five years battling for socially-critical scenarios, only to make in the end the stylistically rather traditional work, *The Joke,* a classical political film about grave injustices and cruel revenges. The paradox of an artist in a paradoxical time, as Jires himself realised while working on *The Joke* in 1968: " 'Engagement' in the form of an exposé will probably disappear. But the exposé of scandals does not constitute a true artistic value in itself, it is merely a symptom of an unhealthy society. When art must concentrate on uncovering the diseases of society—as was the case in recent years—art is tragically diminished. Such a period, when the main artistic value is courage, represents a dark age. Anyway, the only kind of courage that exists is tolerated courage. You are always restricted to filming those things which are permitted. Real courage manifests itself in public life*, where it is needed more. . . . Art alone can never win against brute power. People who hold machine guns either laugh at the man with the pen, or else they shoot him down."

The Cry was a simple story narrated in a highly complex non-chronological pattern. The finesse of treatment given to the simple events provided the film with great subtlety. Two young people meet, marry, and expect a child which is born. Jires proved to un-

*Here Jires points to a frequently neglected fact that not only the leading personalities in art and philosophy, but also the tens of thousands of unknown democratically-thinking common people, provincial intellectuals and functionaries, deserve credit for the liberalization of Czechoslovakia. Without them there might have been a palace revolution, but never the tremendous mass movement of 1968.

Eva Limanova (now a U. of T. professor's wife) in Jires's The Cry.

derstand life as it is, and to have completely avoided the motifs which, anachronistically, began to be required after the conference in Banska Bystrice—such as the superiority of "public affairs" over private ones, such as giving birth to a child. It was Jires' misfortune that, along with his film, came others which offended the socialist-realist norms far more than by simply concentrating on private, but nevertheless "fundamentally positive" motifs. The political manipulators reverted to an old trick: instead of trying to subdue the "noxious" by the "good", they began fighting it by using the "less noxious". In fact it was a reflection of an older socialist-realist theory about the battle between the "good" and the "better". They went to war against Schorm's "pessimistic" *Courage for Every Day* using Jires' "optimistic" *The Cry* as their weapon. Jires at that time imitated the President in the latter's affection for the ceiling position.

Pushed by the unwanted countenance, he feverishly began to tackle political themes *par excellence.* In the assumed role of a political philosopher he wrote on the subject: "Everything is a question of the human qualities of the people in leading positions being greater than the positions themselves. . . . I believe that this is the problem inherent in the building of socialism, which as a system is more viable than capitalism, as long as the leadership is able to creatively exploit the true principles of development. Whenever a

184

person who is unable to wisely utilise power manages to attain it, the advantages of a controlled system turn into negative obstacles. I would be interested in reading a study: The Effects of a Public Office on the Dehumanization of the Human Being."

Together with Arnost Lustig, the Jewish author who provided the New Wave with outstanding material such as *Diamonds of the Night* and *Transport from Paradise,* he wrote a screen-play based on Lustig's novel *White Birches in the Fall.* It dealt with the life of the so called "black units", which were military units made up of "unreliables". Men were sent to the units because the degree of their "unreliability" did not warrant sending them directly to the concentration camp. The life in the "black units" differed from the "uranium" camp about as much as the prison in Solzhenitsyn's *The First Circle* differed from the camps in Northern Siberia. It was not the worst, but certainly not the most pleasant, set-up; the mass presence of drafted priests provided at least some guarantee in case of the worst emergencies.

The screen-play was rejected on grounds of amorality, and dabbling in morass and dirt. The cultural overseers then advised Jires of the theory according to which the artist must carefully assess the "impact" of the truth he is proclaiming—that is, will the truth harm socialism. In view of the revealed circumstances surrounding the murder of Kirov and similar cases, the theory sounded somewhat archaic, but they nonetheless adhered to it. As the maxim to be followed by the artists they chose, "If the enemy praises you for something, you were wrong." This slogan was supposed to be coined by Stalin, and it is indeed true that the generalissimo's less advertised Siberian accomplishments were praised only by his sycophants, the Beria's and Rusanov's.

Jires, disgusted with the futility of his efforts reasoned uncompromisingly, "It is necessary to believe in the power of truth; and it is just as important to realize that there is never enough truth. The theory which claims that up till this point it is a useful truth, but from there on it is useless is absurd and dangerous, because every expurgated truth immediately becomes a lie.... If we succeed in saying the truth about a person, irrespective of its external 'impact' or 'utility', this has an immense social importance, although the truth itself might well be negative. The very fact of its disclosure is in itself positive and indicates a healthy society."

I would run into him at meetings where he fluttered from table to

185

The Joke: *the soldier-artist with his mural that was found "indecent" by the military ideologues.*

table and spoke enthusiastically about socialism. While others made films, he was turning into a kind of a tribune of the New Wave, and an artist turned into a cultural-political theoretician, whether through his own fault or not, tends to become a little ridiculous and people begin to doubt his talent. What Jires was lacking was not talent but opportunism; at least that mild form of it which enables artists to turn out bitter attacks on injustices perpetrated abroad, at a time when the home-supply of injustice is quite adequate. Assisted by the author Karel Michal (*Honour and Glory, The White Lady*), Jires embarked on another quixotic venture, and told me about it once in Brevnov, in the garden where Menzel and I had invented the Kill Kitten Klan. I think it was an excellent idea and I hope that one of the young radical American film-makers, at least, borrows it from him. The film was to be called *Azure Rapids,* and Jires later wrote about it: "It was supposed to be a film about the totalitarian method of thinking. I was interested in the way Nazism utilized so-called 'good, decent citizens', who actually make up the backbone

186

of every totalitarian system. I wanted to show how big and beautiful words can be exploited to fool the public. For the purpose of examining totalitarian deception I chose Nazism deliberately, for this system had already been clearly judged by history and everyone knew its nature."

This does not disclose how Jires wanted to do it, which is exactly where the greatness of the idea lies. It was to be an UFA-Film, Berlin Production, or so it would have said in the credit. Just as Orson Welles pretended to be serious when he broadcasted the sham report about the Martian Invasion, this was to be an exemplary Nazi film produced by Goebbels' manufacturers for the exemplary Nazi audiences: something in the style of Veit Harlan or Leni Riefenstahl. The almost imperceptible microscopical transformations of emphases were to eat away the shiny veneer of the propagandistic product, as if you edited into one film three frames from a different film, here and there. Thus the film would gradually reveal to the audience the lies behind the Truth, horror behind Nobility, inhumanity behind *Gemütlichkeit* of the Nazi show pieces.

Naturally, the idea was of the category of Michael Romm's later *Ordinary Fascism* and they threw him out with it. He flew for two years until he finally landed in the studios in 1968 with the screenplay of *The Joke*. He based it on a novel by Milan Kundera (it had already appeared in English, and it was in a sense a partial return to the motif of the "black battalions" from the *White Birches in the Fall*). "The Joke" in the title is a slogan "Long Live Trotsky!", written by a young philosophy student on a post-card to his girlfriend: he wanted to needle her for being an ardent Communist of the stalinist era. The post-card is intercepted by the Faculty's Party Secretary Zemanek, who takes the joke seriously: the student is thrown out of school and sent to the "black units". Years later, when the storm has blown over and the protagonist has managed to achieve a fairly good position, he gets an opportunity to revenge himself on Zemanek by seducing his wife. The revenge fails. Too late, the hero discovers that Zemanek and his wife are being divorced, and that Zemanek, who has turned from a radical stalinist into an equally radical liberal, is marrying a beautiful young student (Mrs. Kresadlova-Formanova). The importance which the story has for some people in Eastern Europe might be difficult to comprehend for the average Westerner.

Jires intended to achieve maximum authenticity by a completely

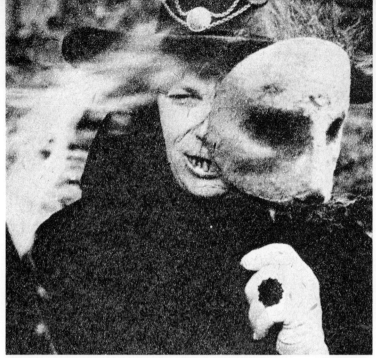

Valerie and the Week of Wonders: *the creators know where to turn "but they simply don't want to"*.

unorthodox and unusually naturalistic method. He gave the part of the seduced wife to Jana Ditetova, an actress who in her younger days had made a name for herself as an avid warrior of the Communist Youth—a perfect case of type-casting. Mrs. Ditetova accepted the bitter role and did an excellent job. For the part of Zemanek, Jires wanted the poet and playwright Pavel Kohout. The latter entered literature with poems and verse plays in which the temporary insanity of his time reached an unusual degree of concentration: then, shaken by the political trials, he wrote a play, used later by Jasny as a basis for *September Nights*. At the Writers' Congress in 1967 during the last days of Novotny's era, he publicly supported Israel, and later involved himself in a prolonged friendly polemic with Gunther Grass in which he defended liberal-revolutionary Communism against the latter's social-democratical approach.* After the Invasion he hastily produced *The Diary of a Counter-Revolutionary,* a work which was symptomatic of the mood of many Party members; by doing so he placed a noose around his own neck, which he further tightened be giving permission to a theatre in Vienna, Austria, to produce his play *War on the Second Floor* which has never been done in Prague. In spite of his admirable courage, he found the part of Zemanek in *The Joke*

*It was published in book form as *Gunther Grass, Pavel Kohout: Briefe Uber die Grenze,* Letters Across the Frontiers, 1968.

188

untenable and refused it. The shooting was interrupted by the Invasion, but despite that the film was completed and with tremendous success distributed in Czechoslovakia, where they knew what it was about.

The history with the racket surrounding *The Cry* repeated itself. Milan Kundera, the author of the novel, was at that time branded as one of the intellectual leaders of the creeping counter-revolution. Nevertheless, Jires was not. As during Dubcek's era, he avoided going to meetings because he was shooting at last. Jan Kliment, the chief theoretician of the Banska Bystice conference in 1959, and a trusted servant of Novotny's cultural department in all its developmental phases, decided once again to peruse the "noxious" to fight the "ultra-noxious", and wrote a review which could have served as a paradigm of sophistry. He commended Jires for correctly maximizing the "positive" traits of the story in his film, thereby countering the "basically negativistic" attitude of the novel.

Jires first wanted to follow the past presidential practice and hang on to the rafters, but then he had a better idea. Following the maxim, "If the enemy praises you for something, you were wrong", he blasted Kliment by declaring that if the film failed to transmit the intentions of the novelist it was bad, and he did not wish to be applauded for a bad film. The kind Mr. Kliment must have been hurt by such blatant ungratefulness, and he soon proved that he would not let Jires get away with it.

Only then did Jires get the opportunity to do work befitting a person of his poetic and sensitive nature. Together with Ester Krumbachova, he wrote and later shot a film based on the "black" novel of the greatest Czech surrealistic poet, Vitezslav Nezval, *Valerie and the Week of Wonders*. In it Jires finally rose from the swamp of the world and entered the realm of beauty, which is—or should be—an important part of being human.

The film won the Grand Prix at the 1970 Bergamo Film Festival. Jan Kliment, who was sent there as the Czechoslovakian representative, made the rounds of the ecstatic reporters, expressing disdain at their bad taste. He was undoubtedly acting on the basis of the necessity to distinguish the "bourgeois" and "proletarian" brands of patriotism, using the "class" approach as his guideline. Upon returning to Czechoslovakia, he produced another brilliant burgeoning of his elastic soul. In it he qualified the one-time praise of *The Joke* by observing that "the film outgrew the obvious efforts of its creator,

189

The Joke: *the less poetic side of the "class justice" – the "unreliables" of the "black units".*

(i.e. Jires) and *against* his will [the emphasis is mine] aimed not only at the deformities of socialism, but also attacked the various Adamek's (sic) who although they once fully supported those deformities, years later set themselves up as idolized leaders of the fanaticized young people, and began to criticize what they themselves had once perpetrated."

In the original review of *The Joke* he still attributed this merit to the director; now he discovered that it was thanks to—it is not quite clear to what, maybe the novel?—and that the director desperately but unsuccessfully tried to prevent it from happening. This discovery, of course, helped Kliment to understand how the seemingly "true marxist-leninist" Jires could produce *Valerie,* a film which transgressed two of the main canons of socialist realism: it was too erotic and totally incomprehensible. Kliment masterfully by-passed the treacherous shoals of the fact that the novel was written by the great Communist, Nezval, by pointing out that "the revered poet wrote the book at a time when he was overcoming the feeling of loneliness... in the year when he visited the Soviet Union. This greatly affected him." Kliment, unfortunately, forgot to mention whether Nezval visited Russia before or after he got those feelings. This was a mistake, as someone might have placed the events into an incorrect chronology. Kliment rectified the oversight in his weighty conclusion: "Although the subject (of the film) is a

190

The Joke: *Jana Ditetova as the seduced one-time avid warrior of the Communist Youth. "A perfect case of type-casting."*

surrealistic novel by a great poet, this is no reason why it should today prove through its existence that its creators don't know where to turn. Or they do, but they simply don't want to."

Another great poet, Vladimir Mayakovsky once wrote in a poem called " Incomprehensible to Masses" the following lines:

> I ask
> the writers
> who pall with fear
> Quit
> spewing poems
> for the beggar's ear.
> Concerning art
> the working class
> Is no less smart
> than you.

Mayakovsky, however, debased his work by a pessimistic suicide, motivated supposedly by unhappy love. Kliment's notice was sent to me by an American Czech, a film afficionado and a retired railway-man, who visited the Old Country at the time when *Valerie and the Week of Wonders* opened. On the margin of the clipping he added in his shaky handwriting: "In my opinion the best film in the history of Czech cinema. Made so well that Felinni (sic) in comparison

191

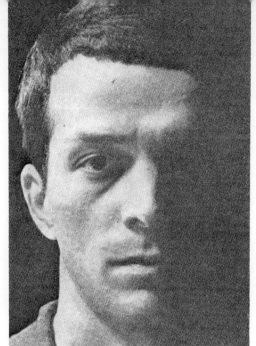

Pavel Juracek

comes out as a bungler. I saw it 2x in a single day, and I would go again if I had an opportunity."

Of course a retired railroad man cannot match the aesthetic class insight of Jan Kliment.

The second man who stood at the sources, but for a long time remained in the background, is Pavel Juracek. He worked for several years as a screen-play writer, and when it finally seemed that he might become a director after all, he accepted the position of artistic director of a new Barrandov production unit. The whole of the New Wave was to be concentrated into this single unit; however the Invasion killed it before it could produce anything.

It was Juracek who once so dreadfully argued with Vera Chytilova over the screen-play of *Ceiling,* that he forbade her to include his name among the credits. (I don't know what the fight was about.) His thesis screen-play, *Black and White Sylva,* directed by another graduate of the Film Academy, Jan Schmidt, was a somewhat immature work, but indicative of the current militant mood at the Film Academy: it parodied the one-time popular films which "made the workers' arms ache" and its heroine, a comely female bricklayer, Sylva, was an unswerving optimist and a shock-worker to boot.

After that, Juracek was drafted, and became one of the ghost-writers for General Sejna, a military man who continued in the peculiar tradition of the admirer of coloured breeches, General

192

Cepicka. Instead of introducing sabres and multicoloured pants into the Army, this high-ranking officer wanted to become a writer. He had great potential: a major influence in the Army, all the necessary connections in the Army press; the only thing that he was missing was talent. This was easily provided by Private Juracek, and others, who in exchange for furloughs provided the General with manuscripts, which the latter published under his own name in the military press. He was well under way towards literary fame when, at the turn of 1967, he became entangled in the military and political machinations of President Novotny, so that when Dubcek arrived the good General was confronted with some black-market activities related to large quantities of industrial seeds. The General, accompanied by one female student of directing from the Film Academy (who a year before had made an appalling film based on a rather good screen-play written by my wife), and with a large number of secret documents belonging to the Warsaw Pact, fled to the United States, where he resumed his literary career by contributing to the *Reader's Digest.*

Fortunately the General ran away a long time after Juracek had finished his military service and returned to Barrandov, where he produced the scenario to a successful science-fiction movie *Ikaria XB-1* as well as to the *Jester's Tale,* which was an original story from the Thirty Years' War written for the famous director Karel Zeman, whose films combine animation with live acting, as well as film tricks and special effects. (*An Invention for Destruction, A Journey to Primeval Times, Baron Munchhausen, The Ark of Mr. Servadac,* and others). In 1963 he wrote the scenario to a medium length film *Joseph Kilian,* which the authorities first contemplated for a year and then rejected, after Nikita Khrushchov delivered his oration on culture. The Czechoslovakia of 1963 however, was not the Czechoslovakia of 1953. Nikita's speech had effects contrary to his intentions, and the scenario was finally rehabilitated. Then another problem arose: Juracek wanted to direct the film himself but, according to some regulation, trained screen-play writers were prohibited from doing so. He joined forces with his old friend Jan Schmidt and they made the film together; Juracek acted more as a theoretician, while Schmidt looked after the practical side of the movie. In the credits only Schmidt was listed as the director. "He really risked more than I did," Juracek later wrote. "If Kilian would have been a failure, he would have been solely responsible, and

Josef Kilian: *"Where Orson Welles failed, Juracek succeeded. . .*

nobody would have been interested whether I got him into it."
Finally Juracek paid Schmidt back by writing the script for
Schmidt's first feature film, *The End of August at the Hotel Ozone*
(1966).

Josef Kilian is one of the best known works of the New Wave's
early tide: it won the Grand Prix in Oberhausen, and both the
Western and Czech critics recognized in it purely Czech,
Kafkaesque characteristics. It is essentially a satire on bureaucracy,
which is indeed in the Kafka tradition; despite all its philosophical
interpretations, *The Castle* may also be read as a joke about the
Austro-Hungarian bumble-dom. While walking through Prague
streets, Josef Kilian, whose initials are of course identical to those of
the hero in *The Trial*, notices a strange store which bears the sign:
Cats for Rent. He enters and rents a cat; just like that, without
thinking why. The next day he wants to return it, but the store has
meanwhile disappeared. As the rental fee doubles each day, Josef
Kilian, with dubious assistance from the bureaucracy, tries
desperately to locate the mysterious store, without success. Juracek
really managed to create a Kafkaesque atmosphere—one Swiss

194

... It is a film worthy of Kafka."

critic went as far as to write that "where Orson Welles failed, Juracek succeeded. It is a film worthy of Kafka."

Encouraged by success Juracek reached into his military experiences (not the literary ones), and made his first feature, *Every Young Man* (1965); it consisted of two unequally successful stories. The first was really an experiment with silent film, that is "naturally" silent. And old hand is ordered to escort a recruit to a military hospital. Being profoundly against such activities, he takes his anger out on the recruit by completely ignoring him, and not saying a single word throughout the journey. The other story was a somewhat expressionless conglomerate of episodes revolving around manoeuvres; it ended with a story about soldiers who organized a dance to which the girls didn't arrive in sufficient numbers. A four-year pause followed; Juracek organized his production unit in 1968, and after the arrival of the tanks he still managed to complete *A Case for the New Hangman* (1970), to which he wrote his own scenario based on the third book of Jonathan Swift's *Gulliver's Travels*. Juracek maintains that it is not a satire, but rather a film "about the certainty and security provided to the stupid by stupidity". During his travels, Gulliver encounters a large number of politically diversified people. As a foreigner he divides them only into the most fundamental categories—the good or the bad. Whatever higher interests they might serve is outside of his horizon, and therefore does not concern him. The film is conceived as a dream and, although it is not supposed to be satire, it contains a

195

Juracek's The Case for the New Hangman: *"A very strange type of a humane hero."*

few of the most scathing scenes that can be seen (or rather, currently cannot be seen) in Czech cinema. One of the best sequences is called "The Ceremonial Execution". A group of condemned people is brought to a crowded stadium where they are to "test" a new executing machine. The Executioner, a servile civil servant fearing his professional reputation might be damaged, stops the girl who is to be executed first, and says, "I'll save you for the end Miss, when I'll know what the machine does." He reveals similar humanitarian consideration a minute later when a condemned poet, before putting his head into the machine, cries out, "Friends! Long live the...." The Executioner courteously waits, but the poet cannot remember who is supposed to live. The Executioner gently beckons him towards the machine, and the poet cries out again, "I shall die, but...", and again he forgets the "but". The Executioner amiably steps aside; for a few moments nothing happens, then the Executioner puts his hand on the poet's shoulder, and the latter yells, "I am happy to die because...", but he does not know why he should be happy to die. The Executioner shuffles, the crowd murmurs restlessly, and the considerate civil servant politely whispers to the poet, "Excuse me, sir, are you going to do any more proclaiming?"

I am not at all surprised that this type of humane hero was not entirely to the liking of the Barrandov censors in the spring of 1970.

196

The Case for the New Hangman reportedly* joined the *Seventh Day, Eighth Night,* and *Skylarks on A String* in the spacious Barrandov vault. Pavel Juracek once wrote: "Nonconformity is not counter-revolution, because it does not reject the ideal, but rather questions the practice. It sometimes happens that practice negates its ideal, and this can often be tragic."

Juracek's friend, Jan Schmidt, was born in my home town of Nachod where his family belonged to the greatest exploiters, or so it would seem from Schmidt's later difficulties with the interpretation of his class origins. His Dad was an absolute ogre. Being the county's medical examiner he would year after year reject my under-

---

*It is almost impossible to find out with absolute certainty which films were banned, which were withheld and which may have slipped through the Big Ban in the spring of 1970. My data may not be entirely correct, and so I run the danger that this may be used against me in Prague when my book is described there in the usual terms as defamatory, slanderous, misrepresenting the facts, etc. Such an incorrectness, however, must not be blamed on me but on the absolute absence of any kind of, even relative, freedom of press in my country. When this is the case and when the official sources keep silent about the exact size of the Big Ban of 1970, rumours and private information remain the only source of knowledge. According to the *International Film Guide 1971* the following finished features were banned: Schorm's *Seventh Day, Eighth Night,* Menzel's *Skylarks on a String,* Kachyna's *The Ear,* Sirovy's *Funeral Rites* and Jakubisko's *Birdies, Orphans and Fools.* According to the same source the fate of Bocan's *The Decoy,* Balada's *Pavilion No. 6* and the Czechoslovak-Bulgarian co-production by Vulchanov, *Aesop,* were questionable (Vulchanov's film had already been banned in Bulgaria). *The Decoy,* however, was only half-finished in the spring of 1970 and, according to very reliable sources, Bocan was not allowed to complete it. Another unfinished film of promise was certainly banned (my wife wrote one of the three sceenplays, so she should know): *The Visits,* a three-story feature which was to be the debut of three young graduates from the Academy, Vladimir Drha, Otakar Fuka and Milan Jonas. Another certainty in that category is *How Bread Is Made* by Ladislav Helge. Drahomira Vihanova's *Killed Sunday* was reportedly withdrawn from public showings. Approximately twelve features were stopped before completion, in addition to the five or six films banned after completion. "Within a single year," writes Jan Zalman, the author of the entry in *International Film Guide 1971,* "there have been more bannings than during the whole twenty-five-year period after the war—yet in no other period has (the Czechoslovak film industry) produced so many outstanding works as in 1969-70. After the *International Film Guide 1971* was published and the employees of the Ministry of Interior, entrusted with following western publications, read Jan Zalman's assessment of the newest trend in the cultural politics of the Party, Mr. Zalman (the pen-name of Dr. Antonin Novak) was duly relieved of his post as editor-in-chief of the *Film&Doba* Magazine, and replaced by a hack whose name, another interesting *nomen omen,* makes me feel that the perhaps non-existent but certainly sardonically just God has a significant sense of humour. The new editor-in-chief's name, Jiri Hrbas, associates strongly with "hunchback". Add to it the Messrs. Jodas, Jack-in-the-Box, Cop, Purs (the new general manager of the Barrandov Studios whose name means, in military slang, "The officer's bootblack") etc., and there can hardly be any doubt that the same ironical force is active here which made only three readers of the *World Literature* Magazine protest, when we printed there, in 1957, a "decadent" novel by Françoise Sagan; their surnames were Posmourny, Protiva and Lokajicek, or Messrs. Murky, Nasty and Little Lackey.

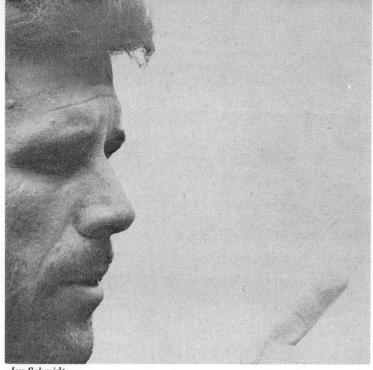

Jan Schmidt

handed attempts to obtain a medical certificate exempting my lazy body from gym classes. For this I cordially hated him. In 1950, when the ogre's son thought he would be going to college, I gave him private English lessons. Naturally they did not accept him, and so he played professional soccer, then made a living as a musician and in the theatre; in 1957 he finally managed to wheedle his way into Film School.

For a long time following *Black and White Sylva* and *Josef Kilian,* he could not get started, until finally in 1966 he made *The End of August at the Hotel Ozone,* an extremely cruel vision about a group of girls who are the only people to have survived the nuclear holocaust, and are wandering through the radioactive desert looking for a man. Its effect in 1966 was somewhat anachronistic; after *On the Beach* and similar dark prophecies people became accustomed to the A-bomb. This of course was not altogether Schmidt's fault; the screen-play was submitted to the Studios in 1958 and went through the usual prenatal complications. Immediately after the premiere, Schmidt accepted Barrandov's offer to make *The Lanfieri Colony* (1970), based on a romantic short story by the Russian novelist Alexander Grin, who died in 1932.

The End of August at the Hotel Ozone: *"An extremely cruel vision about a group of girls who are the only people to have survived the nuclear holocaust . . .*
. . . which was submitted to the studios in 1958 but made only in 1966, due to the usual prenatal complications."

198

HO-4

It was supposed to be a purely Czech film, but required high mountains and the sea. After long negotiations, a co-production with the Soviet Union was arranged. The Soviets were to provide the mountains, the sea, and actors according to the director's consideration, but an argument developed about the script. "The dramaturgical unit 'Junost'," wrote Schmidt, "wanted to emphasize the adverse effects of gold on the character and morale of an individual. On the other hand, old Mr. Zarkhi, the Chief Director of the unit, doggedly insisted on a single thing: 'I ask you to remember that this is to remain Grin.' Grin of course does not contain the emphases required by the Soviet Dramaturgists."

Schmidt and Zarkhi won the argument, but the shooting was interrupted by August the 21st 1968, and "the film ceased to have a meaning. I finished it only for the sake of finishing it," says the director. The news of the Invasion caught the Czechs high up in the mountains. Schmidt describes the ensuing events: "At 5:30 a.m. Prague time, which was 8:30 a.m. local time, we stopped shooting and told them we wanted to go home. It was a strange situation, with the Russians maintaining that we had doubtful information. By tuning the radio to every conceivable station available in the mountains we proved the opposite, but they still insisted on the doubtfulness of our information, and waited for orders from above. This we could not accept and together with my cameraman we went that afternoon to Suchumi, where we were officially assured by the highest Party authorities that not only was there no shooting in Czechoslovakia, but that everything was in the best of order. Meanwhile all the members of the Czech staff arrived at Suchumi; the Russians stayed behind in the mountains, hoping we would return. We tried unsuccessfully to phone Prague. We were worried about our families, while they were disturbed over the millions invested in the unfinished film... After endless negotiations, cameraman Machane and myself were summoned to Moscow to resolve the situation at Mosfilm headquarters. Before a committee of all parties, including the Communist Party, I had to justify the interruption of the shooting. Finally they decided: They understood that we were worried about how those counter-revolutionaries were carrying on at home. They let us go, but could not guarantee plane transportation. Finally we managed to secure it ourselves, and all of us arrived in Prague on August 29th."

Later they returned to the Soviet Union, "because agree-

200

One more Jana: in Schmidt's The Bow of Queen Dorothy.

ments completed before August according to the Moscow pro-
tocol* had to be honoured; so in order not to encourage further
conflicts we completed the film. What happened with it later I
don't know. In the Soviet Union it will of course be shown."
    It was even shown in Prague, but I don't know with what
response. At that time Schmidt was making his next feature *The
Bow of Queen Dorothy* based on Vancura's short stories. This was
one of his earlier plans, which he postponed because both Menzel's
The Capricious Summer and Vlacil's *Marketa Lazarova,* which
were simultaneously in production, were based on Vancura's prose.
    Before he started to work on *The Bow of Queen Dorothy* he ap-
proached me with an offer. He wanted to film my *Song of the
Forgotten Years*†, a story about a jazz singer whose life takes a
radical turn for the worse when the band she sings with decides, as a
joke, to present a swing adaptation of the Russian military song
"Marshal Budenny". An interviewer wondered whether the whole
affair wasn't more related to my own rather than to Schmidt's

*That is: a friendly, voluntarily reached agreement between some abducted repre-
sentatives of a smaller nation and the government of a larger nation, reached in the
capital of the larger nation after the armies of the larger nation and its allies attacked
and occupied the territory of the smaller nation (Ambrose Bierce).

† It was published in English in the anthology *Writing Today in Czechoslovakia*
(Penguin Books).

201

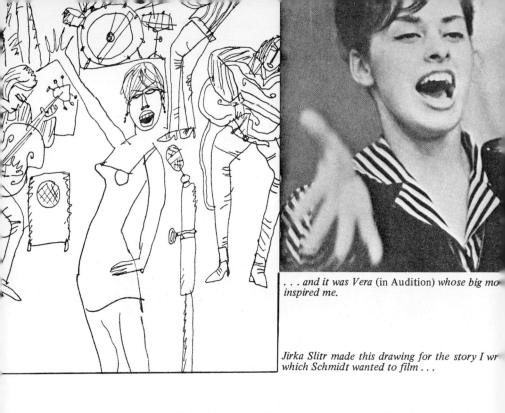

. . . and it was Vera (in Audition) *whose big mo*
inspired me.

Jirka Slitr made this drawing for the story I wr
which Schmidt wanted to film . . .

generation. (Schmidt is exactly ten years younger than I am, which means that at the time of the Budenny affair he would have been only fifteen years old.) Schmidt's reply was characteristic. "In a certain phase this might have meant a certain generation. Nowadays, in view of the present situation, it seems to concern more than one generation. It no longer pertains to that one only, but also to many others."

Obviously, I am not in any position to grant anything to anybody in present-day Czechoslovakia, although I would be delighted to place my story in Schmidt's hands. He is an unassuming and honest artist with a great future. "I don't compare myself to any of the world-renowned personalities," he said, "that is if we don't consider Schorm, Menzel, Forman or Juracek world-renowned. I just want to make films in such a way, so that the other fellows wouldn't say: 'What's that you made, you idiot?' "

Another script-writer-turned-director is Antonin Masa; for those who are so inclined, he may be labelled the politican of the New Wave. One of the side effects of the artificially created inflation of political themes in the fifties was an audience trauma, which instinctively upheld the ageless superstition that "politics have no place in art". This superstition was strangely enough maintained even by some of the realists without the epithet, who otherwise opposed the

Antonin Masa

socialist-realist limitation of the permissible subject-matter, justifying their position by Terentius; "Homo sum: humani nihil a me alienum puto." For years Masa carried on his relatively lonely battle for the recognition of the fact that some people really do live, that is suffer and rejoice, principally through politics. That is what his, until now, last film, *Looking Back* (1969), is about.

It was preceded by a script-writing career which reached its zenith in the screen-play for Schorm's *Courage for Every Day*. Masa's independent directorial debut was the film *Wandering* (1965), which reminds one somewhat of Antonioni in the way it creates an atmosphere. In a story related to the generation gap, he in effect returned to the subject of the betrayal of ideals, or at least their suspension. Then, as if deviating from his own trend, he made the non-realistic, slightly absurdist *Hotel for Foreigners* (1966), a dream play about incarnations of love. It starred Miss Savonarola from *The Crime in the Girls' School,* and it spoiled her so that she didn't feel like doing small parts anymore. The "problems" that Masa expereinced with the screen-play of *Women—Our Fate* were

203

Masa's Looking Back: *"for those who lived through the times a moving and purifyingly relevant fil*

of the usual variety: the rejection of this once again unrealistically oriented film was explained on aesthetic grounds, but the reversal of the decision after January of 1968 convinced Masa that "the real reasons lay elsewhere". (I cannot help remembering the banning of my chaste, yet political, novel, *The End of the Nylon Age,* in 1957 for being "pornographic".) Before he started on *Women . . .*, Masa read Milena Honzikova's novel *Looking Back,* and was so taken by it that he dived headlong into the current, so well known to him.

Looking Back is a political statement *par excellence.* The story, which is formally based on a brutal combination of time sequences, is a confrontation between the life experiences of two lovers: an authoress approaching middle age, and a considerably younger screen-play writer who is supposed to convert her novel into a film. The heroine lived through Gestapo prisons, fought in a guerilla unit, witnessed the killing of her father by the Nazis, and also the deport-ation of some of her guerilla comrades to Siberia by the NKVD after the victory over Hitler.* When the war ended, she

---

*The Soviet soldiers who fought in the guerilla units were frequently escaped POW's. After the war, Stalin declared all soldiers who were taken prisoners to be "traitors".

enthusiastically participated in Party work, in the Communist take-over and the first years of the building of socialism. Obviously a historial period well known to people in the Socialist countries. The hero was ten years old when the Communists came to power: the socialist state is the only reality he knows. In keeping with the ageless laws of human nature he opposes the *status quo* and, besides that, personal problems, particularly emotional ones, play a much more important role in his life than they once played in the life of the heroine.

I don't know whether this film would appeal to an audience who knows all of this only from reading or hearsay, but for those who lived through the times it is a moving and purifyingly relevant film: it tells the story of the events that gave birth to the "creeping counter-revolution" (as Walter Ulbricht of East Germany called it), which I cannot help considering a hesitant, error-laden, threatened-from-abroad, attempt at a music of the future, resembling nevertheless in its deadly sincerity, the first stage of socialist revolution. "Godard fascinates me above all by the degree of freedom and courage which he permits himself, and which is tolerated in his country," said Antonin Masa in an interview. "Godard is a child of fortune. As a romantic he is so free, that even responsibility burdens him. The difference between Godard's romanticism and that of the Czech films lies in the fact, that—besides a certain Slavic heaviness—we have also the disadvantage or advantage that whether we like it or not we consider ourselves much more responsible for the fate of our country. I know that these are big words, but despite that I believe that it is true."

The most inconspicuous member of the New Wave is Hynek Bocan. He is a true child of film; when he was thirteen he played the leading child part in *The Leaden Bread,* which featured another debutante in the eleven-year-old Jana Brejchova. After graduation he worked for a long time as an assistant director (for instance in Nemec's *Diamonds of the Night*). He did not produce his first feature film until 1965, when he made *Nobody Shall Be Laughing,* based on a story by the author of *The Joke,* Milan Kundera; the screen-play was written by Pavel Juracek. The ironic story combines spiteful anti-feminism with the motif of a struggle against human stupidity, and it would not be liked by either the Women's Lib or those who

205

Hynek Bocan

believe that after an accomplished revolution people should adopt the slogan *Maul halten und weiter dienen**.

Then Bocan, in keeping with his admission that he is unable to invent his own story and that his goal is to shoot epic works of other authors, filmed Vladimir Paral's novel, *Private Windstorm* (1967). The novel is a very experimental work affected to some extent by the French *roman-nouveau*. By comprising the text from repetitive particles with an almost imperceptible degree of variation (in dialogue, characteristics, and paragraphs), Paral created the atmosphere of the mechanical monotony of modern life, which relentlessly deadens everything including sex life. The film version lost the experimental touch, and what remained was a clever comedy, which filled cinemas in Czechoslovakia, and got some acclaim even abroad.

For his third film, *Honour and Glory* (1968), Bocan used a novel by Karel Michal, the writer, who together with Jires once wrote the model UFA-Film. *Honour and Glory* takes place during the Thirty Years War, after the Catholic armies of the Habsburgs had defeated

*Shut up and keep on serving!

Bocan's Private Windstorm: *"a clever comedy which filled cinemas in Czechoslovakia and got some acclaim even abroad".*

Bocan's Honour and Glory: *the director is not to blame for the malicious interpretations to which the film may now be subjected.*

the Czech Protestants at the Battle of the White Mountain in 1620, and the, until then independent, Kingdom of Bohemia became a subservient part of the Habsburg empire. The battle, however, did not end the war; it started it, and the English, the French, but particularly the Swedish, armies for thirty years, successfully fought the Catholic monarchs of Europe. For the defeated Czechs, the prolonged war was a source of hope that the Catholics would in the end lose and the Kingdom of Bohemia would regain its independence. Bocan's film is a microscopic picture of that macrocosm; it tells the story of a poor Czech nobleman, who is contacted by two emissaries of the Czech Exiles. They try to persuade him to arm his subjects and rise against the Habsburgs, promising that the Czech uprising will be synchronized with an offensive of the Protestant Armies in the West. The lord finally agrees—but at that moment the news arrives of the peace treaty which ended the thirty years of hostilities, and according to which the Kingdom of Bohemia remained a vassal of the Habsburg monarchy. But the knight has decided and will not withdraw: abandoned by all at home and abroad, he leads his sorry troops to fight the Habsburg Empire.

The film was completed in the summer of 1968, before the Invasion. Bocan cannot help the malicious interpretations to which it is now subjected. His next film was to be a Schweikian comedy based on my novel, *The Tank Corps*. The publication of the novel written in 1955 was several times rejected, postponed, and set aside; a few excerpts from it appeared, and a shortened version was read on the radio in 1968, by Miroslav Hornicek. In the fall of 1969 it was finally set, corrected and prepared for publication, and then once again postponed, this time indefinitely. So far it has only been published by Gallimard in Paris, and so unless Bocan goes and makes the film there. . . .

Somewhat apart from the New Wave stands its immediate predecessor and brilliant fellow-traveller, Frantisek Vlacil. Age-wise, he belongs to the generation before the New Wave (born 1924), and unlike most others (except Ester Krumbachova and Jaroslav Papousek) he did not attend the Prague Film Academy. He studied aesthetics and the history of art in Brno. In the fifties, he got into film and collaborated on a large number of puppet and popular science films. Beneath the popular scientist lived an aesthetician, who finally came to the surface in 1960 with a film called *The Dove*. It was a

Frantisek Vlacil

visual poem heavily dependent on various Western formal influences, but in the Czech context which, except for Radok's *The Long Journey* and Jires' short *The Hall of the Lost Footsteps,* was totally devoid of that type of film, it appeared highly innovative. Vlacil made the film in accordance with Chytilova's maxim, "If formalism—then beautiful", and was protected from the wrath of the vigilantes-against-incomprehensibility by the fact that the symbol of the peace dove, popularized by Picasso, was understood by everybody. With his next feature, *The Devil's Trap* (1961), he even gained support from the sombre overseers, mainly because this time they really misunderstood him. A simple miller from the "time of darkness", i.e. counter-reformation, uses his own findings gained by the study of nature to fight against clerical dogmatism as it was proclaimed by the disciplined and well-organized Jesuits. Formally it was a very sombre film, and the parallel to the other, more contemporary dogmatism, was still somewhat timid. But the motif of anti-dogmatism remained in Vlacil's work and later he twice returned to it. After *The Devil's Trap,* the aesthetician and art historian once again came into prominence. He tackled a historical novel of momentuous importance in the history of Czech literature. In the genre, which was up till that time filled with "patriotic" historical portrayals, this was the first "non-ideological" story, thoroughly permeated with the spirit of the Middle Ages. It was written by the Communist writer and one of the first director-artists of Czech film, Vladislav Vancura, and it was called *Marketa Lazarova.*

209

The shooting of The Devil's Trap: *"the parallel to a more contemporary dogmatism".*

Vlacil's struggle with *Marketa* lasted some four years, and it almost killed him. At the beginning he was thinking of a two-part film, but then as if seized by the same madness as his medieval highwaymen, he shot endless miles of footage; the film swallowed millions, and it began to look like four parts instead of two. Vlacil deteriorated, reinforced himself with alcohol, and broke down; he turned into a bearded skeleton. With similar vengeance he began editing, and he cut and cut until he ended up with two parts consisting of the most beautiful and wild spectacle in all of Czech cinema. Its only equivalent might be found in the early superfilms of D. W. Griffith, or Bergman's *Seventh Seal,* (and in my own opinion in Fellini's *Satyricon*).

It is the story of a family of highwaymen who in the twelfth century revolted against God and the King; the cruel action of the film suffused Christianity with the remnants of pagan ritual, with unrestrained love and, even more uninhibited, death. The fiery beauty of Vancura's narrative was not always translatable into visual imagery, and the film arose, like a phoenix, from a gigantic editorial undertaking; this is why it consists of a progression of barbarously independent sequences, each preambled by commentaries from

Marketa Lazarova: "no ideology, or even 'an idea' in the literary sense. . . . . .but simply the most perfect evocation of the Middle Ages".

210

Antonin Prazak in Vlacil's Valley of the Bees: *a 13th century crusader discovers unpleasant contradictions between the dogmas of his order and real life.*

Vancura's text (which one American reviewer took for fragments of a medieval legend). It has no ideology, or even "idea" in the literary sense. It is simply the most perfect evocation of the Middle Ages ever achieved in Czech film: a four-hour-long intense revitalization of a long forgotten age; herein lies the film's sole purpose.

It cost an incredible amount of money and, as a malicious Barrandov rumour has it, Vlacil had to make another "medieval" film to pay for the cost of costumes and buildings. However, in the *Valley of Bees* (1968), Vlacil returned to the motif of *The Devil's Trap* which he this time utilized in the story of a thirteenth-century crusader who discovers unpleasant contradictions between the dogmas of his religious order and real life. Meditations on a similar theme save Vlacil's last film, *Adelheid* (1970), from triteness; in it a demobilized officer of the World War II Czech Army in Britain falls in love with a daughter of a Nazi war criminal; the story also contains murder and suicide. The trademark of Vlacil's art is that he did not reduce this potential banality to a soap-opera.

Somewhere here the so-called New Wave ends. A few names could be added, but they either stopped producing after promising debuts, or they failed to live up to the expectations. Among those we might name, Cestmir Mlikovsky, who after a fairly original, although not overly successful, *Cucumber Hero* (1963), quit film altogether and became a custodian at a castle in Southern Bohemia; Miroslav On-

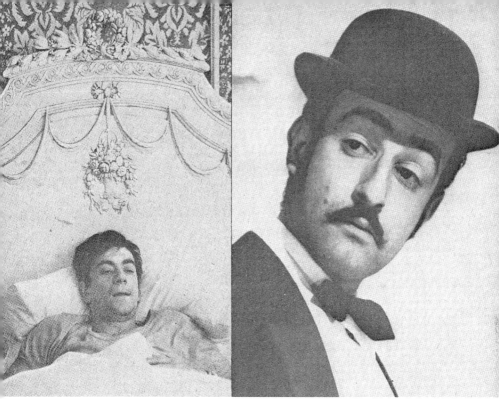

Adelheid: *a potential soap-opera, saved by Vlacil's art.*

Juraj Herz in The Lame Devil

dracek, who first directed a charming medium-length *Slippers* (1962) and then after a feature experiment, *The Final Stretch* (1962), in which he combined the style of reportage with drama, went into television; or Zdenek Sirovy who has so far produced a poetic short feature *The Boy and the Roe,* followed by a flop called *The Dealers* (1963) and an average psychological drama *The Finnish Knife* (1965), and whose latest film *Funeral Rites* was banned by the censors in the spring of 1970.

A director who certainly belongs to the New Wave although he has so far directed only short documentaries, is Karel Vachek. His *Moravian Hellas* (1963) unmasked the fraudulent hocus-pocus surrounding folklore so ruthlessly, that it shocked even a number of the supporters of the New Wave. It was fully defended only by Zbynek Brynych ("I admire that bomb-attack") and by Jiri Menzel, who refuted the objection that Vachek mocked the folkloristic conmen with excessive cruelty by saying, "I am all in favour of fair play, but only with fair people." In 1968, Karel Vachek authored another bomb attack: a head-long, completely unadorned, but all the more convincing documentary about the democratic revolution of Czechoslovakian socialism called *Related through Choice.*

Finally one ought to include Juraj Herz (another one of those who

213

did not attend the Prague Film Academy), although he himself says, "I cannot say that I have the sense of belonging to the Wave, I rather feel that I am at one with certain individuals—with Jires, or Schorm, but not with the Wave." Nevertheless, Herz participated in the Wave's Manifesto, *The Pearls in the Abyss* and, like Menzel and Forman, co-operated closely with the Semafor theatre. After the socially-critical detective story, *The Sign of the Crab* (1967), which pilloried anti-intellectualism then officially nurtured, he made, directed and starred in (he looks a bit like Groucho Marx) a musical revue, *The Lame Devil* (1968). His major contribution to the film history of the blessed sixties is the macabre *The Cremator of Corpses* (1969), made after a novel by Ladislav Fuks. It is a phantasmically deranged tale of a man who having been impressed by National Socialism decides to increase the productivity of the crematorium where he works. The film is made in a grotesquely horrific style which brings back memories of *The Cabinet of Doctor Caligari*. Together with Schorm's *End of a Priest* and Jasny's *The Countrymen, The Cremator of Corpses* was the best attended art film of the post-invasion year. For the time being, Herz seems to be the only one of the New Wave directors who, though he remains in Prague, is allowed to make films. The price, of course is the well known Time Machine, heading for the past. After *Sweet Games of Last Summer* (1970) based on Maupassant's story *The Little Fly,* he is now working on *The Kerosene Lamps* from a novel written in 1935 by Jaroslav Havlicek. This remarkable writer certainly was not a model of socialist realism: other -isms, like psychologism, naturalism and a predilection for decadent themes, all of them pejorative in the socialist realist vocabulary, are better applicable to his work. But he has one advantage. He has been safely dead since 1943 and did not get himself involved in any counter-revolutionary nonsense, such as the New Wave.

Juraj Herz starring in his own The Lame Devil.

Herz's The Cremator of Corpses: *"I feel that I am at one with certain individuals – with Jires and Schorm, but not with the Wave."*

The young men and women of the New Wave carried out an aesthetic-philosophical revolution in the Czech socialist cinema. "The young fool", that is how a middle-aged director, well known in the West, spoke (in a private conversation) about Milos Forman's stubborn early efforts. The older man had always played it safe with the authorities and now he wanted to make Milos co-script a mildly anti-war scenario which would be acceptable to the Czech ideological supervisors, and yet remain saleable to the Western merchants of fashionable film topics. Milos refused. Revolutionaries, however, have always appeared as fools to members of establishments, the stalinist establishment being no exception. Yet these fools set new standards at Barrandov, in view of which it was not only no longer possible to survive on uninspired hack-work but not even on the traditional craftsmanship. The Wave overshadowed even such solid middle-aged artists as Jiri Weiss or Jiri Krejcik; it forced the old pioneer Otakar Vavra* into a new creative upsurge, which resulted in the films *The Romance for the Fluegelhorn* and *The Hammer Against Witches*. It also inspired several middle-aged men to become better directors than they possibly might have been without the competition.

Above all there is the somewhat enigmatic Zbynek Brynych, the author of some of the best and some of the worst films of the sixties. The critics explain the unbelievable vacillation by his "never ending searching"; I tend to believe that it is rather the result of Brynych's nature, which he himself did not always respect.

He produced several total disasters: an imbecile attempt at a screwball comedy, *Every Crown Counts* (1961), a somewhat sickening flirtation with the socially-critical trend, *Don't Hide When It Rains* (1961), and an embarrassing attempt at a parody of James

---

*Some of his overly talented pupils finally cost Vavra his job. One of the foreign students at the Department of Direction of the Film Academy reportedly made in 1970 a thesis film called *The Unwanted Guest*. The story goes as follows: an uninvited guest suddenly moves into a household occupied by a newlywed couple, and refuses to leave. He shares their table, and even sits by their bed observing them. The newlyweds timidly suggest that he might want to go home, but the goodnatured guest encourages them not to pay any attention to him and carry on as if they were alone; he doesn't mind it in the least. The film was seen by an informer, and the students were investigated by the Secret Police. As the director was a foreigner paying in hard currency, old Mr. Vavra was selected for the scapegoat. Although the circumspect artist publicly proclaimed himself in support of the new Barrandov leadership, the Ministry of Culture, the Party, and the Nation, he was nonetheless fired from his position of Chairman of the Film Academy—the school whose founding he proposed in 1939, whose guidelines he secretly worked out during the Nazi occupation, which he founded in 1947, and where he brought up all those clever artists.

Zbynek Brynych directing

Bond movies called *Transit Carlsbad* (1966); (with reference to the last film it should be mentioned how peculiar it was to expect an audience to appreciate a parody, since no James Bond movie was ever shown in Czechoslovakia). Had Brynych only made films of that quality he probably would have been through filming by now.

If he had only made films like *The Local Romance* (1958), *The Spider's Web* (1959), or *A Place in the Crowd* (1964), which were poetic studies of working class environment, or if he kept on producing good, albeit politically rather black and white, thrillers such as *The Skid* (1960), or even continued with slightly Formanesque comedies, *Constellation of the Virgo* (1965), he would belong to the solid average film-makers, and even be patted on the back once in a while. Since he also made *I, The Justice* (1968), the expressionistic *The Fifth Horseman Is Fear* (1964), and above all *Transport from Paradise* (1962), he fully deserves to be counted among the important modern Czech directors.

Brynych's best three films have two important common characteristics: they are all inspired by the Nazi period, and two of them deal with its political principle—brutal dictatorship—on a general and non-realistic level.

The least successful is *I, The Justice,* based on a novel by a good Czech novelist of the older generation, Miroslav Hanus. Hanus

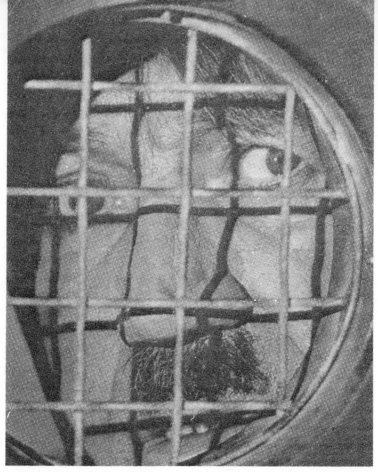

I the Justice: *"a strange anti-utopia".*

wrote the book during the Nazi era and published it after the war. It is an unusual political fantasy: at the end of the war Adolf Hitler does not die, but is kidnapped by a group of German officers who realized that Nazism had been a crime against humanity. They condemn Hitler to death, but they want to kill him slowly and painfully, because only such death complies with their perverted ideas of justice. As well as Hitler, they kidnap a Czech doctor, of whom they demand the invention of some especially painful method of slow torture. However the doctor is a humanitarian: he cannot reconcile himself to the idea of repaying sadism with sadism, and he gives Hitler an injection of a fast-acting poison.

At a first glance, this moralistic parable does not appear attractive, but the film really isn't bad: moreover, its central idea reflected among other things the ideology of the unique Club 231, an organization of released prisoners of the Stalinist era camps founded in 1968, whose programme was in effect a reconciliation with their former jailers. The cold, highly modernistic camera of this strange

218

Brynych's The Fifth Horseman Is Fear: *"I am convinced that fascism is an international disease; its symptoms may be traced . . . even in our own country."*

anti-utopia creates an unreal and oppressive atmosphere of a nightmare, and covers some of the naïveté of the plot by a suggestive semi-darkness.

The same atmosphere, based on the creative camera work of the cameraman Jan Kalis, is the prominent feature of *The Fifth Horseman Is Fear.* The birth of this film is interesting. It was made from the novel by Hana Belohradska (author of the screen-play for Herz's *The Sign of the Crab) Without Beauty, Without a Collar.* The novel submits a realistic portrait of a Jewish family, in a country which was forced to follow the Nuremberg Laws. The original scenario written by Belohradska and Brynych, was also realistic. They situated it in Prague, with typical Czech and Nazi characters. Then Brynych got an idea, and with the help of Ester Krumbachova, he rewrote the scenario, eliminating all historically realistic elements. The representatives of the totalitarian regime in the film do not wear Nazi uniforms, the city is not Prague, and the impunity of the Nazi public notices is exaggerated into a paradoxical grotesque. *(By a timely denunciation you are assuring your own security.)* Rather than achieving a simple condemnation of Nazism, they managed to create a parable: a legend that attacks the disease

219

called Fascism, of which Brynych says, "I am convinced that it is an international disease; its symptoms may be traced in countries other than Germany; even in our own country."*

The strictly controlled stylistic unity of this excellent film is broken by a single inexplicably long sequence from a Nazi military brothel. It first presents about twenty completely naked prostitutes taking showers. The Prussian rigidity of the highly contrasting camera, suddenly turns into an erotically evocative and lyrical mellowness, which indulges in long caressing shots of wet breasts and bottoms, After some time, the scene is invaded by German soldiers in realistic uniforms, who have come to satisfy their needs with the Jewish prostitutes (which in reality undoubtedly would constitute a flagrant violation of the Nuremberg Laws). After this, the film returns to its hallucinatory vision and strict stylization.

When I first saw the film in Prague, this rather nice, yet unfortunately quite illogical sequence was not included. Later I saw it again in Toronto, and suddenly abracadabra, it was there. Then I remembered Belohradska telling me once that a foreign distributor wanted Brynych to shoot some additional footage, and I realized that the naked bottoms were the contribution of Mr. Ponti, who had

*When the friendly tanks came, Brynych accepted offers from West Germany and in 1969-1971 directed six TV films and three feature films in the Bundesrepublik. Of the TV films, two are serious work: Kafka's *America* and Remarque's *A Night in Lisbon.* The rest are parts of a crime-series. *Oh, Happy Day!,* the first of the three feature films, is a psychological analysis of a teenager; *Angels Who Burn Their Wings* tells a social-psychological story of tenants in a big apartment house, and *The Little Women* is a horror film with an international cast. Maybe Brynych, the director of *Transport from Paradise* and *The Fifth Horseman Is Fear,* will spend most of his time in the near future as a successful entertainer of the West Germans. But he probably won't. The official Barrandov bulletin for the fall of 1970 announces that Brynych will direct the first Czechoslovak 70mm superfilm *Oasis,* a psychological story set in the African Desert during World War II. The gist of the story is a conflict between groups of soldiers of the French Foreign Legion and Nazi troops. It is to be shot on location, in the Republic of Mali. According to a Prague underground story, Brynych negotiated this deal himself while still in West Germany, in order to be able, upon his return to Prague, to leave immediately again for Africa. Some recent political developments in Mali, however, endangered the project and shattered completely Brynych's dream of spending the next year in the African desert rather than Prague. But he wasn't allowed even that: in repentance for his West German kafkaesque sins he was forced to accept a commission and is now shooting something somewhere in the deserts of Russian Asia. This, of course, is just a malicious underground yarn which reached these shores through channels which—for obvious reasons—I cannot disclose. It may very well be that it is of the category of tales the Good Soldier liked to tell under the picture of the Emperor, desecrated by Mr. Palivec's flies. But because the Bretschneiders—be their names Kliment, Toman or otherwise—are so busily alive in Prague, Josef Schweik, too, was risen from the dead. His stories, after all, even if sometimes they were utter fiction, told the most profound truths about his times.

220

Transport from Paradise: *"the combination of nightmare with semi-documentary style"*.

not been stimulated by the beauty queen of *The Firemen's Ball*. I hope he had a good time, this time.

Despite this absurd intermezzo it is a great film, full of intense human situations in which death threatens all the protagonists. The intensity of the situations is conveyed by equally intense means. The expressionistic label is in this case quite appropriate, and Brynych himself accepts it. He said, "I have been criticized for being expressionistic. I am. I don't deny it. I don't believe that this style is outdated."

Strong expressionistic elements appear in Brynych's best film, *Transport from Paradise*. The combination of nightmare with a documentary or semi-documentary style*, brings back the memories of Radok's *Long Journey* (although these are much stronger in relation to *The Fifth Horseman Is Fear*). Both Brynych's and Radok's films take place in the Terezin ghetto in Northern Bohemia.

The result is a truly marvellous film—whole sequences give a documentary impression, which elevates the urgency of the drama

---

*I first encountered the idea of an artificial documentary when I began writing with Forman one of his unrealized scenarios. It was to be a film about the tragedy of Lidice (a village which was totally destroyed by the Nazis, and whose male citizens were all murdered). Milos wanted to shoot the film in 16mm, with a hand-held camera, and then blow up the print to 35mm to get the impression of an old newsreel. This was sometime in 1960, and we never did complete the screen-play.

221

written by a witness of the Nazi purgatory, Arnost Lustig.*The action captures one of the maddest periods of Terezin's history— the time when the Nazis expected a visit of the International Red Cross Committee. For a short while, the inmates of the ghetto were permitted or rather forced to play and attend soccer matches, promenade along Terezin's main street and visit a café which even featured The Ghetto Swingers, a Jewish swing band. (One of its members, Erich Vogel, survived and is now an American Jazz critic.) The minute the Red Cross leaves, the party is naturally over, and the Nazi commandant orders the Council of Jewish Elders to compile a list of people who will be transported from the Terezin "paradise" to the Auschwitz hell. The Head of the Council, an aged scholar, refuses to participate in the selection of his own people for the slaughter-house, and is himself included in the transport. The film ends with an unforgettable scene, during which the victims of this unfathomable dehumanization of civilization line up to await the embarkation towards death.

Despite all his vicissitudes and failures, Brynych is a serious artist—serious in every sense of the word. He has something to say, and what he has to say is not meaningless. He tried to be humourous and failed. He attempted to be mildly entertaining and failed again. His power lies in tragedy. It is no meagre power and has its place

*This excellent writer, having been traumatized by his youthful Auschwitz experiences, tried for a long time to play it safe with the authorities (who had similar establishments at their disposal), and carefully avoided contemporary themes. But in 1968, when a Slovak writer, with obvious antisemitism and discarding the essential difference between battlefield casualties and old women and children murdered in concentration camps, commented that "Jews were not the only ones who died in the war; there were also our soldiers", the writer finally came out of his hiding. In a brilliant article in the Writers' Union weekly he defended the case of the Jews, arguing in mostly unpolitical and purely humanist terms and disclaiming any allegiance to Zionism. After the Invasion, Lustig, a typically Czech Jewish boy from Prague, whose jewishness is of that special brand that was represented by Hugo Haas and by Mr. Naceradec, (the character Haas so masterfully embodied in *Men Off-Side,* see page 19) fled the country for Israel, with his wife and two children. Soon, however, he left the Jewish state—a Prague underground anecdote has it that he did so because in the strictly religious community he was not able to get pork and dumplings with sauerkraut, his favourite food and also the Czech national dish. He went to Yugoslavia, where he took part in a Writers' Conference. The Prague underground joke was then surpassed by an article in the stalinist press; according to it, Lustig finally revealed his true character—which is that of an Israeli spy—by appearing in Belgrade in the uniform of an Israeli Army officer. The alleged uniform, however, was an old battledress which Lustig, short both of money and warm clothing after his escape from Prague, purchased in Haifa in a second-hand dealer's shop. In the same battered battledress he, Ahasver-like, arrived in 1970 at Iowa City where he is currently a member of Paul Engle's International Writing Programme.

222

Kadar (right) and Klos (left).

in the context of Czech art, because its moral values are absolute.

The works of Kadar and Klos, the makers of *The Shop on Main Street,* the first Czech film ever to receive an Oscar, is not as variegated as that of Brynych; they never reached Brynych's lows but, despite the Oscar, they probably never reached the level of *Transport from Paradise* either. They worked together from 1952 (*The Hijacking*) till 1969 (*Adrift:* released 1971). Before and after that, Kadar made one film on his own; the older Klos had written screenplays and worked in film since Vancura's times. The duo belongs to the generation of artists who began directing in the early fifties, were always highly above the average, and after the New Wave's aesthetic revolution were stimulated towards the creation of their best works. Kadar and Klos are above all excellent craftsmen, who are careful to select material of topical and temporal significance. They term their approach to the medium as "film-discussion": usually it is simply called *cinéma engagé.*

One could not describe them as formal experimentors; theirs is a more or less traditional narrative method, although they obviously like the modern camera approach. Also one would be hard pressed to find in their work traces of neo-realism, *cinéma vérité* or of expressionistic vision. Indeed they do not rely on purely cinematic elements, but rather on "a good story well told", and often base their films on plays or prose work.

Kadar began his directorial career earlier: he made his first film, the comedy *Cathy,* in 1950. It was a propagandistic film, tributary to the socialist-realistic explosion of that time; the story of a young village girl who goes to the city to work in a factory and under the influence of the workers gradually—or rather rapidly—changes from a primitive villager into an energetic builder of socialism. However, the film for some reason survived in the memories of the audiences. It must have had some freshness, a flash of more than just propagandistic truth, maybe a glimpse of art. The collaboration of Vratislav Blazek on the scenario may have contributed to the success or the presence of a charming new actress, Bozena Obrova. Anyway, the fact remains that the film was one of the few products of the early socialist-realistic school which did not make one's hands ache.*

In 1952 Kadar for the first time collaborated with Klos; the result of this first common effort was far more dubious than *Cathy. The Hijacking* was one of those shallow and malicious films, where the authors pretended that everything in the world is either black or white, or that anyone who for any reason opposed anything that was going on in Czechoslovakia at that time (the year of the Slansky trial), was a traitor—unless he finally repented and accepted the whole and indivisible truth. Desperadoes hijack a Czechoslovakian plane to West Germany and its passengers are subsequently submitted to furious inducement, and even blackmail, on the part of the American and West German officials, to stay in the West. The passengers are predominantly class-conscious people, who demand permission to return, which is finally granted. There are a few wavering characters but, if I remember correctly, only one of them succumbs to the temptations: a young zoot-suited type with a jazz trumpet. He wavers for a long time until he hears the music of an American swing band playing in a nearby restaurant, and decides

* And yet this—if my memory does not fail me entirely—perfectly sweet film did not meet with too much official enthusiasm. Shortly after it was finished, the government decided that it was bad policy to advise villagers to move into towns and become factory workers. The curious logic of those in power held Kadar responsible for disregarding this new order although it was given only after *Cathy* was ready for distribution. As a result of this and other crimes the Slovak Jew, Kadar, had to leave Slovakia for Prague, and thus became a "Czech" director.

to betray his country for the sounds of swing. One can detect the motifs of the ex-capitalist secretly indulging in Count Basie, while the proper young proletarian vigorously whoops it up to the sound of a dulcimer. At that time of course jazz meant "many things" besides music, but if there was one connotation that its young *aficionados* did *not* assign to it then, it was capitalism.

Both the authors were highly praised for *The Hijacking,* but only after an intervention from the old veteran of the very old glorious days of early Soviet cinema, Vselovod Pudovkin. Before he came to their rescue, when they approached him in despair, they were subjected to sharp behind-the-screens attacks from the Party even for this very subservient Black-and-White-Sylva of a tale. The official logic, which in this case escapes me entirely, had it that some scenes in the very red thriller were "bourgeois-objectivistic". If it were not for the angel Pudovkin, Kadar might have been forced to leave Bohemia for—well, Moravia? There is little film industry in Moravia, mostly animated films. And Kadar would hardly have been able to make *Shop on Main Street* with puppets.

Anyway, the two near-culprits joined forces again with the dubious Vratislav Blazek and produced what they hoped not only the people but even the most equal among the more equals would like: a musical comedy *Music from Mars* (1964). If one recalls the jazz-motivated traitor from *The Hijacking,* this film appears almost as a repentance on the part of the directors. Not only does its title hint at memories of one of the biggest Czech hits of the swing era, the foxtrot *Music from Mars* by Kamil Behounek (who actually left the country after the takeover to escape the pogroms on jazz), but one could, for the first time in years, detect in this rather feeble tale about the troubles of a factory band a few timid and very con-voluted, but nevertheless syncopated, songs. But before the musical was released some industrious official soul came to the conclusion that the slightly comical hero, a factory director, was in fact an indirect, and therefore particularly dangerous, attack on the most equal among the more equals. All publicity for the premiere was stopped overnight, and it took complicated behind-the screen diplomacy before the film was released. It had, of course, a very successful run, although the audiences did not recognize the cloaked insults of the Highest Comrades.

Next, the two directors dared a psychological drama, *At the*

225

The Accused— *"a warped Antigone theme that unpleasantly touched upon the basic logical contradiction of the Stalinist justice".*

Terminal Station (1957), which included a suicide attempt. Surprisingly enough, all was quiet on the Party front: the film did not include any "public" problems and remained fully in the sphere of individual love troubles which did not bother the Central Committee. The real catastrophe erupted in 1958, when they released *The Third Wish.* It became the main target of the conference in Banska Bystrice, and brought both Kadar and Klos a two-year suspension.

The pause stretched to five years and the couple's next film did not appear until 1963, when they made a guerilla epic based on Ladislav Mnacko's novel *Death Calls Itself Engelchen**. It was an excellent work, unsentimental and naturalistic to the point of brutality, which portrayed the guerilla war during the Second World War, in the Slovak mountains. Cinematically it is probably their best work.

In 1964 they produced the best example of what they call a

---

*Mnacko, the *enfant terrible* of Slovak literature, parted with Novotny's political system at the time of the Arab-Israeli conflict. He wrote a novel called *The Taste of Power,* which was published in several Western countries, and went to Israel, to return only during Dubcek's era. After the Invasion, this old partisan and Communist (well known for his correspondence with Rolf Hochhut, the author of *The Deputy,* in which he defended the concept of communist socialism in a style similar to Kohouts' polemic with Grass), left the country.

Ida Kaminska in Shop on Main Street.

Shop on Main Street: *a recreation of the atmosphere of the fascist Slovak state.*

226

"film-discussion": it was a court-room drama called *The Accused,* traditionally conceived with an untraditional plot, based on a screen-play by Vladimir Valenta.* Most interesting is a thematic comparison with the socialist-realistic approach. An indoctrinated and selfless power station manager is brought to trial for paying bonuses and extra wages to rebellious workers, although he was not authorized to do so. During the procedings, it becomes increasingly evident that the director committed the financial "misdemeanours" quite unselfishly and in a higher interest, in order to complete the construction of a large new power plant and thus save the country millions of crowns. The Court "plays a smart game" and gives the accused a light suspended jail sentence. The accused, however, finds himself not guilty and refuses to accept the sentence; he demands a new trial and complete exoneration.

Evidently a warped Antigone theme, a work that touched unpleasantly upon the basic logical contradition of the stalinist justice, which in "higher interests" often neglected the law. This however, was tolerated only when the "higher" interest was approved by the "higher" places—and the accused manager, deserted by the higher places, who originally promised to back him, acted entirely according to his conscience.

Shop on Main Street (1965) is a combination of an excellent theme (a novel by Ladislav Grosman), screen-play, outstanding actors, intimate knowledge of the environment, and a passionate involvement with the artistic questions submitted by the form. All of these elements are chiseled into a classical shape by the great experience of the authors, who managed—like Vlacil in *Marketa Lazarova*—to revive the past. They created the atmosphere of the historical nightmare in the independent fascist Slovak State, which

*The name of this screen-play writer is connected with several important Czech films, all of which in one way or another contradicted the official trend. He began with the scenario to the "existential" *Conscience* (1949), directed by Jiri Krejcik. He spent the next few years in a concentration camp, as one of the victims of "the personality cult", and returned to film by collaborating with Vojtech Jasny on the screen-play for *Desire* (1958). The public knows him as a character actor. Among his parts are the pigeon-raising station master from *Closely Watched Trains,* the police chief from *The Crime in the Night-Club,* and the farmer from the *End of a Priest.* He in currently working in Canada as an actor (CBC-TV series "Manipulators": as guest star in *Nobody Business,* 1970; in *Promised Land,* directed by René Bonnière, 1970) and screen-writer (*And the Son,* directed by Raymond Garceau, with the star of the Magic Lantern, Maruska Stankova, in the leading role, 1971; *Truckdriver,* directed by Bill Reid, 1971).

Vladimir Valenta as the station master in Closely Watched Trains

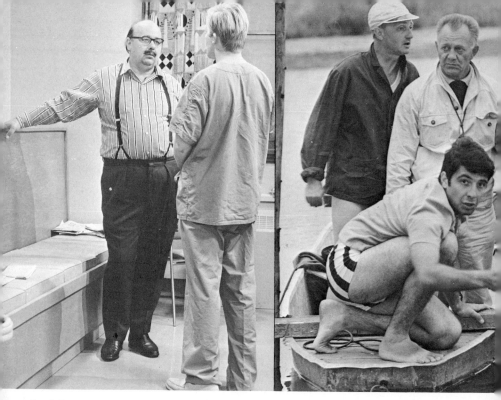

Landed immigrant Valenta in CBC's Nobody's Business · *Karel Kachyna directing*

in the years between 1939 and 1945 reproduced a gruesomely grotesque miniature of the apocalypse of the Third Reich.

In 1968-69, Kadar and Klos made *Adrift,* a Czech-American co-production after a novel by the Hungarian novelists Lajos Zilaly, with American, Czech, Yugoslavian and Hungarian actors. Such a motley cosmopolitan mixtures had never been successfully handled by any Czech director, since the time of Gustav Machaty, however, the film is surprisingly good, especially if one considers that the shooting had to be interrupted for almost a year due to the coming of the tanks and Kadar's subsequent departure for the United States where he used Bernard Malamud's story to shoot *The Angel Levine* (1970). I am afraid that in this film he has met with about as much American success as the maker of *Extasy.*

In the summer of 1971 Kadar decided not to return home. In Prague, in the meantime, his *magnum opus, Shop on Main Street,* has been labelled "zionist" by some and so it would be hard to expect that the anti-zionist Government of today's Czechoslovakia would have any work for a dirty Jew. The logic of subservient minds has, however, turned another interesting somersault: if *Shop on Main Street* is zionist propaganda then

230

what stands in the way of a rehabilitation of *Parteigenosse,* Veit Harlan's *magnum opus The Jew Süss?* Kadar is currently preparing *Lies My Father Told Me* to be shot in Montreal from a script by Canadian Ted Allen, with Zero Mostel in the lead.

Yet another couple created an interesting middle-aged parallel to the efforts of the New Wave. Only one of them is a director; he is Karel Kachyna, one of the first graduates of the Prague Film Academy. In the fifties he collaborated with Vojtech Jasny. In 1954, he co-directed a military-espionage thriller *Everything Ends Tonight* (which is probably the best film of this genre made in the first half of the fifties), and he gave the impression that he was going to specialize in adventure movies—(*The King of the Bohemian Forest,* 1969). Then he met Jan Prochazka, an amazing adventurer of the Czech cinema, literature and finally even of politics, whose rise and fall borders on the incredible. Together they made a few films which deserve to be called artistic, with a capital A.

Jan Prochazka appeared from nowhere at the end of the fifties and, as a protegé of President Novotny, he quickly made his way not only into film, but also into the top echelons of the political hierarchy, until he became a candidate member of the Central Committee of the Czechoslovakian Communist Party. It is not known why Novotny, who had a phobia towards intellectuals, took a liking to him. According to one version of the story, he originally confused him with another Prochazka (which is one of the Czech equivalents of Smith or Jones); this would indeed be in the tradition of Good Soldier Schweik. Another version has it that Prochazka was delegated to a congress of Communist Youth, where he attacked an important official, not knowing that Novotny himself was getting ready to liquidate the wretched comrade. In the middle of Prochazka's philippic, Novotny entered the hall, listened to the speech and, when it ended, kissed Prochazka on both cheeks in front of the whole audience: this is how Prochazka received the attribute which distinguished him from other Prochazkas: Jan Prochazka P P , (President's Pet).

It probably is a folk legend. The fact remains that, under Novotny, Prochazka really "made it". I don't know whether he took part in the regular Thursday card games at the Castle, which were allegedly Novotny's substitute for the philosophical meetings with writers given before World War II by the first Czechoslo-

231

vakian president, Thomas Garrigue Masaryk, every Friday. Anyway Novotny was the godfather, or rather the atheist substitute for god-father, of Prochazka's daughter, and Prochazka himself produced what might be the most remarkable work of political servility in modern Czech history. He wrote a *feuilleton* about an afternoon spent at the President's summer estate in Lany, in which he not only described the head of state as a walker with the endurance of a marathon champion, but also as a captivating intellectual orator. Novotny might have been a walker, but he will always remain in the memory of the people as being, among other things, one of the most stammering deliverers of typed-out speeches who, on the few occasions when he tried to improvise a speech, turned into a national joke. After this journalistic coup, someone coined the following proverb: "Like Masaryk, like Capek." To understand its meaning one has to remember that the important pre-war Czech author Karel Capek *(The War with the Newts, R. U. R., English Letters,* etc.), following the example of Boswell or Eckermann, wrote a book about his meetings with the first Czech President, called *Discussions with Masaryk.*

Yet this man, who bore all the signs of a political brigand, was also an interesting, and sometimes outstanding artist. His output and general ability were amazing. After some very ordinary comical scenarios *(Bitter Love,* 1958, *The Wandering Cannon,* 1959) he entered the literary scene with the novel *The Green Horizons* (1960), and the decade of the New Wave with a film *People Just Like You* (1960). This movie about foundry workers was kind of a swan-song of socialist realism. From then on, year after year, throughout the decade, he spouted novels, short stories, film scripts, *feuilletons,* and political essays as if he knew that his time was short. Simultaneously, he managed to head one of Barrandov's production units, sit on the Party's Central Committee and later to preside over the Writer's Union. There were years when up to six films would be made from his screen-plays (1963), and relatively little of that multiproduction turned out to be completely trashy. In 1961 he joined forces with Karel Kachyna, and through this collaboration both of them produced their best works: the magically lyrical and thoroughly Czech *Worries* (1961), the impudent "anniversary" film *Long Live the Republic!* (1965), the beautifully macabre *The Coach to Vienna* (1966), and the formalistic study of a very realistic

232

The star of Valenta's first Canadian screenplay Et du fils *is Maruska Stankova, the girl from Radok's Magic Lantern.*

affair *The Night of the Bride* (1967) about the class struggle in the village.

The President probably really enjoyed Prochazka's first films: the one about the collective farmers (*The Green Horizons,* made in 1962 by Ivo Novak, the director of Forman's *Puppies*), the love story from the Spartakiada* (*Waltz for a Million,* director Josef-Mach, 1960), and especially the one about the three generations of steel-mill workers dedicated to the Twelfth Congress of the Communist Party (*The Black Dynasty,* director Stepan Skalsky, 1962). He certainly enjoyed the one about the anti-Batista Cuban "barbudos" (*For Whom Havana Dances,* directed by Vladimir Cech in Czech-Cuban co-production); he probably liked the one about the passionately enamoured co-operative farm girl (*Vertigo,* director Karel Kachyna, 1963), and he may have even found some merits in the one about the hooligan, positively influenced by a collective of workers (*On the Tight Rope,* director Ivo Novak, 1963), although the last opus had a little too much drinking and womanizing, and it also was a bit too formalistic. The Head of State probably didn't

---

*The Spartakiada is a nation-wide gymnastic event, which culminates in a mass exhibition in Prague.

Long Live the Republic!: *The president, for the first time, hit the ceiling. When the same tanks appear again in* Marathon, *the president was no longer a president and his protege was the chief counterrevolution*

care too much for *Hope* (director Kachyna, 1963), a love story of a whore and an alcoholic, framed in an appropriate frame of "A Great Socialist Construction Project", or the mildly morbid *The High Wall* (Kachyna, 1964), in which the eleven-year-old Jitka goes to visit a sick youngster, who is separated from the world by the hospital wall. But after all, the President still remembered *Worries,* for which he gave Prochazka and Kachyna the State Prize for 1963; this was a delicate story about the affection of an adolescent girl for a beautiful horse, and it was set in the amiably melancholic countryside of Southern Bohemia. The President was therefore evidently prepared to tolerate many of his protégé's undertakings, but in 1965 when Kachyna and Prochazka celebrated the twentieth anniversary of the nation's liberation by making the two-part *Long Live the Republic!,*the President, for the first time in relation to his favourite, hit the ceiling.

Prochazka and Kachyna carefully observed the New Wave and the formal experimentation going on in the West; first they produced a cultivated combination of the new methods with the required environment and optimistic conclusions, and from there they gradually worked towards a sense of tragedy, which smacked of pessimism.

234

The enthusiastically political title of *Long Live the Republic!* at first glance promised a dignified proclamation celebrating the rounded anniversary—but instead even the President must have realized the irony inherent in the title. The film presented a psychological drama of a child in whose mind the term "liberation" was forever connected with images of hoarding and sadism.

Prochazka, who despite everything remained the President's protegé, began to play the part of the film-makers' "fifth column", or Barrandov's "our man" at the Castle. Whenever the President climbed the walls or chewed the carpets, up came Prochazka—sometimes with considerable effort—to help him down or prop him up, whatever the situation required. As far as I know, he acted the role of the good samaritan for *The Party and the Guests,* in which Mr. Vyskocil so unfortunately resembled Lenin. He may have also intervened on behalf of *Daisies,* which Deputy Jack-in-the-Box so poignantly pointed out to the Ministers of Agriculture and Interior. He managed to placate the President over the issue of *Long Live the Republic!* too, but his credit at the Castle started to diminish soon after this and his usefulness to the film-makers became questionable.

The Coach to Vienna (1966) was probably the couple's best film: it is a cultured study of human reactions under the most extreme conditions. Two German deserters force a peasant woman, whose husband was killed by the Nazis, to take them to Vienna. The woman first wants to kill the deserters with an axe, but then one of them makes love to her, and she changes her mind. The group is ambushed by partisans who brutally murder the woman's new lover. The crime novel compression of the improbable turn-abouts of emotions and plot was neutralized by Kachyna's brilliant direction, and by the equally excellent, almost spectral, camera. It was probably that which facilitated the recognition that this essentially realistic drama was an attempt at a "synthesis of all wars, which this world ever experienced" (Czeslav Michalski).

It is difficult to expect, however, that such syntheses should be understood by politicians. The film did not contain much criticism of the Nazis; this was contrary to the norm applied to the war genre. The partisan who brutally finished off the wounded deserter said, "No point in letting him suffer. After all we aren't Nazis, are we?"

Funny Man – *Prochazka's bitter good-bye to life.*

This sounded even more ironical than the title of the anniversary film.

In 1967, the two of them came up with another contemplation of a decisive moment in history: in *The Night of the Bride,* they treated the more or less compulsory collectivization of the countryside. In an almost gluttonous exploitation of magical photography, the film sets some great hatreds against each other: the rich peasant stands against the village pauper, while the religious fanatic ("Christ's bride") despises the Party officials and vice versa—yet no one seems to be judged. All the characters are victims of the times—chessmen moved by uncontrollable passions. This of course was the case in real life, but only seldom since Sholokhov's *The Quiet Don* has the truth been presented in such an unexpurgated fashion. The distance covered by Prochazka and Kachyna since *The Green Horizons* was indeed astronomical.

To commemorate the twentieth anniversary of the Communist takeover the National Film Corporation opened a prize competition, and Prochazka submitted a scenario. For reasons beyond my knowledge, it was not made by Kachyna, but by Ivo Novak, who was Prochazka's collaborator on two earlier ventures. *Marathon* turned out to be an incredibly melodramatic and expensive kitsch about the liberation of Prague by the Red Army*, crowded with Distinguished Artists, portraying Soviet Generals, and awkwardly imitating the bathos of the Russian language. At least one armored division must have participated in the film: upon seeing the movie one could not avoid remembering Schorm's assessment of the belief that "any nonsense...turns into a work of art...if it employs only trained Distinguished Artists".

It is doubtful whether Mr. President ever got to see this superfilm. As a matter of fact, very few people ever got to see it because, except for a private premiere at Barrandov (where I was present), the film as far as I know, was never released. To show on the screen the arrival of Russian tanks after the arrival of Russian tanks could have seriously endangered the projection equipment.[†]

The second historical arrival of Russian tanks ended Prochazka's career. For a few months after the Invasion, he stubbornly persisted in publishing anti-invasionary articles in youth magazines. Earlier he had gotten very deeply involved in Dubcek's cause, and his journalistic career marked a new high in a panegyric article on T. G. Masaryk—another astronomical distance covered from the eulogy on Novotny. Together with Kachyna they managed to complete their two last films: a comedy *Christmas with Elizabeth,* 1968, and a strange, neurotic nightmarish story about a mortally ill patient recovering after a complicated heart surgery. In this depressing drama *Funny Man* (1969) the patient, suffering from nightmares

---

*The nature of the plot was as follows: one brother arrives in Prague as a soldier of the Red Army only to find his younger brother, who stayed home, shot during the last moments of the war by the SS. The beautiful maid, Jana Brejchova, went the same way.

[†] According to the official *Czechoslovak Film 1945-1970, Marathon,* after all, was released, on December 31, 1968. If this is correct, it must have been released and shown exclusively outside Prague because at that time I was still there. Anyway, the same source gives the figures for the number of spectators who saw the film by December 31, 1969 as 94,035. To realize what a trifling audience this is one has only to compare it with Jasny's *All Those Good Countrymen* which, though released more than half a year later (on July 7, 1969) reached, by December 31, 1969, 948,372 spectators. Even more illuminating are the data about Zdenek Podskalsky's *The Men About Town,* written by Vratislav Blazek. This swan song of my old friend from Nachod was released as late as October 10, 1969, and yet by the end of that same year it was seen by 827,464 people.

237

caused by several years in a Stalinist concentration camp, sees one day a girl through the window of his hospital room. She is feeding pigeons. The next day the girl fails to appear and the patient is obsessed with the idea that something has happened to her. He runs away from the hospital, and with superhuman effort reaches the fifth floor, knocks down the door, and indeed finds the girl dead. She has committed suicide. The patient's heart could not withstand the exertion of climbing the five flights of stairs and fails. The doctor, who writes the death certificate, remembers that the dead man had a daughter, who publicly disclaimed him after he had been sentenced for "treason" during one of the political frame-up trials of the fifties. The "traitor" was later fully rehabilitated and the daughter committed suicide.

After Dubcek's removal, Prochazka was among the main targets of the ideological fire. He became the subject of an extremely dirty intrigue which, although it is probably unprecedented, should not surprise anyone living in the present world. The secret police bugged the apartment of the non-Communist university professor, Vaclav Cerny, and from the tape thus obtained they fabricated a scandalous programme in which Prochazka unflatteringly and in rather obscene terms describes not only his past protector, but also the new President, and all the leading personalities of the "Czechoslovakian Spring". Prefaced by an idiotic story that the tape "was sent to the secret police by an unknown person from Paris" the impressively edited "document" was broadcasted on Prague television. The psychological consideration underlying this legal and constitutional egregiousness is obvious: such a blatant transgression of a citizen's privacy cannot harm the secret police, because everybody hates it anyway. It can only harm the popular image of an important and militant representative of "socialism with a human face"*. Prochazka publicly protested—his letter must have been one of the

*The trick belongs to the same category as the one played on Marta Kubisova—the singer who kissed Dubcek. A photograph (which was in fact a paste-up) circulated through Prague, showing a naked couple making love. It was supposed to be Marta and Dubcek (who is incidently a married man). The psychological intention was once again elementary: the picture was supposed to elicit moral indignation among the common people who do not grant their saints the right of human lapses. The case further presents an interesting example of "jurisprudence" in neo-stalinist Czechoslovakia.

Marta Kubisova started a court action, but the court refused to hear the case claiming that "the perpetrator was not apprehended". Marta then launched a new case, this time against the director of the international concert agency *Pragokoncert*,

last published expressions of dissent. (The reasons were again clearly tactical: *audiatur et altera pars,* since the harm was done and could not be undone.) In the letter he also apologized to the representatives, whom he had called on the tape "kind-hearted idiots". It was expected that after the disclosure he would be jailed, but instead he was taken to the hospital where he underwent a serious operation. His last film, again directed by Kachyna, *The Ear,* fell victim to the Big Ban of 1970. Prochazka then died, in February 1971. Pavel Kohout spoke at the funeral, and although the police closed the roads leading to the Kosire cemetery and tried to prevent people from attending, a large crowd assembled, including the playwright Vaclav Havel and such leaders of the Czechoslovak Spring as Josef Smrkovsky and Frantisek Kriegel.

In Prochazka departs a picturesque, but significant, figure of a *va banque* gambler and artist whom God endowed with art, but not with self-criticism, or with prudence. Whoever may be judging him will have to consider on the positive side—besides his considerable literary achievement—at least three very important scripts: *Worries, The Coach to Vienna,* and *The Night of the Bride.*

Every brief historical survey is necessarily unfair; it neglects certain people who do not deserve to be neglected. In this book I have omitted, for instance, such excellent directors of comedies as Zdenek Podskalsky (*Where the Devil Cannot Go,* 1959, *The White Lady,* 1965, *The Men about Town,* 1969), and Ladislav Rychman (*The Hop-Pickers,* 1964, *The Lady on the Tracks* 1966). I realize that many underestimate comedies, and some don't even consider them art. I am not guilty of either of those crimes, since I know how difficult they are to make and, after all, four of my five feature films are comedies. But Czech comedy would simply require a separate book, and it would necessarily have to be very different from this one. The same is true of Czech

---

who showed the pictures to several people as an explanation as to why the agency cannot represent Marta. At the trial the director of *Pragokoncert* testified that he received the photographs "from an unknown anonymous person". He was followed to the witness stand by Vaclav Neckar who told the director to his face what the latter had told him. The discreet gentlement had confided to him that the pornographic pictures were provided by the "state authorities".

After Neckar's testimony the judge adjourned the case indefinitely. As far as we know the trial has so far not resumed; however soon after the first hearing Neckar began to appear less and less frequently until he vanished from the TV screens altogether.

animated and puppet film, created and revolutionized by people like Jiri Trnka, Hermina Tyrlova, Bretislav Pojar, Jiri Brdecka, and many others; and of documentaries, made by Bruno Sefranka, Pavel Hobl, Kurt Goldberger, the brothers Jiri and Frantisek Papousek, Vaclav Taborsky, and also by such feature film directors as Evald Schorm and Jaromil Jires, often during their times of "difficulties". I would like to include all that—but *ars longa, liber brevis.*

This then is the story of Czech* film as I saw it and partially lived it. It would seem that the decade of the New Wave is a completed chapter, with the present outlook not too good. After the changes in Barrandov's leadership a seemingly more catastrophic repetition of the Banska Bystrice events took place: the Big Ban in the spring of 1970. The five existing autonomous production units with their script advisory boards, consisting mostly of prominent directors and writers have been abolished and seven "workshops" without any rights to make autonomous decisions have been established. The scripting and production plan for 1970 has been cancelled and replaced by a new plan in which detective stories and costume and light comedies altogether prevail. The chiefs of the old production units, and many members of their advisory boards, were fired and replaced by new ones; among them men like Vojtech Cach, one of the notorious representatives of ancient socialist realism, who when westerns of this type ceased to be fashionable † , tried his luck with a detective story; Karel Cop, a screen-play writer of two successful detective movies; Bohumil Smida, an actor whose biggest claim to art is the portrayal of a petty thief in one of Cop's detective films; Vojtech Trapl, a film critic of the Kliment variety, who left an indelible impression of the minds of the public by

*I did not include any Slovak film makers in this book. A few Slovak films were made before the Second World War, but the real upsurge of Slovak cinema came only after the war, and particularly in the sixties. From that time on, a number of Slovak directors achieved a high level of artistry, and the work of some is fully comparable with the best products of the Czech directors. We can name for instance Juraj Jakubisko (*Christ's Years,* 1967, *Deserters and Wanderers,* 1968, and *Birdies, Orphans and Fools,* 1969: the last two banned in 1970), Stefan Uher (*The Sun in the Net,* 1962, *Organ,* 1964), Peter Solan (*The Boxers and Death,* 1962. *Before this Night Is Over,* 1965), or Stanislav Barabas *The Bells for the Poor,* 1965). The present day Slovak cinematography is so vast that it would require a history of its own, and then, this is a personal history, and I know the Slovak directors only superficially.

† I use the term because the formula of a cheap pulp-magazine western is surprisingly similar to the formula of a degenerated socialist realistic novel. In a western there is a county with a big ranch and a pretty rancher's daughter (or local school teacher), with an incompetent sheriff, with a bunch of lazy indifferent cow-hands and with a band of desperados, stealing cattle from the good old rancher. Out of nowhere arrives a stranger, gets a job at the ranch, becomes the leader of the roused cowboys, fights the desperados and, in the end, either marries the pretty daughter, or goes away to some other neglected county, undoubtedly to repeat his good deeds there. In socialist-realistic "builders' novels" you get a factory with an incompetent director, a bunch of indifferent, wavering workers, a small band of reactionary desperados and an even smaller, and therefore helpless group of honest progressives—usually a pretty doctor (sometimes even a schoolteacher). Out of nowhere comes a stranger, gets a job at the factory, wins over the wavering workers, so that they stop drinking and become shock-workers. Then he fights the reactionary desperados and in the end either marries the pretty doctor (teacher) or goes to some other neglected factory, undoubtedly to repeat his good deeds there.

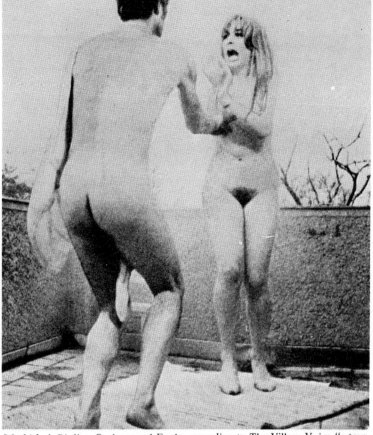

Jakubisko's Birdies, Orphans and Fools: *according to* The Village Voice *"a tour-de-force of creative camera work and montage which whirls us through a mad surrealist universe".*

his solo attack on *Peter and Paula,* at a time when such things were no longer taken seriously. The new director of the Barrandov studios announced far-reaching changes; while in the past only six of the total of approximately thirty films made per year were coloured, in 1971, the Czech audiences will have the opportunity of seeing no less than seventeen colour films made in Czechoslovakia. The 70mm super-screen, which has so far been supplied exclusively from the West (*Cleopatra, Spartacus*), will receive its first Czech products; Barrandov in co-production with other countries will manufacture its first super-films—a thing that Czech directors so far had not dared to undertake.

Barrandov seems to be leaving the road taken ten years ago by the young graduates of the Film Academy, and stepping out in the direction of Hollywood. At first glance, this is catastrophic. But only at first glance; learning from history we can read between the lines. *Panta rei.*

He who would have dared to point out in the fifties that the em-

242

peror's new clothes reveal his private parts would have risked being included in one of the numerous categories of high treason (Zionism, social democraticism, Titoism, revisionism, cosmopolitism, anti-socialism, slander, anti-Communism, Trotskyism, pornography, decadence, counter-revolution, pessimism, modernism, formalism, disorientation, psychologism, freudism, influencialism, structuralism, fascism, racism, lack of ideology, naturalism, bowing to the West, etc, etc.) and becoming a personal target of heavily concentrated fire; he would then go through all kinds of experiences, none of them too good. Banska Bystica preserved the tradition of personal attacks, but it replaced the traditional vocabulary lifted out of the criminal code for a more civilized collection of terms (such as anti-organical influences of neo-realism, being atypical, black vision, excerption of partial deficiencies from the complex totality, and their magnification, etc.); the apprehended criminals were simply suspended, and consequently suffered from an increased intensity of "problems". The inquisitions of 1970 so far have not reverted to attacks on individual artists—if we disregard the lunatic fringe which took over the radio*, and are simply repeating some of the Moscow attacks on the zionist (i.e. non-aryan) Forman, or the pornographer Menzel. "Unhealthy Occurrences" at Barrandov are condemned on very general terms, and even the old hatchet-men such as Kliment (the attack on *Valerie* was a settling of an old account, and while it assaults the film on the grounds of incomprehensibility, it acknowledges the high quality of Jires' direction) carefully emphasize that there were only a few "seducers" among the filmmakers, while the others were simply "seduced" little fools. Notwithstanding the warped "Marxism" of such a theory (similarly it is said of the nation: an infinitesimal number of saboteurs seduced the completely idiotic masses to all-absorbing enthusiasm), it is certainly more pleasant than if it were interpreted truthfully, that is the other way around. In my estimate the "little fools" will include everybody from the bearers of international laurels to those who

---

*The main speaker of these Aryan warriors is a Mr. Karel Janik (supposedly the pen-name for a group of authors). The level of his writing is best assessed in the following sample: to celebrate the first anniversary of the Invasion he (with a Mr. Banik) published a paper-back called *They Did Not Pass*. Among the pictures of police dispersing the demonstrating youth with the help of tanks and water cannons, there is a photo of a group of long-haired youngsters giving the internationally known V-sign. Mr. Janik's caption below this picture of one of the counter-revolutionary "groups that were directing the provocations" reads: "The sign they agreed upon: In two minutes we shall start the attack."

really only imitated the New Wave; they should, strictly speaking, include even Kliment, as he was induced to praise (with reservation) many an offensive counter-revolutionary work at the time of Novotny's decline and fall. The seducers will probably include Prochazka, too deeply involved with the President who was thrown overboard by his own "Kliments", they may also include some of the critics and dramaturgists who fought on the side of the New Wave, and whose names, devoid of international acclaim, may disappear more easily through the trap-door. Of course the list will be headed by those who left the country—which may also be the manifestation of a praiseworthy intention to alleviate the predicament of those who remained within the reach of the stalinist tough guys.*

The new manager-director of Barrandov also stressed that the confiscated films will not be destroyed, but only "put on ice", for eventual future release, but less than six months passed and he himself was put on ice, and Miroslav Fabera, a fairly good author, and as far as I know a decent person, was appointed new director of the Barrandov Studios.

The announced production formula is of course typical for a certain type of socialist country; a type which is different from either the Czechoslovakia of the period of Novotny's decline, or of the short era of Dubcek. History took a somewhat ironic stand towards the old revolutionaries who once assumed that the socialist state would necessarily facilitate the creation of never-dreamt-of products of revolutionary artistic endeavour. Instead of the fulfillment of this ideal the trend of the announced works can be described by a single word (which at the time of ancient socialist realism belonged to the list of treacherous activities): escapism. The programme is

---

*Thus I was uncovered by the Communist Party daily paper *Rude Pravo* of February 1, 1971, as the man who, together with Ludvik Vaculik, Dr. Jan Brod, A.J. Liehm and Professor O. Wichterle, initiated and wrote the notorious *2000 Words Manifesto.* Up till then I tried to keep this a secret by maintaining that I read the Manifesto only after it had been criticized by the Party Conservatives, and only then, out of solidarity with Vaculik (whom I admire as a writer rather than as a politician) did I attach my signature to it. Well, now the truth is out, and I might as well alleviate my own predicament by confessing the *whole* truth about the famous document; after all, so many before me did confess even more than the whole truth, and why should the innocent suffer? *Rude Pravo* has wrong information on this point: Vaculik, Brod, Liehm and Wichterle were *not* my co-authors. I wrote the *2000 Words* with Yvonne Prenosilova, the pop singer, now in Western Germany (she typed it), with Jaroslav Brodsky, a triple-agent for the CIA, ICI and CPUS and founder of the Club of Former Political Prisoners in Czechoslovakia (K231), now in Canada; further with Herr Graf von Razumowski of the *Frankfurter Allgemeine,* now in Western Germany, and with Eldridge Cleaver, now in Algiers, who in the summer of 1968 visited Prague incognito, disguised as a correspondent for a John Birch Society paper.

*The socialist film-makers' escapes: Rangel Vulchanov's from Bulgaria
to Czechoslovakia in* The Face under the Mask . . . .

*. . . and Karel Kachyna's from Czechoslovakia to Australia via the
Austro-Hungarian Empire in* I Can Jump Puddles.

dominated by comedies and detective thrillers*, those well-trodden paths used to circumvent the true reality, and by films from ancient or more recent ancient history. Soviet art began to take this type of evasive action during the thirties, when Stalin and Zhdanov set forth the eternal laws. For instance, nowhere in the world would it be possible to persistently produce as many books and films about war (Second World or the Revolutionary one of 1917-1920) as in the Soviet Union. The quality of these products in comparison to those in other thematic areas is far superior. Practically all of Soviet crime novels are either spy stories, or they are related to the Nazi invasion of the USSR, because the only legitimate, (i.e. accepted by socialist realism) murder motive in socialist society, is the elimination of a witness of one's collaboration with the Nazis. I don't know what the Soviet crime novelists will write about, when the generation of those who remember World War II dies out.

Other voices typical for the culture of socialist realism have been heard sounding off around Prague: they complain about the inadequate number of "great, artistically strong and truthful works depicting our times", and so on. These "voices calling in the desert" can

*Of the "serious" films announced in the official film bulletin for the fall of 1970, the most remarkable promises to be *Factory of Illusions,* a back stage view of the Barrandov studios, in the old muckraker style. It was written by the new Chief Dramaturgist of Barrandov, Ludvik Toman (according to a Barrandov underground story his main dramaturgical accomplishment to date is the suspension of a new Nazi occupation film on the grounds that the protagonist's first name is Moritz: the Chief Dramaturgist is dead set against "Zionist" names for heroes of the Czech resistance.) *The Dream Factory* is supposed to take place during the time of "the terror of snobs", (which is the name given to the sixties by Stalinists). A young graduate of the Film Academy, bursting of creative desire arrives at Barrandov, where he is shocked to find the famous directors drinking and whoring instead of filming. As nobody bothers to give him any work, he watches the films of his older depraved colleagues in the projection room. (I hope the story will explain where they found the time to make them with all the drinking and whoring.) The viewing in the projection room is to be the experimental part of the opus: it will provide most of the footage and it will be a montage of authentic shots and scenes from the decadent films of the New Wave, including the last ones, banned in the spring of 1970. After a prolonged exposure to such indoctrination the young candidate also succumbs to whores, booze, and general counter-revolution. The perverts of the New Wave have claimed another decent young person. It's probably unnecessary to add what a moving socialist-realist film could be obtained by a clever editing of scenes from Luis Trenker's *The Rebel,* 1933, or from the folkloristic dramas (*The Blue Light,* 1932) made by Leni Riefenstahl before her famous party film, *Triumph of the Will,* 1936. Anyway, whatever changes and embellishments this story (I recount it from underground sources) may undergo before the film is released, it is undoubtedly in good hands. Dramaturgically it is supervised by Dr. Trapl (for whose qualifications see pages 79 and 254) and by Mr. Rudolf Cerny, one of the original members of the antisemitic ultrastalinist Jodas group. So far, Mr. Cerny has been probably the only jodasist who suffered at the hands of the censors. Shortly after the Invasion he was the first to publish a muckraking booklet, according to underground sources, on the "creeping counterrevolution".

246

be heard throughout the Socialist bloc—in some countries permanently, in others periodically—since the advent of Stalin. As recently as the Twelfth All-Russian Drama Congress in 1970, the well-known voice intimates that, "there are unfortunately few new plays about the Soviet Man". Of course, whenever new works bearing at least one of the above mentioned criteria do appear, the same voices attack them, and if a sufficient power is on hand, they liquidate them. In the intervals between the periods the menacing and melancholic voices pretend that they don't know the reason for the paucity. Since the official cultural stand made it impossible to truthfully explain the mass escape from the present into history, war, degenerated genres and questions surrounding private sexual activities, a strange tradition developed: not the artists themselves, but the editors and dramaturgists receive a periodical drubbing from the bureaucratic spokesmen, for having failed to "discover" enough great and truthful works. This is supposedly caused by laziness; instead of going out to places where "the sources of real life" can be discovered, they sit in their comfortable armchairs in Moscow (Prague, Warsaw, Berlin, and, who knows, maybe even Tirana).

The chief villain of this opus was allegedly Mr. Jiri Hajek, a well-known party-hack and a rubber-man of ideology. He was assigned this sinister role by Mr. Cerny because of an old personal feud. Years ago, Mr. Cerny had been discovered by Mr. Hajek as a new literary genius. His subsequent fiction, unfortunately, was rather less than mediocre, and so Mr. Hajek, who has always tried to appear as a literary arbiter of deep insight and great analytical abilities, revoked his judgement and disclaimed his protégé. Mr. Cerny's description of Mr. Hajek's activities was, however, not unfounded, if by "preparing counterrevolution" we mean efforts to aid the liberalisation of the humanitites. In the early fifties, Mr. Hajek was one of the chief theoreticians of socialist-realism; then he developed, and in the sixties he tried to lead the field once again by eulogizing Kafka, Camus, Sartre, Garaudy and others of the same sort, and by opening the pages of the *Plamen* magazine to the chief ideologues of communist liberalism. After Novotny's counter-attack in the Fall of 1967 he lost his nerve and tried to shift his position safely towards the Novotny boys. Soon after that Novotny fell and Hajek was fired as editor-in-chief of *Plamen*. During the Dubcek period he remained cautiously silent, but regularly attended meetings, listening and taking notes. Soon after the Invasion he joined the ranks of the "true leninists". Being however, unlike the unswervingly faithful stalinist Mr. Cerny he did not side with Jodas but became what is known as "centrist" or "moderate". As such—and also because of his "liberal" international reputation—he was more useful to the forces which decide in today's Czechoslovakia, and so poor old ironguard Mr. Cerny had his book quietly withdrawn from circulation while Mr. Hajek had his similar book published and translated into several languages. Mr. Cerny, in just wrath and an inebriated condition, knocked down another former socialist realist Mr. Stern while the latter was giving a pro-Dubcek speech at a writers' meeting. Later he turned his wrath against Jan Prochazka and maintained that far from being ill the former President's favourite tried to save his skin by simulating cancer. I have no doubts that Prochazka's death appeared to this dangerous innocent as another trick committed by the film-maker for the sole purpose of giving the surviving counterrevolutionaries an opportunity to assemble at his funeral and thus provoke the true marxists.

The editors and dramaturgists are presented as mushroom-pickers. If they want to gather a lot of mushrooms they have to venture after them deep into the forest; they cannot remain on the edge where there aren't any to be found. Art is the mushroom, growing somewhere, probably in secret drawers of unknown Solzhenitsyns. But what will happen to the mushroom-pickers if they pull something from out of the drawers?

It is, however, indeed ridiculous to ignore what the Marxists call the super-structure: although he was no Marxist, we must recall the famous words of Abraham Lincoln about who can be duped, and how long it can last. The intellectuals, particularly those involved in the humanities and arts, act as a seismograph of injustices, and revolutionary art is largely a cry of *J'accuse!* The revolution sometimes removes the most flagrant injustices: unemployment, hunger, blatant poverty. But the spectrum of injustices is colourful, and the revolution does not change the intellectuals according to Plato's wish from a seismograph of injustices into a gauge for the measuring of the nation's love for their representatives. It would be betraying its own principles. There is no more hunger and incredible poverty, but there are unjust convictions, concentration camps, encroachments in personal assessments, "class" approach to children. Too often we see what Milan Kundera in his play *The Cock and Bull Story* calls "the reign of fools over the clever, of the spineless over the idealists." Also: "there at the bottom of all those great works, are the injustices, which no social order will eliminate" (Forman). This leads to "pessimism" and "the mucking around with atypical exceptions" and so forth, which is how the socialist realists express the fact that "all that which is noble and which has remained in art and literature since ancient times...always concerned itself with injuries and injustices perpetrated against the individual" (Forman).

People, who are no longer hungry and do not have to fear hospital bills, and yet are forced to live in a spiritual climate created by the spirit of the Kliments, will not remain endlessly contented with television serials of the "I Love Lucy" quality in a socialist rendition. Their ageless cultural tradition going all the way back to the Middle Ages, far too often resisted simplifications and officious obedience and will not permit them to accept stupidities particularly when they live a life dominated by political repression, which makes culture an important outlet for them. In Czechoslovakia, films and literature are not just entertainment on different levels of

248

Smluvené znamení: za dvě minuty začne útok.

Yellow Journalism in action: the caption under this photo of Czech Peace-sign greeting youths reads: "The sign they agreed upon: In two minutes we shall start the attack." *From Messrs. Janik & Banik masterwork:* They Did Not Pass.

sophistication, nor are they the subject of snobbish conversation, as is all too frequently the case in the West. They play an important part in the lives of wide masses. Aeneas Silvius Piccolomini, later Pope Pius II (1458-64), declared once that any Czech old woman can quote the Bible better than a Roman Cardinal. Similarly, an average Czech bank clerk, not to mention doctor or nuclear scientist, knows his Fellini better than many an American film producer.

The socialist state nationalized film and gave the film-makers much better potential opportunities than other regimes. Not that they were better paid than Western directors or film stars, certainly not. That, however, was not what they wanted. They did not have to seek financial backing for their intentions, or struggle to subsist—as employees of the Studios they received a permanent salary. Even the tedious arguments between the directors of the New Wave and Novotny's bureaucracy were in a sense more dignified than the quarrels of the same directors with some of their Western profit-oriented patrons. They argued aesthetico-political approaches, and nobody was terribly concerned about the box-office profit, at most some bureaucrat despaired about the safety of his position. The graduates of the Film Academy, if they were worth anything, had an open and direct road towards a career.

The Maecenas State, or rather its cultural bureaucracy, expected in return from the artists a mass production of adult fairy-tales, which would be enjoyed by the powerful in this world. This was something that the artists—I use the word in a qualitative sense, not

249

as a mere professional label—could not do. Historically, they always felt the necessity to be loyal to what they considered to be the truth, rather than to their patrons. No revolution can change that, because if it succeeded in doing so, it would, in my opinion, cease to be revolutionary.

Thus another type of uniformity appears in the cinematographies of socialist states. It is different from socialist realism, because it is unimposed. The ranks of governmental story-tellers and bureaucratic managers are slowly infiltrated by artists and their friends. It might even reach the point when the artists take over the leading positions in the arts altogether; which is what happened, or almost happened in Czechoslovakia. A strange paradox arose: the State was financing its own critics*. This was of course pointed out by the well-known angry voices after the Invasion, in a manner symptomatic of the feudal souls among the socialist-realistic theoreticians. But it is natural that in a socialist society the critics are paid by the state. Who else is supposed to finance them? Unless of course we were dealing with a brand of socialism which does not wish to be criticized. That type did exist: it was called National Socialism, and operated on the so called *fuhrerprinzip*. To prove that the dissatisfaction with the status quo is one of the basic characteristics of mankind is, I think, unnecessary. If we did not have the need to criticize we would still be eating caterpillars.

The infiltration of creative intellect into the various levels of cultural bureaucracy is a natural developmental tendency in socialist states. It is an important and redeeming infiltration, because the "socialist system is more viable than capitalism, as long as the leadership is able to creatively exploit the true principles of development. Whenever a person who is unable to wisely utilize power manages to attain it the advantages of a controlled system turn into negative obstacles" (Jires).

Sometimes the infiltration takes place too rapidly, in which case the artists end up with bloodied noses: this happened to some extent to the Polish "Black Wave", it happened to brave individuals in the

---

*In this connection it is necessary to define the term "criticism". I hope it is evident from what I have written, that the New Wave was not only a socially critical trend. Social criticism probably was not even its most important feature. Naturally the Kliments and Jack-in-the-Boxes found the New Wave's social involvement its most annoying feature. But they were just as displeased by the New Wave's revolt against the aesthetic regimentation. In the world of socialist realism, surrealism is almost as terrible as espionage and, after all, "everything is interdependent" (Stalin): a certain aesthetic system with a certain political system.

250

Soviet Union (Kalatozov, Chukhray), and it took place twice within a relatively short time period, and with great intensity, in Czechoslovakia. But the creative spirit always comes back. When it becomes impossible for an art form which requires backers, such as film, to attack the "heart of the matter", there is a fantastic improvement in the quality of comedies, (Wajda: *The Innocent Sorcerers*—if one may label this delicate study with this epithet), of psychological drama (Szabo: *Father*), and excellent war films are produced (Kalatozov: *The Cranes Are Flying*). This will happen even in such seeming cultural wastelands as Bulgaria (Vulchanov: *On the Little Island,* or *Sun and Shadow*; Zheljazkova: *The Attached Balloon*). The retreat into the times of the October Revolution (Chukhray: *The Forty First*) or into more distant history (Kawalerovicz: *Mother Joan of the Angels*) is carried out with formal brilliance, and to make it completely clear, someone like Andrzej Wajda, in Prague in 1970, declares: "Very many plays and novels, which deal with historically distant events, frequently possess a greater topicality than many works set in the present. . . . This is a common occurrence." Excellent compilation documentaries may be created, which at face value propagandistically attack a defeated enemy, but which also elicit a memory of Brynych's quotation: ". . .it is an international disease; its symptoms may be found. . .even in our own country" (Romm: *Ordinary Fascism*). Next to the Kalatozovs and Chukhrays who are having "difficulties", works relatively undisturbed, the excellent Kozintsev, utilizing materials from Shakespeare and Cervantes; in the border republics appear various Ibragimbekovs, who might not be risking political dissent, but whose aesthetics are anything but the official code periodically ayed by the cultural congresses, which as a sideline intermittently sanctify or excommunicate Nobel Prize winners. When the aesthetics become a little too overpowering, they go and make their movies in a friendly socialist country, which reprimands its own artists for comparable work, but a foreigner who does not belong under that country's critical control, is permitted to shoot whatever he wishes. (Vulchanov: *The Face Under the Mask,* produced at Barrandov in 1970, after which Vulchanov was reportedly ordered to return to Bulgaria.) On the other hand if the dramaturgist-censor rejects "unsuitable" original subjects from local life, because—to quote the old expert Kliment—their author "knows which way he should take, but simply doesn't want to"—the director may reach out for a theme all

251

the way to the antipodes. This was done by Karel Kachyna, after the involuntary severance of his collaboration with Prochazka. His film *I Can Jump Puddles* (made at Barrandov in 1970)* is based on a charming autobiography by Alan Marshall, an Australian author so far neglected by Hollywood. In Prague he has the reputation of a "progressive" due to his friendship with left-wing Australian writers, and consequently no servile spirit dares to object against this Anglo-Saxon import; though he may against the importer.

The roads are numerous and varied, but all of them carefully avoid the thruway of socialist realism, which is, as far as the stalinist cultural commissars are concerned, the only right route, The feud between reality and dogmatic fixed ideas about reality sometimes erupts into a bloody massacre, yet a few years later a Miklos Jancso produces *The Red and the White,* a highly formalistic drama of a revolution "seen through the eyes of a horse" (a description given to it by an influential Western aesthetician), which Rakosi's theoreticians would have condemned as persiflage. Even artists learn tactics, and they combine the organizational infiltration with an aesthetic indoctrination. Whereas during Stalin's era the socialist-

*The title under which it was released reads in translation: *I Am Jumping Muddy-Puddles Again.* This is—without any doubt unintentionally—a rather *nomen omen* of a title indeed, if one considers Kachyna's career.

And to add a finishing touch to the portrait of the vigilant Mr. Jan Kliment. In a vitriolic article attached to an interview with Kachyna he reminds the director that he has never "satisfactorily explained" his long collaboration with the late Jan Prochazka, and urges him to "tell us who, in your present opinion, profited from such films as *The Coach to Vienna* and *The Night of the Bride?* Who would have profited from *The Ear* which, most rightly, was banned from showing?" And finally: "What is comrade Kachyna's present opinion of the *2000 Words Manifesto* which he, too, signed?"

Whenever I read about the unceasing exploits of Mr. Kliment I cannot help remembering how I first met him. That was in the early sixties; I was still pretty notorious and the times were just ripening for the second round of the struggle for liberalization. One day I went to see an editor in her office in the Radio Building. On opening the door I saw her listening to a one-eyed man and grinning uncertainly. As soon as she saw me, she interrupted the narrator and introduced him to me: "Meet Comrade Kliment." Behind his back she blinked furiously as if something had fallen into her eye. I did not know then which of the several Kliments he was—the name is pretty common—but the pathological blinking identified his kind beyond any shadow of a doubt. I sat down and he resumed his interrupted story. In a second he was shooting away a fiercely anti-soviet anecdote, and then another and another, with the speed and atrocity of a well-oiled machine gun. After each anecdote he laughed and remained silent for a while in the hope we would add some funny story of our own. Every Czech is well-supplied with news from Radio Yerevan—the mythical Soviet station that spreads slander within the Soviet Union—but the situation smacked too much of the first chapter of *Schweik* in which Mr. Bretschneider hopes the Good Soldier will insult the Emperor. We held out and did not join the reactionary feast; we just grinned politely, trying to make the grins look a little disapproving. That's how I met Mr. Jan Kliment.

252

A reminder of Report on the Party and the Guests *(see page 121): In the 1972 Barrandov feature,* Black Wolf, *the Czech lover of a West German spy (killed earlier by the vigilant frontier gunmen), is justly torn to pieces by a crossbreed of wolf and German Shepherd (a breed raised by the Czech frontier police). For the sake of human interest, a love affair between the doggie and a bitch from across the border is thrown in.*

realistic overseers handed the artists over to the secret police and ten years later still arranged firings and suspensions, nowadays they generally restrain themselves to cursing or grumbling. Whether they like it or not, they are slowly forced to accept the elements of the aesthetics and philosophy which they continually try to suppress*. Following the example of Orwell's Big Brother they will of course maintain that they always held these views, and only objected against their "misuse". Unlike Orwell's Big Brother they are unable to reprint all the old newspapers.

And so I hope and believe, indeed I am convinced, that Czecho-slovakia will take the same road. The professors of socialist realism

---

*Typical of this process is an interview with one of the new production chiefs, Vojtech Cach, a man who went from socialist-realistic dramas of the fifties (*The Duchcov Underpass,* 1950, *The Most Strike,* 1953), through light comedies and children's books all the way to detective story (*Who Will Collect the Loot,* 1968). In an interview Cach declared among other things: "For instance, we should not renounce certain attributes offered by the theatre of the absurd—such as irony, sarcasm, nonsense, shocking, provocation and maybe even paradox. It would be a political luxury if our society permitted the publication of anti-social literature...but this does not mean that I opt for a literature "in attention", for a tamed and really "public" art; for the good of literature we must avoid the canonization of one opinion, or one poetic system." The question, of course, is how much of the "shocking, nonsense and provocation" will Cach be able to put through in practice.

253

among the film-makers are few (or more accurately: I rather doubt there are any,*) just as there are few worshippers of permanent dictatorship in a nation, which throughout its history fought a long and difficult battle for democracy, and did not forget it after thirty years of dictatorial regimes. The official ideology theoretically encourages the artists to honesty and "creative searching"—although in practice the artists usually get their hands slapped for such activity. Nevertheless, if theory fights against practice, instead of providing it with help, it is waging a hopeless war. The length of such a war is naturally questionable, but even Marx was convinced of its hopelessness, and although he was frequently wrong, he was also frequently right.

As far as the future of Czech film is concerned, I am optimistic. Unfortunately, I cannot be so optimistic about the future of some of its creators (including myself). *Vita brevis.* There are traumas which a person cannot overcome, and sometimes there is just so much that one can take in a single lifetime. It is said, "That is revolution! In a revolution it can't be otherwise!" Man has become what he is through dissatisfaction, which in the end has always made him do everything differently than it was supposed to be done.

Toronto, Fall 1970 — Spring 1971

*The term itself re-appeared at a meeting of film-makers in Moscow in the Spring of 1971 in a rather significant way. The Czechoslovak delegates, Mr. Trapl (the same who once had attacked Forman's *Peter and Paula* for pessimism) and Professor A. M. Brousil of the Film Academy tried to prove to a predominantly Soviet audience that the refusal of socialist realism by the New Wave was "unnecessarily radical" — which is a cautious way (they had to go back to Prague) of saying that we should have stuck to zhdanovism as it does not encourage any funny new ideas. Whereupon some Soviet delegates rose in protest, demanding, on the contrary, a new and radical approach to socialist art. This should lay down some very broad conceptual foundations of a radically new method which would only "utilize the traditions of socialist realism" and could be described as "post-socialist realism" or "neo-socialist realism". Which reminds me of a rather nice Soviet writer who at a literary conference in the West, in the mid-sixties, after having proclaimed himself a true and faithful socialist realist, found room enough, within the zhdanovite esthetical framework, for everybody from Franz Kafka to James Joyce to Evelyn Waugh.

Alain Resnais, Milos and Ivan in a winter night in New York, 1971. Far away from the barrel of sauerkraut, but also far away from home . . .

254

CHRONOLOGICAL LIST

OF THE MORE INTERESTING CZECH FEATURE FILMS 1898-1970
(with the Names of Their Directors)

Some dates may slightly differ from those given in other reference books. Such discrepancies occur even in official publications by the Czechoslovak Film Institute, and are due to the fact that some sources give the year of production while others the year of release. In a few instances the difference may be several years; this usually indicates censorship difficulties. The number after the year indicates the total number of features produced that year.

1898 / 3 features

DOSTAVENÍČKO VE MLÝNICI (Rendez-vous at the Grinding Room) *Jan Kříženecký*
PLÁČ A SMÍCH (Laughing and Crying) *Jan Kříženecký*
VÝSTAVNÍ PÁRKAŘ A LEPIČ PLAKÁTŮ (The Exhibition Sausage Vendor) *J. Kříženecký*

1899—1909 / no features made

1910 / 3 features

ARTUR SE ŽENÍ (Arthur Gets Married) *Antonín Pech*
SEN STARÉHO MLÁDENCE (The Bachelor's Dream) *Jan Kříženecký*

1911 / 5 features

RUDI NA KŘTINÁCH (Rudi the Godfather) *Emil Arthur Longen*
RUDI NA ZÁLETECH (Rudi the Seducer of Women) *Emil Arthur Longen*
RUDI SPORTSMANEM (Rudi the Sportsman) *Emil Arthur Longen & Antonín Pech*

1912 / 11 features

FAUST / *Stanislav Hlavsa*
PĚT SMYSLŮ ČLOVĚKA (The Five Senses of Man) *Josef Šváb-Malostranský*
ŠATY DĚLAJÍ ČLOVĚKA (Clothes Make Man) *Max Urban & Jára Sedláček*
　　(based freely on Shakespeare's Much Ado about Nothing.)
ZUB ZA ZUB (Tooth for Tooth) *Antonín Pech*

1913 / 14 features

CHOLERA V PRAZE (Cholera in Prague) *Alois Jalovec*
ESTRELLA / *Otakar Štáfl & Max Urban*
KONEC MILOVÁNÍ (End of Lovemaking) *Otakar Štáfl & Max Urban*
PAN PROFESOR, NEPŘÍTEL ŽEN (Our Professor, the Enemy of Women) *Jiří Steimar*
PRODANÁ NEVĚSTA (The Bartered Bride) *Max Urban* (memorable for being a silent movie based on the opera by *Bedřich Smetana)*
ŽIVOT ŠEL KOLEM (Life Passed By) *Rudolf Mejkal*
ZKAŽENÁ KREV (Rotten Blood) *Alois Wiesmer*

1914 / 14 features

NOČNÍ DĚS (Night Horror) *J. A. Palouš*
ZAMILOVANÁ TCHYNĚ (Mother-in-Law in Love) *Antonín Pech* (memorable as the first film appearance of *Josef Rovenský)*

1915 / 2 features

AHASVER / *Jaroslav Kvapil*

256

257

MRTVÍ ŽIJÍ (The Dead Are Alive) *J. S. Kolár*
ZLATÝ KLÍČEK (The Little Gold Key) *Jaroslav Kvapil*

1923 / 8 features

ULIČKA HŘÍCHU A LÁSKY (The Street of Sin and Love) *Václav Binovec*
ÚNOS BANKÉŘE FUXE (The Kidnapping of Banker Fux) *Karel Anton*

1924 / 17 features

BÍLÝ RÁJ (The White Paradise) *Karel Lamač*
PÍSEŇ ŽIVOTA (The Song of Life) *Miroslav J. Krňanský*

1925 / 25 features

DO PANSKÉHO STAVU (Becoming Middle-Class) *Karel Anton*
JEDENÁCTÉ PŘIKÁZÁNÍ (The Eleventh Commandment) *Václav Kubásek*
KAREL HAVLÍČEK BOROVSKÝ / *Karel Lamač & Theodor Pištěk*
LUCERNA (The Lantern) *Karel Lamač*
VDAVKY NANYNKY KULICHOVÉ (Nanynka Kulichová's Marriage) **M. J. Krňanský**

1926 / 33 features

DOBRÝ VOJÁK ŠVEJK (Good Soldier Schweik) *Karel Lamač*
KREUTZEROVA SONÁTA (Kreutzer Sonata) *Gustav Machatý*
OTEC KONDELÍK A ŽENICH VEJVARA (Father Kondelík and Bridegroom Vejvara)
    Karel Anton
POHÁDKA MÁJE (The May Story) *Karel Anton* (the first film role of *George Voskovec*)
VELBLOUD UCHEM JEHLY (Camel through the Needle's Eye) *Karel Lamač*
WERTHER / *Miloš Hajský* (based freely on a novel by *J. W. Goethe*)

1927 / 23 features

BAHNO PRAHY (The Bog of Prague) *Miroslav J. Krňanský*
BATALION / *Přemysl Pražský*

1928 / 26 features

PÁTER VOJTĚCH (Father Vojtěch) *Mac Frič* (directorial debut of *Frič*)
POHORSKÁ VESNICE (The Mountain Village) *Miroslav J. Krňanský*
ŽIVOTEM VEDLA JE LÁSKA (Love Lead Them through Life) *Josef Rovenský*

1929 / 34 features

EROTIKON / *Gustav Machatý*
PLUKOVNÍK ŠVEC (Colonel Švec) *Svatopluk Innemann*
SVATÝ VÁCLAV (Saint Wenceslas) *J. S. Kolár*
TAKOVÝ JE ŽIVOT (That's Life) *Karl Junghans*
VARHANÍK U SV. VÍTA (The Organist of St. Vít) *Mac Frič*

1930 / 8 features

C. a K. POLNÍ MARŠÁLEK (The Field Marshal) *Karel Lamač* (first Czech sound comedy,
    first talkie of *Vlasta Burian*)
KDYŽ STRUNY LKAJÍ (When the Strings Weep) *Friedrich Fehér* (first Czech talkie)
OPEŘENÉ STÍNY (The Feathered Shadows) *Leo Marten* (from a story by *E. A. Poe*)
TONKA ŠIBENICE (Tonka, the Gallows) *Karel Anton*

258

1931 / 19 features

KAREL HAVLÍČEK BOROVSKÝ / *Svatopluk Innemann*
MUŽI V OFFSIDU (Men Off-Side) *Svatopluk Innemann*
PUDR A BENZIN (Powder and Petrol) *Jindřich Honzl* (first film of *Voskovec + Werich*)
ZE SOBOTY NA NEDĚLI (From Saturday to Sunday) *Gustav Machatý*

1932 / 24 features

EXTASE (Ecstasy) *Gustav Machatý*
PENÍZE NEBO ŽIVOT (Money or your Life) *Jindřich Honzl*
PÍSNIČKÁŘ (The Songster) *Svatopluk Innemann*
PŘED MATURITOU (Before the Matriculation) *Vladislav Vančura* & *Svatopluk Innemann*

1933 / 33 features

DŮM NA PŘEDMĚSTÍ (A House in the Suburbs) *Miroslav Cikán*
NA SLUNEČNÍ STRANĚ (On the Sunny Side) *Vladislav Vančura*
ŘEKA (The River) *Josef Rovenský*
REVISOR (Government Inspector) *Martin Frič*
SVÍTÁNÍ (The Dawn) *Václav Kubásek*
U SNĚDENÉHO KRÁMU (The Eaten-Up Shop) *Martin Frič*
VRAŽDA V OSTROVNÍ ULICI (Murder in Island Street) *Svatopluk Innemann*
ZÁHADA MODRÉHO POKOJE (The Mystery of the Blue Room) *Miroslav Cikán*
ZEM SPIEVA (The Earth Is Singing) *Karel Plicka*
ZE SVĚTA LESNÍCH SAMOT (For Forest Loneliness) *M. J. Krňanský*
ŽIVOT JE PES (A Dog's Life) *Martin Frič*

1934 / 31 features

AŤ ŽIJE NEBOŽTÍK! (Long Live the Loved One!) *Martin Frič*
HEJ RUP! (Heave-Ho!) *Martin Frič*
MARIJKA NEVĚRNICE (The Unfaithful Marijka) *Vladislav Vančura*
POSLEDNÍ MUŽ (The Last Man) *Martin Frič*
U NÁS V KOCOURKOVĚ (We at Krähwinkel) *Miroslav Cikán*
ZA RANNÍCH ČERVÁNKŮ (The Rosy Dawn) *Josef Rovenský*

1935 / 25 features

A ŽIVOT JDE DÁL.. (Life Goes On) *Carl Junghans*
GOLEM / *Julien Duvivier* (made for a Czech company, with Czech technical staff, screenwriters and a mixed Czech-French cast)
JÁNOŠÍK / *Martin Frič*
JEDENÁCTÉ PŘIKÁZÁNÍ (The Eleventh Commandment) *Martin Frič*
MARYŠA / *Josef Rovenský*

1936 / 26 features

JÍZDNÍ HLÍDKA (The Mounted Patrol) *Václav Binovec*
TRHANI (The Ragamuffins) *Václav Wasserman*
ULIČKA V RÁJI (A Lane in Paradise) *Martin Frič*
VELBLOUD UCHEM JEHLY (Camel Through the Needle's Eye) *Hugo Haas, Otakar Vávra*
VOJNARKA / *Vladimír Borský*

1937 / 45 features

BATALION / *Miroslav Cikán*
BÍLÁ NEMOC (The White Illness) *Hugo Haas*
FILOSOFSKÁ HISTORIE / *Otakar Vávra*
HLÍDAČ Č. 47 (Watchman No. 47) *Josef Rovenský*

259

LÁSKA A LÍDÉ (Love and People) *Václav Kubásek & Vladislav Vančura*
LIDÉ NA KŘE (People on the Iceberg) *Martin Frič*
MRAVNOST NADE VŠE (Morality Above All) *Martin Frič*
NAŠI FURIANTI (The Swaggerers) *Vladislav Vančura & Václav Kubásek*
OTEC KONDELÍK A ŽENICH VEJVARA (Father Kondelík and Bridegroom Vejvara)
    M. J. Krňanský
PANENSTVÍ (Virginity) *Otakar Vávra*
SVĚT PATŘÍ NÁM (The World Belongs to Us) *Martin Frič*

1938 / 40 features

CECH PANEN KUTNOHORSKÝCH (Guild of the Maidens of Kutná Hora) *Otakar Vávra*
POD JEDNOU STŘECHOU (Under One Roof) *M. J. Krňanský*
SVĚT, KDE SE ŽEBRÁ (The World of Beggars) *Miroslav Cikán*

1939 / 39 features

DÍVKA V MODRÉM (The Girl in Blue) *Otakar Vávra*
EVA TROPÍ HLOUPOSTI (Eva Is Fooling) *Martin Frič*
HUMORESKA (Humoresque) *Otakar Vávra*
HVĚZDA Z POSLEDNÍ ŠTACE (The Star of the One-Night Stands) *Jiří Slaviček*
KOUZELNÝ DŮM (The Enchanted House) *Otakar Vávra*
KRISTIÁN / *Martin Frič*
OHNIVÉ LÉTO (Fiery Summer) *Fratišek Čáp & Václav Krška*
TULÁK MACOUN (Macoun the Tramp) *Ladislav Brom*
VĚRA LUKÁŠOVÁ / *E. F. Burian*

1940 / 32 features

BABIČKA (The Granny) *František Čáp*
ČEKANKY (The Waiting Girls) *Vladimír Borský*
DRUHÁ SMĚNA (The Second Shift) *Martin Frič*
KATAKOMBY (Catacombe) *Martin Frič*
MUZIKANTSKÁ LIDUŠKA (The Musicians' Liduška) *Martin Frič*
PACIENTKA DR. HEGLA (Dr. Hegl's Pacient) *Otakar Vávra*
POHÁDKA MÁJE (The May Story) *Otakar Vávra*
TO BYL ČESKÝ MUZIKANT (He Was a Czech Musician) *Vladimír Slavinský*

1941 / 19 features

ADVOKÁT CHUDÝCH (The Lawyer of the Poor) *Vladimír Slavinský*
JAN CIMBURA / *František Čáp*
NOČNÍ MOTÝL (The Night Moth) *František Čáp*
PALIČOVA DCERA (The Arsonist's Daughter) *Vladimír Borský*
PRAŽSKÝ FLAMENDR (The Prague Gallivanter) *Karel Spelina*
ROZTOMILÝ ČLOVĚK (A Charming Man) *Martin Frič*
TĚŽKÝ ŽIVOT DOBRODRUHA (The Difficult Life of an Adventurer) *Martin Frič*
TURBINA (The Turbine) *Otakar Vávra*

1942 / 11 features

BARBORA HLAVSOVÁ / *Martin Frič*
MĚSTEČKO NA DLANI (The Village in your Palm) *Václav Binovec*
VALENTIN DOBROTIVÝ (Valentin the Good) *Martin Frič*

1943 / 8 features

EXPERIMENT / *Martin Frič*
ŠŤASNOU CESTU (Farewell) *Otakar Vávra*
ŽÍZNIVÉ MLÁDÍ (The Thirsty Youth) *M J. Krňanský*

260

1954 / 13 features

FRONA (The Sisters) *Jiří Krejčík*
HUDBA Z MARSU (Music from Mars) *Ján Kadár & Elmar Klos*
STŘÍBRNÝ VÍTR (The Silver Wind) *Václav Krška* (banned; released in 1956)

1955 / 14 features

CESTA DO PRAVĚKU (A Journey to the Primeval Times) *Karel Zeman*

1956 / 18 features

DĚDEČEK AUTOMOBIL (Grandfather Automobile) *Alfréd Radok*
HRA O ŽIVOT (Life Was the Stake) *Jiří Weiss*
NEPORAŽENÍ (The Unvanquished) *Jiří Sequens*

1957 / 21 features

LEGENDA O LÁSCE (Legend of Love) *Václav Krška*
ROČNÍK JEDENADVACET (Born 1921) *Václav Gajer*
ŠKOLA OTCŮ (School of Fathers) *Ladislav Helge*
ŠTĚŇATA (Puppies) *Ivo Novák*
TAM NA KONEČNÉ (At the Terminal Station) *Ján Kadár & Elmar Klos*
ZÁŘIJOVÉ NOCI (September Nights) *Vojtěch Jasný*
ZTRACENCI (Three Men Missing) *Miloš Makovec*

1958 / 24 features

TOUHA (Desire) *Vojtěch Jasný*
TŘETÍ PŘÁNÍ (The Third Wish) *Ján Kadár & Elmar Klos*
VLČÍ JÁMA (Wolf Trap) *Jiří Weiss*
VYNÁLEZ ZKÁZY (Invention for Destruction) *Karel Zeman*
ZDE JSOU LVI (Hic sunt leones) *Václav Krška*
ŽIŽKOVSKÁ ROMANCE (A Local Romance) *Zbyněk Brynych*

1959 / 28 features

KAM ČERT NEMŮŽE (Where the Devil Cannot Go) *Zdeněk Podskalský*
OŠKLIVÁ SLEČNA (The Plain Old Maid) *Miroslav Hubáček*
PROBUZENÍ (Awakening) *Jiří Krejčík*
VELKÁ SAMOTA (Great Seclusion) *Ladislav Helge*

1960 / 27 features

HOLUBICE (Dove) *František Vláčil*
PŘEŽIL JSEM SVOU SMRT (I Survived My Death) *Vojtěch Jasný*
ROMEO, JULIE A TMA (Romeo, Juliet and the Darkness) *Jiří Weiss*
SMYK (Skid) *Zbyněk Brynych*
VYŠŠÍ PRINCIP (Higher Principle) *Jiří Krejčík*

1961 / 31 features

DÁBLOVA PAST (The Devil's Trap) *František Vláčil*
KRÁLÍCI VE VYSOKÉ TRÁVĚ (Rabbits in the Tall Grass) *Václav Gajer*
PROCESÍ K PANENCE (Pilgrimage to the Virgin) *Vojtěch Jasný*
TRÁPENÍ (Worries) *Karel Kachyňa*

262

NÁVRAT ZTRACENÉHO SYNA (The Return of the Prodigal Son) *Evald Schorm*
O SLAVNOSTI A HOSTECH (The Party and the Guests) *Jan Němec*
OSTŘE SLEDOVANÉ VLAKY (Closely Watched Trains) *Jiří Menzel*
ROMANCE PRO KŘÍDLOVKU (Romance for the Flügelhorn) *Otakar Vávra*
SEDMIKRÁSKY (Daisies) *Věra Chytilová*

1967 / 33 features

HOŘÍ, MÁ PANENKO! (Firemen's Ball)) *Miloš Forman*
JÁ SPRAVEDLNOST (I the Justice) *Zbyněk Brynych*
MARKÉTA LAZAROVÁ / *František Vláčil*
NOC NEVĚSTY (The Night of the Bride) *Karel Kachyňa*
PĚT HOLEK NA KRKU (Five Girls to Deal With) *Evald Schorm*
SOUKROMÁ VICHŘICE (Private Windstorm) *Hynek Bočan*
ZNAMENÍ RAKA (The Sign of the Crab) *Juraj Herz*

1968 / 36 features

ČEST A SLÁVA (Honor and Glory) *Hynek Bočan*
KRÁLOVSKÝ OMYL (The Royal Mistake) *Oldřich Daněk*
KULHAVÝ ĎÁBEL (The Lame Devil) *Juraj Herz*
PENZIÓN PRO SVOBODNÉ PÁNY (Boarding House for Gentlemen) *Jiří Krejčík*
ROZMARNÉ LÉTO (Capricious Summer) *Jiří Menzel*
STUD (Shame) *Ladislav Helge*
ÚDOLÍ VČEL (Valley of Bees) *František Vláčil*
ZLOČIN V ŠANTÁNU (Crime in the Night Club) *Jiří Menzel*

1969—1970 /

(There were about 25 Czech features made in 1969). Some were not shown until 1970. In the spring of 1970 some eight finished films were banned and about twelve unfinished films were stopped. I have marked those films, as far as I was able to establish wath happened to which of them. See also note on page 197.
ADELHEID / *František Vláčil*
AESOP / *Rangel Vulchanov* (BANNED)
DEN SEDMÝ, OSMÁ NOC (Seventh Day, Eigth Night) *Evald Schorm* (BANNED)
ECCE HOMO HOMOLKA / *Jaroslav Papoušek*
FARÁŘŮV KONEC (End of a Priest) *Evald Schorm*
HLÍDAČ (The Watchman) *Ivan Renč*
HRST VODY (Adrift) *Ján Kadár & Elmar Klos*
HVĚZDA (The Star) *Jiří Hanibal*
JAK SE PEČE CHLEBA (How Bread is Made) *Ladislav Helge* (STOPPED)
JÁ TRUCHLIVÝ BŮH (I the Sad God) *Antonín Kachlík*
KLADIVO NA ČARODĚJNICE (Hammer Against Witches) *Otakar Vávra*
KOLONIE LANFIERI (The Lanfieri Colony) *Jan Schmidt*
LUK KRÁLOVNY DOROTKY (The Bow of Queen Dorothy) *Jan Schmidt*
NAHOTA (Nakedness) *Václav Matějka* (BANNED)
NÁVŠTĚVY (The Visits) *Vladimír Drha, Otakar Fuka, Milan Jonáš* (STOPPED)
NEJKRÁSNĚJŠÍ VĚK (The Most Beautiful Age) *Jaroslav Papoušek*
NEVĚSTA (The Bride) *Jiří Suchý*
OHLÉDNUTÍ (Looking Back) *Antonín Máša*
OVOCE STROMŮ RAJSKÝCH JÍME (We Eat the Fruit of the Trees of Paradise)
    Věra Chytilová

264

PASŤÁK (The Decoy) *Hynek Bočan* (STOPPED)
PAVILION No. 6 (Pavilón č. 6) *Ivan Balada* (STOPPED)
PŘÍPAD PRO ZAČÍNAJÍCIHO KATA (The Case for the New Hangman) *Pavel Juráček*
(BANNED)
SKŘIVÁNCI NA NITI (Skylarks on a String) *Jiří Menzel* (BANNED)
SMĚŠNÝ PÁN (The Funny Man) *Karel Kachyňa*
SMUTEČNÍ SLAVNOST (Funeral Rites) *Zdeněk Sirový* (BANNED)
SPALOVAČ MRTVOL (The Cremator of Corpses) *Juraj Herz*
SVATEJ Z KREJCÁRKU (The Saint from the Outskirts of the Town) *Petr Tuček*
SVĚTÁCI (Men About Town) *Zdeněk Podskalský*
TVÁŘ POD MASKOU (Face under. the Mask) *Rangel Vulchanov* (also announced as
Cvoci — The Eccentrics)
UCHO (The Ear) *Karel Kachyňa* (BANNED)
VALERIE A TYDEN DIVŮ (Valerie and the Week of Wonders) *Jaromil Jireš*
VŠICHNI DOBŘÍ RODÁCI (All Those Good Countrymen) *Vojtěch Jasný*
ZABITÁ NEDĚLE (Killed Sunday) *Drahomíra Vihanová* (BANNED)
ŽERT (The Joke) *Jaromil Jireš*

INDEX

271

277

278